Parenting with Reason

Sometimes it feels as though everybody has an opinion on how you should bring up your child – and no two people seem to agree on how it should be done for the best! *Parenting with Reason* cuts through the masses of confusing and often contradictory advice about parenting by providing hard evidence to back up the tough decisions all parents face. Unlike many self-help guides to parenting which are based on the opinion of one author, this book is based on many findings from scientific research, giving you a trustworthy, 'evidence-based' guide to help see your way through parenting dilemmas.

Written by a clinical psychologist, a developmental psychologist and a doctor of family medicine, the book looks at pressing questions such as: 'What should I do when my child acts up?', 'How can I get my baby to sleep through the night?' and 'How do I begin to toilet-train my child?' The authors, who are also parents themselves, debunk common myths about parenting, such as the notion that a healthy baby needs to be able to breastfeed at will throughout the night, or the idea that children who are adopted need specialized counselling. They also cover issues such as how children might be affected by seeing violence on television, how a parent's psychological health can affect their child, what the scientific evidence is for and against circumcision, and how divorce and adoption affect a child's development. The end of each chapter gives you 'The Bottom Line', a handy summary of the key points of each issue.

This book is ideal for new or prospective parents, and paediatricians, family health providers and anyone who works with children and their parents will also find the book's objective, scientific approach useful in their work.

Esther Yoder Strahan taught for a decade as Professor and Chair of the Department of Psychology at Heidelberg College, combined with part-time clinical practice. She has recently moved into full-time clinical practice. She enjoys travel with her husband Jeffrey and two young children, Laura and Isaac.

Wallace E. Dixon, Jr. is Professor and Chair of the Psychology Department at East Tennessee State University. His wife Michele is a clinical child psychologist, and the two struggle to raise their daughters Rachel and Sarah to withstand the stigma of having two child psychologist parents.

J. Burton Banks is a former associative professor of family medicine at East Tennessee State University. His clinical interests include children's health and care of child abuse victims. Dr Banks now practises medicine in southwest Virginia, where he lives with his wife Korina and three children, Trent, Skylar and Tanner.

PARENT AND CHILD SERIES
Edited by David Cohen

This series aims to bridge the gap in parents' understanding of the issues that may affect their children from infancy to early adolescence. These scientifically grounded books will communicate the findings of psychologists and other developmental experts to parents in a user-friendly way.

The books will be brief but comprehensive, accessible and intelligent. Topics will cover both normal development and problem areas, such as nutrition, sexuality, eating disorders, learning disabilities, aggressive children and conduct disorders, drugs and alcohol use, and relationship building. The books will be invaluable for all parents and parents-to-be.

TITLES IN THE SERIES

Cohen/*What Every Man Should Know About Being a Dad*

FORTHCOMING BOOKS IN THE SERIES

Sonna/*First Friends: Nurturing Your Child's Social Development* (Summer 2010)
Toddlers' social issues are as many and varied as children themselves. This book gives parents the tools to teach their children what they need to know: how to get along with others and form healthy, satisfying relationships.

Parenting with Reason
Evidence-Based Approaches to Parenting Dilemmas

Esther Yoder Strahan,
Wallace E. Dixon, Jr.
and J. Burton Banks

Routledge
Taylor & Francis Group

LONDON AND NEW YORK

First published 2010
by Routledge
27 Church Road, Hove, East Sussex BN3 2FA

Simultaneously published in the USA and Canada
by Routledge
711 Third Avenue, New York, NY 10017

Routledge is an imprint of the Taylor & Francis Group, an Informa business

Copyright © 2010 Psychology Press

Typeset in New Century Schoolbook by Garfield Morgan,
Swansea, West Glamorgan
Cover design by Lisa Dynan

British Library Cataloguing in Publication Data
A catalogue record for this book is available from the British Library

Library of Congress Cataloging-in-Publication Data
Strahan, Esther Yoder, 1960-
   Parenting with reason : evidence-based approaches to parenting
dilemmas / Esther Yoder Strahan, Wallace E. Dixon, Jr., and J. Burton Banks.
      p. cm.
   Includes bibliographical references.
   ISBN 978-0-415-41328-2 (hardcover) – ISBN 978-0-415-41329-9 (pbk.) 1.
Parenting. 2. Child rearing. I. Dixon, Wallace E. II. Banks, J. Burton (Jerry
Burton), 1963- III. Title.
   HQ755.8.S767 2010
   649'.1–dc22

                                                        2009018329

ISBN 978-0-415-41328-2 (hbk)
ISBN 978-0-415-41329-9 (pbk)

Contents

Author biographies and acknowledgements

Esther Yoder Strahan

 Born to a French mother and an American father, I grew up mostly in the United States, but I also spent four years of my childhood living abroad, in a variety of countries. These experiences gave me, among many other gifts, an appreciation for how differently people in various cultures approach the same issue. For example, one of my French uncles, Adolphe, would never allow us to open the windows in his car, believing the air currents caused ear infections. This was surprising to us, since we normally drove with the car windows down all summer long and never seemed to suffer from it.

After completing a university degree, I worked for some years as a registered nurse. My professional career really began when I entered a doctoral programme in clinical psychology at Purdue University. The programme was very science-focused, which has become a key ingredient in my clinical practice. Too often, both in medicine and in psychology, we make decisions based on tradition rather than evidence. Just like my uncle Adolphe with his air currents, we often fail to question our assumptions. When I became a parent, I noticed the same characteristic in most parenting books I was reading. It frustrated me that the authors did not clearly distinguish between advice that was simply based on their opinion, and what was based on good evidence.

It was when my daughter was a baby that I turned to my then-colleague at Heidelberg College, Wallace Dixon, to see if he would be interested in co-authoring a book for parents based on scientific evidence. Wally is a cognitive psychologist who studies infant thought and language. I am grateful that he agreed to be a partner in this project. We were joined by Burton Banks, a physician who at the time was on the faculty at a school of medicine. Burt has a deep interest in evidence-based medicine, as well as in issues related to child welfare and safety, and he agreed to write on many topics that were medical in nature. Since we started this project, Burt and I have both left academia to engage in full-time clinical practice, while Wally continues to train a new generation of psychologists at East Tennessee State University. I am also grateful to my colleague Matthew Ziccardi, a neuropsychologist, for his contribution to this book.

Most of all, I would like to acknowledge my deep appreciation to my husband Jeffrey, who willingly shouldered an unfair share of parenting duties so that I could spend many Saturday mornings *writing* about parenting! I would also like to acknowledge time taken away from my children, Laura and Isaac, whose energy, kindness and thoughtfulness fill me with love and gratitude. I would also like to thank my sister Martha and my cousin Kathryn for their ongoing support and advice.

Special thanks are also due to Rebekah Edmondson, Sharla Plant and Lucy Kennedy at Psychology Press. They were most patient throughout the trans-Atlantic process of working with three authors, and I express deepest gratitude to them on behalf of all three authors.

Wallace E. Dixon, Jr.

Although my status as full professor and head of my department may convey an aura of scientific authority, I myself have never been much impressed with *mere* authority. For me, authority only carries weight insofar as it is justified by evidence and sound logical argument. Indeed, I have been a stickler for science and the power of reason for as long as I can remember. I was probably 10 when I conducted my first controlled experiment. At that time, having a long history of seasonal allergies and of using medications to combat them, I became interested in the question of whether it made more sense to take my medication with cold or warm water. Under the assumption that faster dissolving was better, I designed a controlled scientific test in which I placed one allergy tablet in a glass of cold water, and one in a glass of warm water. My results proved beyond doubt that taking medicine with warm water would be better for rapid bloodstream entry. But my study led to the equally important discovery that, alas, drinking warm water was extremely unpleasant. Hence, I learned, even before puberty, that perception often outweighs reality. Psychology – 1, Physics – 0.

Throughout those early years my curiosity wrested many other nuggets of knowledge from the world, often through ill-conceived scientific forays. There was the light-bulb socket event (Chapter 9). There was the time I tried to lift myself up while standing in a laundry basket. And there was the time I explored my primitive conception of torque by testing whether my thumb would be sufficiently dense to prevent the blades of my mum's blender from whirling. Yes for 'stir', no for 'whip'. Physics – 1, Biology and Intelligence – 0. Do *not* try this at home.

But over the years, what became abundantly clear was that much of the world did not work the way people thought it did, and yet this lack of understanding seemed to have little effect on their day-to-day lives. I discovered not only that many people had little interest in correcting their misconceptions, but that sometimes they *actively avoided* disconfirming evidence. Indeed, I would be willing to bet that a major contributing factor for the emergence of 'Superbugs' in the US, ironically, is the fact that nearly half of Americans deny the existence of evolution. If one denies evolution, then one need not follow doctor's orders to completely finish off one's antibiotic prescription. Of course, some of the bacteria being harboured by these people will evolve resistances to antibiotic treatments, but if the patients feel better, the details may not much matter. Diseases – 1, Common Good – 0.

If anything is to be contagious, I would prefer that it be critical, reasoned, evidence-based thinking. As a scientist–teacher, and an academic administrator, I strive above all else to make the point that experience with something is not the same as knowing the truth about it, especially when dealing with people. After my first day as a college professor, a student came up to share that she would *try not to intimidate me*. Clueless as to her implications, I asked her to clarify. It turns out she had four children, and knew pretty much all there was to know about childhood. She only needed to take my course because it was a programme requirement. Thoughtfully, she worried she might embarrass me with her massive child development expertise. Of course, just as experience with nights and days doesn't demonstrate that the earth revolves around the sun, and experience with sitting in a chair doesn't demonstrate that the chair is made of atoms, so it goes that being a parent doesn't automatically demonstrate knowledge of child psychology.

Of course, one doesn't go around challenging and critiquing ideas and beliefs without others taking notice, and so I am regarded by my friends and family as a fairly radical sceptic. But it can't be otherwise because I can't *not* think what I think. I subscribe to *Skeptical Inquirer* to track modern cultural mythologies, and I scour *Consumer Reports'* data before purchasing household items. I am empiricist to the bone. Does this make me hard to live with? It must. But I have been married to my wife Michele for more than two decades, and so at least one person seems to find my way of thinking useful. I imagine my two daughters, Rachel (16) and Sarah (12), must find my ongoing review of their life's goals irritating, especially now, during the prime of their adolescence. But they still let me give them head-kisses every morning before school, which suggests that I haven't bungled things too badly.

I provide these self-disclosures merely as a backdrop against which to read my chapters; it may be helpful for readers to know where I am coming from. However, I would be derelict of conscience if I did not also gratefully acknowledge the context from which my work was produced. Especially central for the preparation of my chapters was my immediate family, especially Michele, Rachel and Sarah. Also, thanks to Bobby Russell for his help in collecting material I used for several chapters of this book. Thanks to Rachel Coykendall and Jodi Polaha for reading through and commenting on selected chapter drafts. Thanks to Tiffany Pempek for helping talk me through the political world of media mythinformation, and for reading and commenting on the associated chapter. Finally, extra special thanks to my co-author Esther Strahan, who not only conceptualized this book, and conceptualized my role as a contributor to it, but also put up with my various rants throughout the process.

J. Burton Banks

 I can remember when reality first struck me. My first child was 4 years old, and our second child was just starting to toddle around. Seemingly overnight both children conspired to destroy the sanity of their parents. Defiance became the rule rather than the exception, and it was clear that the adults had lost all control. Surely the parenting thing could not be this difficult. I had been a perfect child and my own parents seemed to have no trouble at all. At least that is the way I choose to remember it. However, I was convinced that something terrible had happened to my own children – perhaps the obstetrician had dropped them on their heads when I was distracted and looking away, or perhaps a strange and as yet unidentified virus had tragically struck our home and transformed the children into alien beings. While I knew these possibilities did not make logical sense, I was convinced that the fault lay completely outside of me. After all, I was a physician and a faculty member at a medical university. Out of desperation, I began searching for answers and realized there were many inconsistencies in those answers. It was clear that parents could be easily misinformed by advice circulating in the

general public from 'The Experts'. It also became clear that maybe my children were not so abnormal after all, and that I was not alone in my desperation. Now, with three children in the home (and one in full-blown adolescence), I jumped at the chance to participate in the creation of this book, hoping to alleviate some of the anxieties I experienced when I thought I knew everything.

I am a family physician, trained to provide medical care to all age groups and encompassing medical problems related to all organ systems. This gives me a bit of a unique perspective when discussing medical or parenting issues, because I tend to see things from both the child's and the parent's perspective. Having a special clinical interest in child abuse and child sexual abuse gives me yet another perspective, because I see on a daily basis how quickly things can fall apart and how important it is to have every opportunity to enhance one's parenting skills before problems arise.

I am certainly not a perfect parent myself, but the quest is always there; not a day goes by that my children do not point out another area for growth. As a medical educator, I have tried to instil in medical students and junior doctors the importance of questioning tradition and not basing their clinical skills merely on the 'wisdom' of their instructors. What is 'best' today may not be so tomorrow, but experts are generally slow to change their opinions or practices. That is not to say that experience should be completely ignored. When there is no evidence to the contrary, then experience is all we have. This is true for parents as well as physicians. Aunt Hilda may sometimes give good advice, but sometimes there are better alternatives. I hope this book will help cut through some of the myths and give a good basis for enhancing one's parenting skills. The journey is long, but the rewards are great.

My thanks go to my parents who got me where I am; to my wife, Korina, who inspires me to go further; and to my lovely children, Trent, Skylar and Tanner, who push me to the limits – then bring me back again.

A history of science and parenting advice

Strahan and Dixon

Introduction

When Sarah and Chris first hold their newborn son, William, they feel overwhelmed with tenderness and love for this beautiful baby. They resolve to be the best possible parents for him. Three weeks later, Chris and Sarah are exhausted. William has been sleeping very poorly, and they are so sleep-deprived that they feel like zombies. William is only sleeping for ninety minutes at a stretch. Chris and Sarah decide they must be doing something wrong. They begin a desperate internet search to look for advice on infant sleep. This is what they find:

- **Always sleep with your infant:** The attachment parenting websites recommend the 'Dr Sears' or 'family bed' method of sleeping with your infant. They say that this method will help William be better adjusted as a baby, and will help him have better relationships in the future. Further, they suggest that failing to sleep with your infant could lead to permanent brain damage due to the influence of stress hormones on the baby's brain. Finally, they hint that aggressiveness and violence come from insecurely attached children. Hence, attachment parenting practices could ultimately lead to a more peaceful world.
- **Never sleep with your infant:** The Consumer Safety Protection Commission issued an advisory in 1999 warning parents of the dangers of co-sleeping with an

infant, due to the risk of suffocating the baby. This recommendation states that the safest way for William to sleep is in a crib, alone, with minimal bedding. Sleeping William alone in his crib is also recommended by the 'Dr Ferber' method of putting the child to bed awake and allowing the child to cry him- or herself to sleep. Dr Mindell, another infant sleep expert, points out that poor sleeping patterns are far more likely to persist than other child behaviour problems (like tantrums). She suggests that it is much more beneficial for the child to learn to sleep alone, in a crib.

So there you have it – Chris and Sarah can pick a method that will lead to world peace and intact brain structures in their happy baby – if he survives without being suffocated! Alternatively, they can choose a method that will allow William to survive and to have healthy sleeping patterns later in life, although he may be hopelessly traumatized and unable to form friendships.

Confused, they turn to their paediatrician. She recommends they choose whatever approach they are comfortable with, forgetting that by this time they are so sleep-deprived they couldn't choose between a Timex and a Rolex if they were offered their free pick of either.

They get further advice from Sarah's mother, who says her babies did best when they took a bottle of formula at bedtime. She tells them that is really the only way to get a baby to sleep through the night. Sarah, however, is breastfeeding William and does not want to give him formula. Chris's mother, on the other hand, pressures the new parents to put William on the Ezzo 'Babywise' plan, which promotes very strict feeding and sleep patterns. As it turns out, Chris and Sarah had already considered this method until they learned that it can lead to infant malnutrition and possibly childhood depression, according to some paediatricians.

In despair, the new parents give up on seeking advice, and endure several miserable months of sleeplessness. They feel guilty that their chosen approach to William's sleep, which includes some co-sleeping and some crib-sleeping, is either too indulgent or too harsh, and will probably lead to ill effects in the future.

Frustrating scenarios like this comprise the major reason we decided to write this book. When I (Esther) had my first baby, I read a lot of parenting manuals, starting with the ones about infant sleep. At the time, my newborn daughter was waking four to six times per night. Some of the popular childcare books seemed to be full of good advice, but often that advice was based on one writer's opinion alone, and frequently was contradicted by the good advice of another writer.

This experience led to lots of discussions between those of us who got together to write this book. We had been trained as scientists, and we knew that there *was* scientific literature that addressed many of these important parenting questions. It just didn't seem to be consistently making its way into the parenting self-help books. We decided to write a manual on 'evidence-based parenting' as a way of bringing more of that rich scientific knowledge into the world of parenting books. Here is who we are: Dr Esther Strahan is trained in clinical psychology and 'evidence-based' methods of treating psychological problems. Dr Wallace Dixon is a developmental psychologist, who researches infants' cognitive, language and temperament development. Dr J. Burton Banks is a professor of family medicine with a special interest in 'evidence-based medicine' and paediatrics. We believed our areas of expertise would lend themselves well to writing a parenting manual that was grounded in the best that science has to offer.

These are the goals of our book:

- To give parents recommendations on the best available practices in parenting. In some cases those recommendations will be very clear because the weight of the evidence is so strong in favour of one approach. In others, we will simply provide you with the pros and cons of a particular decision, based on current scientific evidence, so that you can make an informed decision, or at least be armed with information to discuss with your healthcare providers.

- To develop a strategy that parents can follow to get the best information when they come across questions we have not addressed. We want to help you become more savvy about how science works, and how to get good-quality information on any topic. But developing this kind of skill takes practice.

Scientists offering child-rearing advice are often accused of advocating a 'cook book' approach to parenting, meaning it is too mechanical and simple-minded. We like the idea of being compared to cooks. It's certainly not because we expect to give you fail-safe recipes for raising your children. That would mean abandoning our principles and pretending to have knowledge that has not yet been developed. We would hope, instead, to provide parents with the sort of guidance offered to people watching cookery shows, who go away with useful general principles that they can use creatively in their own cooking. There is a science of cooking as well as a science of parenting, and those who are most comfortable in their roles have a good idea of the basics.

Culture and child-rearing beliefs

The culture you live in and the values you hold will be crucial in helping you determine what constitutes good parenting. There simply isn't one model of parenting that works equally well for all children everywhere.

Let us start with a rather extreme example. The !Kung people, who live in the Kalahari desert, raise their children on a diet of breast milk supplemented by nuts, grubs, and fibrous vegetables. Obviously, Western baby feeding advice, derived from the study of babies in developed nations, is of little help to these parents. Likewise, we do not expect our advice to be universally applicable, as it is based on research primarily from Western, developed nations. Successful parenting will differ depending on the culture in which the child is raised, and the expectations placed upon the child when she/he grows up. Not only the child's culture, but also the historical era will shape what is adequate parenting.

To illustrate the importance of cultural perspective, let's look for a moment at what might have constituted 'good parenting' over the last few hundred years. We'll draw examples from several English-speaking countries.

Colonial America

Puritans in America saw children as wicked due to the effects of original sin. To save their children's souls, they placed emphasis on obedience and on breaking the child's will. They believed that if the child learned to submit to the parent's will, that child would find it easier to submit to God's will. It is clear from the historical record that many of these Puritans felt great love for their children, but the methods they used seem harsh and unfeeling to us, hundreds of years later. Their writings reveal that they were torn between their affections, and a sense of duty that their children's eternal salvation depended on the parents' strictness.

For example, Jonathan Edwards, the famous Protestant preacher, wrote in the mid-1700s that, 'As innocent as children seem to be to us, yet if they are out of Christ, they are not so in God's sight, but are young vipers, and infinitely more hateful than vipers, and are in a most miserable condition . . .' (Jonathan Edwards, *The Great Awakening*).

It is understandable that parents of that era, with the values they held, would have thought it important to parent in a very different way than we would today. Strict attitudes persisted into the next century. There are many written accounts of the methods used by parents who thought it was necessary to 'break children's wills' in order to help them become moral and productive citizens. The extract below is an example dating from 1831 of a particularly well documented struggle to break a child's will.

It is a quote from *American Baptist Magazine*, written by Rev. Francis Wayland, early president of Brown University.

My youngest child was an infant about 15 months of age, with about the intelligence common to children of that age. It had for some months been evident, that he was more than usually self willed, but the several attempts to subdue him, had been thus far relinquished, form the fear that he did not fully understand what was said to him . . . Still I had seen enough to convince me of the necessity of subduing his temper, and resolved to seize upon the first favorable opportunity which presented, for settling the question of authority between us.

On Friday last before breakfast, on my taking him from his nurse, he began to cry violently. I determined to hold him in my arms until he ceased. As he had a piece of bread in his hand, I took it away, intending to give it to him after he became quiet. In a few minutes he ceased, but when I offered him the bread he threw it away, although he was very hungry. He had, in fact, taken no nourishment except a cup of milk since 5 o'clock on the preceding afternoon. I considered this a fit opportunity for attempting to subdue his temper, and resolved to embrace it. I thought it necessary to change his disposition, so that he would receive the bread from me, and also be so reconciled to me that he would voluntarily come to me. The task I found more difficult than I had expected.

I put him into a room by himself, and desired that no one should speak to him, or give him any food or drink whatever. This was about 8 o'clock in the morning. I visited him every hour or two during the day, and spoke to him in the kindest tones, offering him the bread and putting out my arms to take him. But throughout the day he remained inflexibly obstinate. He did not yield a hair's breadth. I put a cup of water to his mouth, and he drank it greedily, but would not touch it with his hands. If a crumb was dropped on the floor he would eat it, but if I offered him the piece of bread, he would push it away from him. When I told him to come to me, he would turn away and cry bitterly. He went to bed supperless. It was now 24 hours since he had eaten anything.

He woke the next morning in the same state. He would take nothing that I offered him, and shunned all my offers of kindness. He was now truly an object of pity.

He had fasted 36 hours. His eyes were wan and sunken. His breath hot and feverish, and his voice feeble and wailing. Yet he remained obstinate. He continued thus, until 10 o'clock, a.m., when hunger overcame him, and he took from me a piece of bread, to which I added a cup of milk, and hoped that the labor was at last accomplished.

In this however I had not rightly judged. He ate his bread greedily, but when I offered to take him, he still refused as pertinaciously as ever. I therefore ceased feeding him, and recommenced my course of discipline.

He was again left alone in his crib, and I visited him as before, at intervals. About one o'clock, Saturday, I found that he began to view his condition in its true light. The tones of his voice in weeping were graver and less passionate, and had more the appearance of one bemoaning himself. Yet when I went to him he remained obstinate. You could clearly see in him the abortive efforts of the will. Frequently he would raise his hands an inch or two, and then suddenly put them down again. He would look at me, and then hiding his face in the bedclothes weep most sorrowfully. During all this time I was addressing him, whenever I came into the room, with invariable kindness. But my kindness met with no suitable return. All I required of him was, that he should come to me. This he would not do, and he began now to see that it had become a serious business. Hence his distress increased. He would not submit, and he found that there was no help without it. It was truly surprising to behold how much agony so young a being could inflict upon himself.

About three o'clock I visited him again. He continued in the state I have described. I was going away, and had opened the door, when I thought that he looked somewhat softened, and returning, put out my hands, again requesting him to come to me. To my joy, and I hope gratitude, he rose up and put forth his hands immediately. The agony was over. He was completely subdued. He repeatedly kissed me, and would do so whenever I commanded. He would kiss any one when I directed him, so full of love was he to all the family.

Indeed, so entirely and instantaneously were his feelings toward me changed, that he preferred me now to any of the family. As he had never done before, he moaned after me when he saw that I was going away.

Since this event several slight revivals of his former temper have occurred, but they have all been easily subdued. His disposition is, as it never has been before, mild and obedient. He is kind and affectionate, and evidently much happier than he was, when he was determined to have his own way. I hope and pray that it may prove that an effect has been produced on him for life.

> ('A Case of Conviction', *The American Baptist Magazine, XI* (1831), pp. 296–298); quoted in Greven 1977, p. 41.

As Britain and North America industrialized, and levels of education rose, science became more respected. Scientists and clinicians began to provide recommendations about how to raise children.

Eighteenth-century England

The London Foundling Hospital, opened in 1741 as a response to the large numbers of deserted and dying infants in the streets of London, provided an informal laboratory on child care. It is reported that, by 1753, over one hundred babies a day were brought to the hospital. William Buchan, who trained at another foundling hospital, used his experiences to write *Domestic Medicine*, an early book including advice to parents, which was a huge success (having been published in eighteen editions and translated into numerous languages). An excerpt from Buchan's book follows:

WHEN we say that mothers are not always in a condition to suckle their own children, we would not be understood as discouraging that practice. Every mother who can, ought certainly to perform so tender and agreeable an office. But, suppose it to be out of her power, she may, nevertheless, be of great service to her child. The business of nursing is by no means confined to giving suck. To a woman who abounds with milk, this is the easiest part of it. Numberless other offices are necessary for a child, which the mother ought at least to see done. Many advantages would arise to society, as well as to individuals, from mothers suckling their own children. It would prevent the temptation which poor women are laid under, of abandoning their children to suckle those of the rich for the sake of gain; by which means society loses many of its most useful members, and mothers become in some sense the murderers of their own offspring. I am sure I speak within the truth when I say, that not one in a hundred of those children live, who are thus abandoned by their mothers.

Buchan addressed a number of common child-rearing practices of his time, such as that of preventing newborn babies from nursing until the mother's milk came in, often several days after delivery, and of giving the child a variety of drugs in the meantime:

A CHILD, soon after the birth, shews an inclination to suck; and there is no reason why it should not be gratified. It is true, the mother's milk does not always come immediately after the birth; but this is the way to bring it: Besides, the first milk that the child can squeeze out of the breast answers the purpose of cleansing, better than all the drugs in the apothecary's shop, and at the same time prevents inflammations of the breast, fevers, and other diseases incident to mothers.

IT is strange how people came to think that the first thing given to a child should be drugs. This is beginning with medicine by times, and no wonder that they generally end with it.

Dr Buchan advocated giving young children plenty of exercise, limiting or eliminating their consumption of alcohol, not educating them too soon, and giving them cold baths to strengthen their constitution. His book is fascinating for the light it sheds on child-rearing practices of the day (such as his disapproval of teaching children to 'guzzle' ale and liquors at every meal), as well as for the actual advice offered by the enlightened doctor.

A variety of books on child-rearing, written by apothecaries and physicians, sold well in the late eighteenth and early nineteenth centuries. Christina Hardyment's *Dream Babies* documents fascinating examples of parenting advice, and evidence that scientific views on child-rearing were being sought by literate parents several hundred years ago.

America in the early twentieth century

In addition to parents' desire to obtain the best scientific advice, pressures were placed on families who had moved far away from their own families, and began to turn to other sources of information.

There is a wonderful collection of poignant, early twentieth-century letters written by mothers to the American federal government's Children's Bureau and published in a 1986 book by Molly Ladd-Taylor. This collection demonstrates how desperate mothers were for information on pregnancy, childbirth, and parenting. Their narratives reflect a variety of superstitions that were troubling the women. For example, it was commonly held that if a pregnant woman saw a deformed person, her child would also be deformed or otherwise 'marked'. These letters also attest to the difficulty of life in those days. Consider two passages from women requesting informational pamphlets on child-rearing:

(Mrs J.T., Wisconsin, 1927). Please send me a copy of the *Care of Children* Number eight (revised). At the same time could you give specific advice concerning a six month old baby boy weighting twenty-eight pounds perfectly healthy except that he cries three or four times during the night and has to be picked up and walked with. There is no question but what he is spoiled, but he has such a lusty cry that my husband and I are afraid to let him cry long for fear he will rupture himself . . . Have you ever heard of a baby harmed thru crying? Awaiting what ever information you may have I am Very Truly Yours.

(Mrs A.P., Wyoming, 1916). I should very much like all the Publications on the care of my self, who am now pregnant, also the care of a baby . . . I live sixty-five miles from a Dr. and my other babies (two) were very large at birth, one 12-lbs the other 10 ½ lbs. I have been very badly torn each time . . . So many of my neighbors die at giving birth to their children. I have a baby 11 months old in my keeping now whose mother died . . . Will you please send me all other information for the care of my self before and after the time of delivery. I am far from a Dr. and we have no means, only what we get on this rented ranch. I also want all the information on baby care especially right young new born ones. If there is **anything** that I can do to escape being torn again won't you let me know.

The Children's Bureau staff were so moved by the latter mother's plight that they took a donation from their own pockets to send her baby supplies, and sent a public health doctor out to examine her.

Many mothers were so grateful for the advice they culled from the Children's Bureau pamphlets that they wrote letters of thanks to that agency. One woman from New York commented:

When people stop me on the street and ask the whys and wherefores of my so obviously healthy baby I always say 'He's a Government baby,' giving all the credit to your bulletin (*Infant Care*). I was lucky enough not to know anything about babies before and not to have any relatives who thought they did.

'Science' and the 'experts' weigh in on child-rearing

Science has a mixed record when it comes to providing advice on parenting. On the one hand, many attempts to provide scientific parenting advice were greeted with tremendous enthusiasm, as with William Buchan's book in the eighteenth century, or the Children's Bureau examples just mentioned. On the other hand, I must confess that horrendous advice has been given in the name of science.

Some of the most flagrant examples occur when people claim scientific authority by misrepresenting their credentials. For example, Bruno Bettelheim, a man with a Ph.D. in philosophical aesthetics, successfully passed himself off as a psychologist with expertise in the care of autistic children. He claimed that autism was due to poor parenting, and specifically to those 'refrigerator mothers' who were so cold and rejecting that their children withdrew into autism. As a result of his unsubstantiated opinions, untold numbers of parents were made to feel defensive, guilty and/or ashamed for their roles in 'causing' the autism of their children. From a scientific perspective, we know very little about the causes of autism and the rest of the 'autistic spectrum' disorders. However, we do know that, in general, mothers of autistic children are anything but cold and rejecting. Other problems that have come to light since Bettelheim's death include his abuse of the charges under his care, and his blatant misrepresentation of success rates at the Orthogenic School he founded in Chicago. Thus, a man idealized by many as a heroic pioneer of psychological treatment turned out to have been a highly successful self-promoter, one who built an elaborate and compelling fantasy about how to solve our most challenging child-rearing problems.

Another problem with child-rearing advice occurs when legitimate scientists write books based on their opinions, confusing both themselves and the public about how much they really know about the subject in question. Some of these scientists, starting out with good intentions, probably created more problems than they solved. For example, in nineteenth-century America and Canada, parents were expected to provide basic education for their very young children at home. A new movement began, starting in England, in which 'infant schools' were established to help poor children overcome their disadvantages.

Some of these infant schools appeared in the US and Canada, starting in the mid-1820s. North American middle-class parents began noticing the advantages of these schools and enrolled their children. As a result, infant schools spread rapidly until by 1840 nearly half of all 3-year-olds in Massachusetts were enrolled in one. This trend stopped abruptly in North America when a prominent physician, Amariah Brigham, in 1833, promoted the idea that too much thinking at a young age would stunt the brain's development and lead to insanity. His ideas received a lot of attention in the press, and by 1860 few children under the age of 5 were in schools. Thus, based on the unsubstantiated opinions of one 'expert', a promising educational movement was stopped due to fears that it could lead to mental weakness and insanity.

A clear example of this sort of misguided advice-giving occurs later, at the beginning of the twentieth century. There was much concern expressed about the effects of education on adolescent girls' fertility. It was commonly believed that too much education (particularly college education) would destroy women's reproductive health. G. Stanley Hall, a prominent founder of developmental psychology, wrote in 1904 about the dangers of advanced education for girls. His books include statements such as the following one describing what happens to a woman who gets a college education:

> First she loses mammary function, so that should she
> undertake maternity its functions are incompletely
> performed because she can not nurse, and this implies
> defective motherhood and leaves love of the child itself
> defective and maimed, for the mother who has never
> nursed can not love or be loved aright by her child. It
> crops out again in the abnormal or especially incomplete
> development of her offspring . . . These women are often

in every way magnificent, only they are not mothers, and sometimes have very little wifehood in them . . . Some, though by no means all, of them are functionally castrated . . . .

Now, in fairness, Dr Brigham and Dr Hall were simply reflecting commonly held beliefs of their time; in all likelihood, future generations will likewise find today's 'modern' beliefs ridiculous. The good Drs Brigham and Hall apparently based their statements on 'evidence' such as hearing of an educated woman who was unable to nurse her child. Today we would call this form of information 'anecdotal', and give it little weight in our scientific decision-making. The main point is that these professionals were using their credentials to lend weight to assertions that were nothing more than folk wisdom.

A very different use of 'scientific' advice giving that contradicted folk wisdom occurred with Dr John Watson, a prominent psychologist who founded the behavioural psychology movement in about 1913. He conducted some studies on the emotional development of babies, and in particular on how babies acquire fears. He became concerned about the ways in which children were encouraged to become clingy and dependent on their parents. In his 1928 book *The Psychological Care of Infant and Child*, he proclaimed, 'Mothers just don't know, when they kiss their children and pick them up and rock them, caress them and jiggle them upon their knee, that they are slowly building up a human being totally unable to cope with the world it must later live in.' He advocated showing minimal affection to the child, to prevent the child from becoming emotionally dependent on the parent. Thus, many portions of his book represented a misguided attempt to extend advice far beyond the topics he had actually studied in his laboratory. To be fair to Dr Watson, the book also contains much advice that is sensible by present standards, such as advice to have a regular time to talk over questions raised by the child, and a description of how to help the child overcome fears that is surprisingly accurate by today's standards.

Even today, we are not immune to 'experts' giving advice in the absence of scientific data. Consider a case involving an American radio celebrity 'Dr Laura' Schlessinger. It all started with a scientific article published in 1998 by three psychologists named Bruce Rind, Philip Tromovitch and Robert Bauserman. In their study, which represented information collected from tens of thousands of people, they found that people who were sexually abused in childhood or adolescence did not necessarily turn out to have terrible lives. In fact, these authors reported that most people who reported sexual abuse in childhood turned out to be relatively well adjusted later on in life.

Now one might think the findings of this study would be cause for celebration. After all, prior to this major study, common wisdom believed that victims of child sexual abuse would be damaged for life in one way or another. But the events that followed were not celebratory, and an all-out attack on the scientific merit of the study and the moral character of its authors resulted, spearheaded by Dr Laura on the airwaves. Psychologist Scott Lilienfeld describes Dr Laura's public response this way: 'She asserted that as a "real scientist," she had learned that if a study's results contradict conventional wisdom, then the dissemination of these findings should be withheld and the results deemed erroneous.' This claim strikes us as extraordinary and baffling. Science doesn't exist to support conventional wisdom; science exists to *test* conventional wisdom.

Given that Dr Laura's audience at the time exceeded several million listeners, and given that no alternative, science-literate radio talk-show existed to combat her claims, we have to conclude that millions of her listeners harboured the false belief that child sexual abuse causes permanent psychological harm. Dr Laura's comments in this case are troublesome from a variety of standpoints. First, it sends the wrong message to people who experienced childhood sexual abuse that they must view themselves as damaged. Second, it dismisses a major scientific finding simply on the basis that it contradicts conventional wisdom.

Let me give a medical example to illustrate why this kind of reasoning is faulty. For years doctors prescribed hormone replacement therapy (HRT) for menopausal women. This was because they believed that HRT lowered the risk of heart disease to pre-menopausal levels (oestrogen was felt to be one of the protective factors). Now, after the Women's Health Initiative and the tens of thousands of subjects who were studied, it is clear there is a negative effect of HRT on many women's health. Does this finding contradict previous conventional wisdom? Yes. Does this mean that the study's results should be dismissed and physicians should keep prescribing HRT for menopausal women? You decide.

Despite its limitations, science has contributed a great deal to our society and our lifestyles. As the Children's Bureau letters reveal, even flawed scientific knowledge was often a vast improvement over the advice parents were getting before that time. It is through scientific research that we know, for example, that women need sufficient amounts of folic acid in their diet during pregnancy to help protect their children from birth defects. It is through scientific research that we learned of the effects of alcohol consumption on the developing child's brain, and the increased risk for these children of Fetal Alcohol Syndrome. Future chapters of this book will provide other examples of important parenting information generated by science, such as ways to prevent sudden infant death syndrome, or SIDS. Science provides vital pieces of information to any parent. And although it may go without saying, we believe that in most instances, good science offers the best guidance for making decisions. Of course, for scientific advice to be useful, parents should learn to be smart consumers of scientific knowledge.

How to think scientifically about parenting

Anecdotal evidence

'I know a man who smoked three packs of cigarettes a day and lived to be 95 years old, so I don't believe any of that stuff about cigarette smoking and your health.' This is the sort of thinking that makes health professionals want to jump off cliffs. Unfortunately, this sort of thinking is also fairly common. Anecdotal evidence operates on the assumption that evidence from a single case is as valid as the careful study of hundreds or even tens of thousands of cases. This sort of reasoning is rampant in the world of parenting advice. Think of radio talk-show hosts who proclaim that the way to raise a child is the way they raised their children, because they turned out just fine . . .

What is the problem with anecdotal evidence? Quite simply, it is often misleading, because for every case that is brought to bear on one side of an argument, an equally compelling case can be brought up for the other side of the argument. No consensus can ever be arrived at. And in the end, we are no closer to the truth when all the sides have brought to bear all their anecdotal cases. For example, humans can survive an astonishing number of adverse conditions. Consider Frank McCourt, whose autobiography, *Angela's Ashes*, was a huge publishing success. McCourt grew up with an alcoholic father, in desperate poverty, amid high infant mortality. Using the anecdotal method alone, we would be led to conclude that the way to produce children who grow up to be successful is to subject them to alcoholism, death, and near-starvation. Then, if they survive, they will probably be famous writers. Clearly, this is ridiculous. In general, children who grow up amid such desperate conditions are more likely than privileged children to have problems with the law, to do poorly in school, and to have a host of other troubles. We admit this example was deliberately designed to be far-fetched, but let us try an example closer to home for most parents.

Elective Caesarian section births occur at the highest rate in Wales, compared to the rest of the UK. What are the long-term effects on the child of a Caesarian section? Is it, as Dr Michel Odent of London's Primal Health Research Network claims on his website, a procedure that increases the child's risk of developing autism and other illnesses (more on this in a moment)? We would argue that such parenting decisions are important enough that they merit active investigation of what the scientific literature says about such matters.

Correlational studies

So, if science is so great and parenting has been studied scientifically, why don't we have definitive answers to some of the most important parenting questions? The answer lies with the types of research on parenting that are possible. You see, scientists aren't allowed to *experiment* with human parenting the way they might with, say, rat or monkey parenting. With human parenting there are so many moral values to consider, and so many ethical and monetary restrictions on the kinds of research questions that can be asked, that for most of the really important parenting questions, we just can't experiment. This means that the vast majority of studies having to do with parenting are correlational, where children and/or parents are compared on a variety of dimensions, and relationships between these dimensions are assessed.

For example, what if we wanted to look at the effects of poverty on children's IQ? The best way to find out whether poverty lowers children's IQ would be to conduct an experiment on families in which we control how much money parents have, and measure whether children's IQ scores vary accordingly. Of course, we couldn't *really* conduct an experiment to answer this question, because then we would have to randomly assign a group of families to live in poverty conditions and another group of families to live in non-poverty conditions. No ethical scientist would undertake this study.

We are only left with a correlational methodology, then. Using a correlational approach, we would generally measure IQ scores on a large number of children, collect information on their family incomes, and determine whether families with more money have children with higher IQ scores. The problem with the correlational approach is that it cannot separate out the effects of family income from many other factors also known to be related to family income. So smoking, which is also correlated with family income, might be the actual cause of IQ differences, even if poverty and IQ scores are highly correlated.

Not all parenting studies *have* to be correlational. Some experimental parenting studies can be conducted, so long as the experimental interventions are not ethically problematic. Parents could be asked to read more frequently to their children over a six-week period, for example, and then children could be observed to see if their vocabulary underwent a developmental growth spurt as a result of the increased parental reading. Unfortunately, though, for many of the most contentious areas of parenting, including issues related to discipline, experimental studies are rarely possible.

How science proceeds

Many people have a false understanding of the rate at which science happens. Science doesn't happen overnight: it moves slowly. This is really for the best, as there are checks and balances associated with every scientific investigation. This ultimately yields better information, but this keeps researchers from finding quick answers. One researcher's findings always have to be corroborated by another independent researcher's findings before we can place much weight on them. In this way, we say that science is 'self-correcting'. When one scientist occasionally produces a wrong answer, the nature of science is such that another scientist will come along to correct it. For example, answering the question raised earlier of whether Caesarian section deliveries are dangerous to babies is highly complex. In some instances, we know that Caesarian section deliveries are a positive benefit to both mother and child, for example in cases of 'placenta previa', and they certainly can improve babies' outcomes when compared to very difficult deliveries. On the other hand, recent credible scientific reviews have found increased rates of asthma (up to 20 per cent higher) in children born via Caesarian section, and food allergies may also be more common in these children. The autism question is still somewhat less well studied, so we will look for more evidence as the science develops.

Other checks need to be in place if research results are to be convincing. For example, we know that our bodies and minds are strongly influenced by our expectations (the 'placebo effect' is one example of this). If a mother gives her child a medication that she strongly expects to improve the child's behaviour, that mother will generally *see* improvements, regardless of whether there really are any positive changes, simply because she so badly wants to see improvements. For this reason, researchers have to design studies that control for the parent's good and bad expectations.

What does all this mean for the parent struggling to make a decision about the well-being of their child? First, it means *proceed with caution*. The internet is full of stories about amazing cures for autism, obesity, learning disorders, and almost any other childhood malady. Parents can spend huge amounts of money and time on treatments that turn out to be nothing more than 'snake oil'.

If you are seeking information for a particular problem and find something that looks promising, ask yourself the following questions:

- Does it seem too good to be true?
- How much of the evidence is anecdotal? Stories of miracle cures are always compelling, but they are almost never true.
- If it involves a medication or dietary supplement, are there any long-term studies of the safety and effectiveness of the supplement? Maybe something will help your child's behaviour problem but will lead to a variety of medical problems later in life.
- Does my doctor recommend it? If you really think it looks good, check it out with your paediatrician, family doctor, or mental health professional.
- Is my doctor unsure? If so, there are numerous resources you can go to for good-quality information that will balance the pros and cons of the decision you are trying to make. One of these would be the National Institute for Health and Clinical Excellence, at http://www.nice.org.uk, or the American National Institute of Health, whose website includes research conducted by the National Institute of Child Health and Human Development, at http://www.nichd.nih.gov/.

Structure of this book

The three of us (Strahan, Dixon and Banks) have written chapters based on our areas of expertise, looking at a variety of parenting dilemmas. In some of them, there are clear benefits connected with a particular approach, with strong scientific support. Others are less clear. We intend to be honest both about the areas that have strong support, and the other areas where we are making recommendations based on strong theoretical grounds because the research is missing or inconclusive.

At the end of each chapter, we will conclude with a brief section called 'The Bottom Line', using the following questions as guides:

• What are the key dilemmas parents have to struggle with on this topic?
• What does the science say about this topic?
• What do the authors advise?

Smart parenting exercise

This should serve as a way to become more vividly acquainted with some of the pitfalls of seeking information on a scientific topic:

1 Imagine you are the parent of an autistic child. You have heard exciting reports of the benefits of a hormone called 'secretin' in treating autism.
2 Do a general internet search using whatever browser you normally use, inputting the terms 'secretin' and 'autism'. When you get the results, pay particular attention to how you would feel upon seeing the reports you run across.
3 Now, go to the National Institute of Health's website at www.nih.org, enter the term 'secretin', and compare the results of the studies they conducted with what you found before.
4 Repeat this exercise with any other health-related search terms of interest to you.

Recommended reading

Hardyment, C. (1983). *Dream babies: Three centuries of good advice on child care*. London: Harper & Row. A highly readable and entertaining portrait of three centuries of child-rearing in England.

Hrdy, S.B. (1999). *Mother Nature: A history of mothers, infants, and natural selection*. New York: Pantheon Books. Dr Hrdy is an anthropologist and mother who has written a riveting, and sometimes appalling, examination of maternal behaviour across cultures and through the centuries.

Hulbert, A. (2003). *Raising America: Experts, parents, and a century of advice about children*. New York: Alfred A. Knopf. A compelling study of 'hard' and 'soft' approaches to parenting advocated by the most famous American parenting experts, along with glimpses into how their theories were shaped by their own childhood experiences.

Sleep and its controversies
Strahan

Infancy: the first and sleepiest year

The big co-sleeping controversy

In the first chapter of this book we highlighted the controversy surrounding how infant sleep should best be handled. This is an area that provokes much passion. Visit any internet parenting site and examine their 'bulletin board' or chat area on the topic of infant sleep, and you will find yourself in the midst of a pitched battle. The primary opponents in this battle are those who follow the recommendations of behaviourally oriented sleep experts, such as Dr Richard Ferber, and those who follow the recommendations of the Attachment Parenting movement leaders, such as 'Dr Bill' Sears. Below I have copied two sample posts representing these different views (I avoided the most vitriolic examples, where parents on each side insult the others. If you like championship boxing, though, you might enjoy visiting these sites).

I will start with a fairly typical post representing the Attachment Parenting side. These parents have a strong focus on the parent–child bond and often make references to non-Western cultures and to the sleeping patterns of other primates in their arguments for the 'family bed' approach. The more extreme advocates of this position highlight research that links severe trauma to brain damage. Then, they equate infant crying with severe trauma, and go on to predict that parents who do not keep their children in bed with them (or at least next to the parents' bed, within touching distance) are permanently damaging their children's health and emotional well-being. They also refer to research showing that infants who co-sleep are less susceptible to 'cot death' or 'sudden infant death syndrome' (SIDS). This parent's post captures another of the themes running through this parenting philosophy, which is that you should sleep with your children because it is more comforting for the child and it will improve the parent–child bond.

Only in western culture are children expected to be independent before they even know what the word means! At term, a baby is removed from the mother's warm body and placed in a strange environment from that moment forward. No heart sounds, no blood sounds rushing through veins, just voices and lights, etc. I think co-sleeping is a beautiful thing. It is as close as is humanly possible to the womb experience. My child hears my breathing, my heart sounds, and who knows, maybe even the sound of my blood rushing through my veins. I hear his heart, smell his head ('new baby' smell) and oh . . . the wonderful wonderful sound of his breathing. It can't be replaced. It's just sleeping, people. The majority of our children's lives will be spent apart from us. Think about it. Maybe those persons in other cultures have it exactly right: let's ALL sleep in the same space, just an arm's reach from one another. Westerners are so ruined by consumerism and capitalism that it makes sense for them to encourage independence early on – that way, when the time comes, they'll be able to stand on their own two feet. Ridiculous. Once your kids are teenagers and they won't have two decent words to say to you, you'll regret not letting them sleep with you, even temporarily.

Loving that 'new baby' smell

The other side operates from a very practical perspective. Their arguments highlight the long-term health benefits of children learning to sleep on their own, as well as the safety arguments that can be made against co-sleeping. The more extreme advocates of this position, when challenged by Attachment parents about being selfish and putting their convenience before the well-being of their child, reply that modelling our behaviour on other primates would require us eating faeces and fleas. The following post represents a moderate argument for adopting a 'sleep training' or 'Ferber' approach to infant sleep. This approach includes the expectation that the child will sleep in a crib/cot and will learn to 'self-soothe'. This process involves some crying on the part of the child, and some parents consequently refer to it as the CIO ('Cry It Out') or 'controlled crying' method. This parent describes her initial reluctance to adopt this approach, and demonstrates how she came to be a firm believer in it. Notice her comment at the end about her guilt.

I was 100 per cent against the Ferber Method. I bought the 'No-Cry Sleep Solution' and tried everything. From 4 months to 8 months my daughter was waking up crying every 1 or 2 hours to nurse. Finally, driven by sheer exhaustion, I tried Ferber. Before trying it, I bought a Baby Einstein bedtime CD. Every time I rocked her to sleep for 3 weeks I played the music. Then when I decided to try the CIO method, when she was tired, I put her down and played the music. I went in after 5 minutes, then 10, then 15. She was asleep before 20 minutes. I think the trick is to get them in early, and go in and talk to them at increasing intervals. (So they know you haven't abandoned them.) She now goes to bed and sleeps all night long. She sleeps from 7:30 p.m. – 6:00 a.m., nurses, then goes back to sleep until 8 a.m. Babies need to learn how to go to sleep, and yes we all wake up during the night but they should be able to fall asleep without you. After 6 months babies do not need to eat during the night. Crying does not hurt your bond or trust. My daughter is happier than ever. I am thankful I let go of my guilt. After the first night she slept wonderfully. Yea, Ferber!

If you spend any amount of time on these internet battlegrounds, you may also notice something else. Many of the parents' arguments rely on 'case studies' or 'anecdotal evidence', which we discussed in the first chapter. The basic argument goes like this: 'I handled my child's sleep by doing X and she/he has turned out beautifully. Therefore X is the proper way to handle a child's sleep.'

This argument misses a lot of important points. One is that children's temperaments vary. Another is that there are often multiple 'good' approaches to a particular problem. Yet another is that parents' temperaments vary: their parenting philosophy, anxiety levels, and stress tolerance are inescapable parts of the picture. Still another is that their goals for their infants will be quite different – one may place a high value on getting more sleep, while another may place more emphasis on spending time with their child around-the-clock. The 'anecdotal evidence' approach is like the stories about the great comedian George Burns, who died when he was 100 years of age. He was famous for lines such as 'Happiness? A good cigar, a good meal, a good cigar and a good woman – or a bad woman; it depends on how much happiness you can handle.' Relying on this anecdotal evidence would have doctors recommending at least two cigars a day, among other things. Based on anecdotal evidence, parents are routinely given advice by well-meaning friends and relatives on how to best handle their newborn's sleep.

The controversy about whether it is better for the child to co-sleep or sleep separately is complicated by the connections with the breastfeeding literature, as many breastfeeding mothers find it more convenient to keep their children in their beds. Breastfed babies sleep shorter stretches, on average, than bottle-fed babies, so they are more likely to wake up during the night, wanting to nurse. Thus, breastfeeding mothers who can just pick up the baby and nurse him don't have to get out of bed. A storm blew up a few years ago when the American Academy of Pediatrics issued guidelines recommending that parents not share beds with their infants. This was in contradiction to the international Academy of Breastfeeding Medicine's recommendations that infants should either 'bed-share' or 'co-sleep' (either in the same bed or in a crib or cot placed immediately next to the parents' bed) as a way of encouraging better breastfeeding.

Another complication in this debate has to do with what is safest for the infant. Some recommendations from child safety experts say that parents should never co-sleep with infants because of the dangers of smothering them. Other experts, particularly those who study cot death (also known as sudden infant death syndrome (SIDS)), argue that co-sleeping is better for the infant because those babies do not sleep as soundly and therefore are less likely to stop breathing. To make matters more complicated, some studies have shown that co-sleeping can increase the risk of SIDS, particularly when one of the parents smokes. These are powerful fears.

Finally, this whole question of what is best for the child also needs to include considerations about what is best for the family as a whole. Many of the parents on both sides of the argument admit that they are exhausted. This may be why emotions are so raw on this topic. These parents are often trying to work full-time and perhaps having to care for other children while subsisting on very little sleep. Postpartum depression is fuelled by this lack of sleep, and sleep-deprived parents can become irritable with children and spouses. In general, infants who bed-share or co-sleep with their parents are less likely to sleep through the night. When my breastfed daughter was only a few weeks old, I became obsessed with the topic of sleep because for a time she was sleeping for less than two hours at a stretch – I was groggy, sluggish, and had trouble concentrating. I coped by reading everything I could find on the topic of infant sleep. It was also during this time that I made plans to receive some postdoctoral training in sleep disorders, driven by the newly developed conviction that sleep was one of the most important things in life!

Normal infant sleep

It is worth summarizing what we know about normal infant sleep. Newborns have sleep that is broken into 'Active Sleep' and 'Quiet Sleep' phases. 'Active Sleep' involves a lot of twitching, head movements, and eye movements. Researchers are guessing that the purpose of this twitching is to 'map the body' by strengthening connections between body movements, sensations, and brain centres. Infants in 'Quiet Sleep' are very still, limp, and difficult to rouse. Initially, newborns have no clear pattern of day and night sleep. It is not until about 3 months of age that infants begin to develop a more mature pattern of night and day sleep.

One very important point in understanding infant sleep is that, as part of the natural sleep cycle, all of us wake many times during the night. These events are often called 'micro-awakenings', and they are visible on a sleep polysomnograph (a recording of brain waves and body movements during sleep), but generally the sleeper is unaware of them. This is because the sleeper has learned to emerge from deep sleep, move a bit, and descend back into sleep without ever becoming fully awake. So if an infant has learned to 'self-soothe' herself back to sleep, this will lead to the appearance that she slept soundly all night. On the other hand, if the infant has become accustomed to breastfeeding or being rocked back to sleep at each of these transitions, her parent will be doing those things at least twice each night. Some babies, regardless of what the parents do, are natural sleepers, and learn to quickly transition back to sleep, giving their grateful parents a long and peaceful night. These children are known as 'self-soothers'. Conversely, other babies have such difficulty with these transitions that their parents' attempts to teach them to self-soothe are stymied. These children are described in the scientific literature as 'signallers', meaning they cry or call to the parent when they are awake. Most babies fall somewhere between, having the ability to self-soothe at some awakenings, but crying for parents at other awakenings.

Having a schedule is important to children, and sleep schedules will help your child develop strong wake/sleep patterns. I would encourage parents to set up a schedule that suits them, but not to despair if they need to alter it due to changing circumstances. Flexibility is one of the most useful lessons that having children can teach us.

Some of the parenting gurus (e.g. Gina Ford) advocate a fixed sleep and eating schedule. This is certainly helpful in many situations.

However, rigid scheduling is not recommended if the baby is failing to gain weight properly, or when the baby is premature, or born at a very low weight. Some babies who are born prematurely benefit from 'kangaroo care', in which they spend all of their time in skin-to-skin contact with an adult, sleeping on the adult's chest, until they reach a gestational age of 34–38 weeks. Consult closely with your paediatrician about sleeping and feeding arrangements if you have a child who was born prematurely or who has any significant health problems.

The use of a 'transitional object', such as a small stuffed animal, a 'dummy' or pacifier, or a favourite soft blanket, can make it easier for a child to comfort herself at night. In fact, the American Academy of Pediatrics recommends the use of a pacifier, which has been found to reduce the risk of cot death or SIDS. However, this use of a pacifier ('dummy') can create sleep problems, as the child may begin to cry whenever it is lost, which can take a toll on the child and the family as well. As a parent, you must weigh these pros and cons and decide based on your preferences.

The recommendations

If we set aside the heated debates, the parenting gurus' recommendations, and the unfounded assumptions made about infant sleep and look only at the best available scientific evidence, what does research tell us about infant sleep? Some findings do emerge from the literature.

1 The safety questions about where the baby sleeps are still under fierce debate and require much more research. Clarifying the safety issues for any given family will involve careful consideration of the parents' environment, family needs, and the parents' primary goals. For instance, in areas where malaria is prevalent, bed-sharing is recommended as a way to help protect the infant by making better use of scarce mosquito netting.

In some cases, parents choose to bed-share because they are not able to afford a safe crib/cot.

2 If either adult smokes, the infant should definitely not sleep in the same room with the parents. This is probably true even if the parents are not smoking in the sleeping area, although more research remains to be done.

3 Nevertheless, after reviewing the death rates for different sleeping arrangements, three important organizations have recently released statements against the practice of bed-sharing between parents and infants. These are the UK's Department of Health, the Canadian Paediatric Society, and the American Academy of Pediatrics. These organizations do support the practice of room-sharing, which involves the baby sleeping in a crib/cot or specially designed sleeping surface placed in the parents' room.

4 If parents choose to bed-share with their baby, care must be taken that the bed should be firm, the parents should not have consumed any alcohol or drugs or be extremely fatigued, and the child should not bed-share with anyone other than the usual caregiver. Additionally, an adult and baby sleeping together on a sofa is by far the most hazardous combination. In a recent review of data from Canada, 93 per cent of cases of sudden unexpected deaths in infants occurred on nights when a new sleeping arrangement was being used for the first time (that is, a child accustomed to back-sleeping was placed on his stomach to sleep, or an infant was bed-sharing with an adult for the first time, or the baby was bed-sharing with a new adult).

5 The clearest way to reduce the risk of 'cot death' or SIDS is to put your baby to sleep on his back on a flat surface, for each nap and throughout the night. Make sure the sleep surface is firm and that there are no pillows, soft toys, or loose blankets about. This holds true regardless of whether the baby is sleeping with the parent or by himself.

6 Parental anxiety and mental health problems can contribute to babies' and toddlers' sleep problems. There is evidence that parents who are not sensitive to their

child's emotional needs tend to have children with more sleep problems. On the other hand, research shows that parents who are anxious and 'over-responsive' to children's night waking also have children with more sleep problems. One very interesting study on this was conducted by Scher and Blumberg in 1998. They looked at something they called 'maternal separation anxiety', and how that relates to infant sleep. They found that mothers who reported high separation anxiety had children who awoke more frequently and who needed greater parental involvement to calm them down. Much remains to be done on this topic. It would make sense, given the many effects of parents' depression and anxiety on children in general, that children's sleep would be affected by parents' anxiety levels.

7 One clear finding is that providing parents with education about how to use 'sleep training' behavioural techniques can be very valuable in helping children sleep through the night at an earlier age. For example, a group of 610 mothers giving birth in the UK agreed to take part in a study. They were randomly assigned to a sleep approach, which they agreed to follow for the first twelve weeks of the infant's life. The first of these was a 'behavioural approach' group. The Behavioural Group mothers were given instructions that roughly parallel the 'Ferber' approach. For example, these mothers were instructed to feed the baby between 10 p.m. and midnight (awaking the child if necessary for this), to put the baby down to sleep when the baby was still awake but drowsy, to increase daytime exposure to bright light (in the home and outdoors), and after three weeks, if the baby's weight gain was progressing satisfactorily, to begin to increase the times between night feedings.

The Educational Group mothers were given information on a variety of approaches that they could take, without recommending one in particular. The Control Group mothers received standard postpartum care and instructions (without specific sleep instructions). The researchers, headed by Professor Jennifer Sleep (I am not making this up!), took care to ensure that each of the

ntained an equal mix of breastfed and bottle-
s. They found that babies in all three groups
ping much better by the age of 12 weeks than
they had at first. However, the behavioural group of
babies were more likely to sleep at least five hours in a
row than the babies in either of the other groups. Babies
in all three groups showed equal weight gain, which
means that sleeping more soundly through the night did
not deprive the behavioural group babies of food. Additionally, the mothers in the behavioural group reported
that their approach was more convenient and easy to use
than the mothers in the other two groups reported.
Finally, the researchers contacted the mothers when
their babies were 9 months old. The mothers in the
behavioural group reported at that time that they were
more likely to have a regular bedtime routine for their
babies, and they were less likely to have asked professionals for help with crying and sleeping problems
than the mothers in the other two groups. Other studies
have found that parents who received this kind of
education about taking a behavioural approach to infant
sleep felt more competent as parents and were more
satisfied with their marriages than parents who did not
receive such education.

8 Successful breastfeeding is compatible with behavioural
approaches and avoiding co-sleeping and night nursing.
One study looking at children as young as *8 weeks* of age
found that they could sleep through the night without
breastfeeding, and that the babies compensated for this
by having a larger morning feed, so that their total
weight gain was equivalent to that of infants who were
allowed to breastfeed thoughout the night.

9 A number of different behavioural approaches are effective in helping children to sleep through the night. In
general, these approaches require the child to sleep in his
own bed. Some of the terms for these approaches are
'systematic ignoring', 'graduated withdrawal of attention', 'scheduled waking', and 'chronotherapy' (see Dr
Weissbluth's book below). A review of decades of research
shows clearly that, if the parent has a strong desire to get

more sleep at night, there is a clear advantage to sleeping in separate beds and to using a behavioural approach to infant sleep. Sleep disorder clinics can be very helpful in teaching parents how to use these techniques. Books by authors such as Mindell, Weissbluth and Ferber describe these approaches in step-by-step fashion.

10   It is also evident from a review of the literature that 'growing out of it' can work well over time. That is to say, no matter what the parent does, over time most children will learn to sleep well by the age of 5 years. However, children who are having great difficulty sleeping as babies and toddlers should be evaluated by a sleep specialist, as these problems may persist into adulthood if not given proper treatment.

11   The *worst* approach to infant sleep problems is through drugs. Physicians, when faced with desperate, tired parents, sometimes prescribe sleep medications or 'hypnotics' as a quick solution. These result in daytime drowsiness for your child, and do not work over the long term, in addition to posing unknown dangers to the child's health and brain development over time. Additionally, some parents have used alcohol for this purpose, for example by adding brandy to the baby's bottle, which is harmful to the baby's brain development and can lead to future problems with alcohol and drug dependence. The one exception to this may be the use of the hormone melatonin, which acts as a sedative and sleep regulator. It has been found to be helpful in treating sleep problems, particularly in children with seizures or developmental difficulties. In these studies, it was used in combination with behavioural techniques. For children without serious neurological problems, the behavioural approaches usually work well and should be sufficient.

12   A small controversy has developed around the issue of night lights for infants. A study published in *Nature*, a prestigious scientific journal, found that infants who slept with night lights or room lights on were at greater risk for developing myopia or near-sightedness. They

recommended having children sleep in dark rooms for the first two years of life. Other researchers dispute the findings. I would have to say that the evidence at this point is far from conclusive. Still, in weighing the potential costs and benefits, I decided for my own children that I would have them sleep in completely dark rooms. I reasoned that the human eye has adapted to sleeping in dark environments through the millennia, there is no particular benefit to leaving on a light, and there is a potential hazard. A night light is not necessary for checking your baby; simply allowing your eyes to adjust to the darkness so you can see your baby works quite well, and of course your senses of smell and hearing will tell you a great deal about how the baby is doing.

Toddlerhood/preschool years

Common problems

The sleep issues in this age range include bedtime refusal (also called 'settling problems'), jumping out of beds or cribs/cots, and wandering around the house. A lot of toddlers also discover marvellous ways of getting attention, such as removing their clothes. This is the age when fears of 'monsters' and the like begin to capture the child's imagination. It is during this time that parents must rely on creativity, imagination, and good behaviour management skills in order to handle these problems.

Many of these problems can also be avoided by good 'sleep hygiene' (in other words, good bedtime routines and sleep practices). Note that some of these problems would not be present in children still co-sleeping with their parents, although many of these children would still have 'settling problems' unless the parents went to bed with them at an early hour. These problems also might not occur with children in cultures where they are routinely allowed to fall asleep wherever they might be and at whatever hour. Still, it is notable that, in countries as diverse as China, Switzerland, Italy, and the United States, about 25 per cent of all children experience some type of distressing sleep problem.

Problems with sleep during this stage can have serious negative effects on both parents and children. For example, if bedtime becomes a huge battle and parents and children alike lose sleep as a result, parents can become more stressed, parents' driving can become dangerous due to sleep deprivation, and children can become more likely to quarrel or throw temper tantrums. Dr Lyn Quine (see Kent University website, below) provides a helpful checklist for parents in order to determine whether their child has a 'sleep problem'. Her list includes the following signs in your child, which are problematic if they occur more than two or three times per week:

- Refusal to go to bed, bedtime battles, or taking a long time to settle to sleep
- Refusal to go to sleep unless you lie down with him
- Coming downstairs repeatedly or crying or calling out for you
- Progressively later bedtimes
- Waking at night and calling out for you
- Coming into your bedroom or insisting on sharing your bed on a regular basis
- Early waking (before 5 a.m.)

Dr Quine also provides a list of parent symptoms that the child has a sleep problem, including negative feelings toward the child at bedtime, feeling tired all the time, and shouting at the child. She describes the positive benefits to families who receive treatment for a child's sleep problems. These include less stress, happier marriages, less irritability, and less hitting of children. For the children who receive the treatment, they show better concentration, less irritability, and greater happiness and affection-giving.

Recommendations

The best approaches to these problems are preventative. In other words, if the parent has established some clear patterns during the child's infancy, they are less likely to arise. The following recommendations for good 'sleep hygiene' at this age come from Drs Mindell and Owens. These include the following:

- Develop a daily sleep schedule that is regular and pre-dictable and does not include late afternoon naps.
- Encourage use of a security object.
- Develop a bedtime routine (involving calming, non-frightening activities such as bath, story time, or songs), the last two activities occurring in the child's bedroom.
- Set up a consistent bedroom environment that does not include a television. A night light is acceptable.
- Put your toddler to bed drowsy but awake.
- Set limits on behaviours that disrupt good sleep.

Many other behavioural problems at this age can be forestalled with some imagination on the part of the parent. For example, parents who are planning to move a child from a crib/cot to a toddler bed can make the experience positive by throwing a 'big bed party' or by using rewards for the child who makes a successful transition to the bed. For example, the time-honoured 'star chart' works well for this and many other purposes. With a star chart, the child earns a sticker for every night in which he sleeps well in his new bed. After he earns enough stickers (the number to be based on the child's developmental level and the parents' judgement), the child earns a desired reward. One good way to proceed is to start with a small number, for example two or three nights. Once the child has had some success, gradually increase the number of stickers the child needs to earn before receiving his reward. A creative spin on the star chart would be if the toddler or preschooler wants the popular glow-in-the-dark stars pasted up on his bedroom ceiling. He could earn one of them for every good night, until the packet of stars is used up. By that time, the child will likely have established good sleep habits and the reward system can be phased out.

Childhood (6–12 years of age)

Problems

Here I will list a number of troublesome sleep disorders that can occur at any age, including adulthood, but that often appear during the school years. These include the following:

1 Sleepwalking is most likely to be seen during these years, due to changes in sleep 'architecture' (the pattern of brain waves).
2 Night-time fears and nightmares are common at this age. These problems respond well to simple treatments including helping the child talk about what is bothering her, reading books about children who conquered their fears, etc. Relaxation training also works well for this. Some children respond very well to an intervention in which they are encouraged to 'fix' the scary dream. In other words, if they awaken after a bad dream, they learn to recognize that it was just a dream, and to imagine a positive ending in which they defeat the monster, find their missing loved one, or whatever makes them feel most comforted or entertained.
3 Sleep terrors, in which children partially awaken and are inconsolable. This problem, along with many similar sleep problems such as head-banging, tends to disappear as the child grows older.
4 'Over-arousal.' This may be due to excessive caffeine intake, watching thrilling or exciting television in the evening, or not having a regular bedtime.
5 Obstructive sleep apnoea, resulting in snoring, gasping, mouth-breathing, and restless sleep. This disorder requires a medical evaluation.
6 Nocturnal eating or drinking syndrome. This is a pattern in which the child awakens and is unable to go back to sleep without eating or drinking.

Recommendations

Again, I will borrow from Drs Mindell and Owens and their book with recommendations for physicians evaluating children's sleep problems. They suggest the following, along with many recommendations already given for toddlers and preschoolers, such as a regular bedtime routine:

- Maintain a consistent bedtime routine, preferably one that includes some regular parent/child talk time.
- Set up a soothing environment.
- Set limits.
- Turn off televisions, computers, and radios.
- Avoid caffeine.

Other researchers recommend being aware of ways in which parents may unconsciously be reinforcing problems, such as attending to your child only when he wakes up crying and frightened. They also suggest examining the family schedule to determine whether problems getting to sleep have to do with the fact that the child no longer needs to get to bed so early.

A variant of the 'star chart' can be used successfully for the school-aged child who is having problems with spending the entire night in her/his bed. Some sleep specialists use the following technique: begin with buying a packet of 'tokens', poker chips, or similar markers. Each night, give your child one at bedtime. These tokens are redeemable for one night-time request or contact with the parent. When the child redeems the token, for example by making a night-time trip into the parents' bedroom, the parent takes the token. If the child saves up tokens by spending entire nights in her/his own bed, the child can redeem the saved tokens for other valued activities such as a special weekend trip, a longed-for toy, time doing something extra with the parent, etc. Thus, it is in the child's interest to be sparing in the use of night-time visits to parents, but this technique still preserves that option for cases in which the child has had a bad nightmare and really needs comfort from the parents.

Another problem that continues to haunt some children at this age is 'enuresis', or bed-wetting. In addition to being a bother to the parents, enuresis is horribly embarrassing to the child who needs to avoid going to friends' houses, has to make excuses to avoid camping trips, and the like. This problem is sometimes dealt with by giving medication to the child that makes it more difficult to urinate, but that is probably the worst approach. Instead, use of the 'alarm pad' or 'bell pad' will make it possible to eliminate the problem in just a few nights, without drugs. This technique makes use of a moisture-sensitive microchip in a pad placed on the bed, which rings an alarm when the child urinates. This wakes up the child the second he/she begins to urinate, and is much more effective in helping the child gain night-time control over urination than other techniques.

Adolescence

Problems

A number of problems with sleep tend to arise during adolescence, some of them very serious in their consequences. These are as follows:

1 Serious sleeplessness. This can be due to worries and anxiety about school, friends, or sports. It can also be due to excessive late-night use of electronic devices, talking with friends, watching movies, and the like.
2 'Delayed phase sleep syndrome', which is related to the adolescent's brain maturation. A serious mismatch tends to occur in modern society between the adolescent's natural inclination to stay up late and sleep late, and the need to get up early due to school schedules, family routines, etc. This can result in chronic sleep deprivation for adolescents.
3 Psychological disorders such as anxiety, depression, and bipolar disorder can be aggravated by sleeplessness, or they may actually be the cause of either sleeplessness or excessive sleepiness.
4 Use of legal or illegal substances can greatly damage sleep quality. Caffeine is a major problem, but any stimulants, other drugs, and alcohol can all contribute to serious sleep problems. Smoking is often associated with poorer sleep as well.

5 Power struggles with parents can be focused on this topic. In some families, the more parents push the teenager to go to bed early, the less likely that is to happen.

There are many consequences of this inadequate sleep for the adolescent. Most sleep researchers recommend that adolescents get between nine and nine and a half hours of sleep. Not getting enough sleep tends to result in moodiness, irritability, impulsively engaging in risky behaviours, not functioning as well intellectually, poor academic performance, and falling asleep while driving.

Recommendations

Again, here are some of Mindell and Owens's recommendations for this age:

- Maintain a regular sleep schedule.
- Avoid oversleeping on weekends, as it will disrupt sleep during the week.
- Take an early afternoon nap (30–45 minutes).
- Turn off televisions, computers, DVDs, and radios at bedtime, and avoid highly exciting, scary or stimulating activities before bedtime.
- Avoid caffeine, smoking, alcohol and drugs.

Other recommendations include the usual guidelines for dealing successfully with a teenager. First, having established a warm and caring relationship early in childhood goes a long way toward making parent/child relationships work well in adolescence. Second, recognize your teenager's need for increased autonomy and increased involvement in decision-making. Thus, providing the adolescent with more information about sleep and discussing possible alternatives together can work very well.

Remember, too, that teenagers who show marked behavioural changes or who seem very moody may be dealing with psychological problems such as depression or anxiety, or drug use. It can be extremely helpful to talk this over with your adolescent, and to schedule an appointment for them with a competent psychologist or other psychothera-pist. Upon doing that, however, pay attention to the general feelings your child has toward that therapist, because a good therapist/client relationship is essential for effective-ness. If your teenager sees the therapist as cold or distant or otherwise incompetent, find another therapist!

Parent sleep

One last word on childhood sleep is actually about the parents. Parenting is full of challenges, all of which become more difficult when the parent is chronically sleep-deprived. Granted, occasional sleepless nights if your child is ill or has a nightmare are inevitable for any parent. Still, there are some things you can do in order to maximize the amount of sleep that you get. Many of the recommendations for parents are similar to those for children and adolescents. One common misconception among adults has to do with using alcohol or sleeping pills in order to go to sleep. While these drugs do help people get to sleep, they do not work over the long term, they reduce the quality of your sleep, and they can lead to 'rebound insomnia', or worsened sleep when the person stops taking them.

One problem I had, early in my infants' lives, was that I would get up to nurse them, change their nappies, and then be wide awake. This helps me understand why a number of my patients who seek treatment for insomnia first devel-oped the problem when they were parents of newborns. Fortunately, being a clinical psychologist has three bene-fits, and understanding something about human sleep patterns is one of them. I was able to remind myself that it would do me good to lie in bed and just breathe deeply and relax. Another useful technique involved giving myself instructions *not* to go to sleep, as I knew that trying to sleep is the most harmful thing you can do if you are sleepless. Yet a third involved imagining pleasant activities such as hiking in the mountains with friends. These techniques allowed me to drift back off to sleep without any problems.

Several of the major sleep foundations have excellent lists of ideas for how to improve your own sleep. These include the National Sleep Foundation and the Royal College of Psychiatrists, on whose websites you can find information about sleep disorders, sleeplessness, and strategies you can use to improve the quality of your own sleep. Other excellent resources are the Glovinsky and Spielman and Jacobs books on insomnia, which I list below.

The Bottom Line

- **What are the key dilemmas parents have to struggle with on this topic?**
  - Should we co-sleep with our baby?
  - Should breastfed babies nurse ad lib throughout the night?
  - Should babies be rocked to sleep or put to bed awake?
  - Is it a good idea to use a 'dummy' or 'pacifier'?
- **What does the science say about this topic?**
  - Co-sleeping is still controversial, and there are strong cultural biases both for and against it; it requires some safety precautions and should not be done if the parent is obese, or a smoker, or if the parent has consumed alcohol or any medications (including antihistamines) before sleep. Parents who want to co-sleep would be better off to choose the type of baby bed that pulls up next to the parents' bed, so the child can be next to the parent but has a separate sleeping surface.
  - Breastfeeding need not be done ad lib throughout the night past the first few weeks of life.
  - What is incontrovertible is that parents who put the baby to sleep while the baby is still awake, following recommendations of such researchers as Dr Mindell and other behavioural sleep specialists, are rewarded with children who sleep far better. Additionally, children who learn to sleep under these conditions are less at risk for sleep disorders later in life.
  - The 'dummy debate' is still not resolved by science.
- **What do the authors advise?**
  - My personal preference is against using a pacifier or 'dummy', though the science is unclear.

- Definitely teach your baby to go to sleep on his or her own, whether or not you choose to co-sleep most of the time. Unless you take every nap with your baby, this will happen naturally anyway. The process will involve some crying, but most babies make the adjustment very quickly and ultimately everyone in the family will be more rested and less irritable.
- I would also suggest that, since babies are very flexible and can thrive under a variety of circumstances, you decide on an approach without being too dogmatic, see if it works, and consult with your nurse practitioner or paediatrician if your chosen approach is not working.
- Also, keep in mind that children's sleep is quite affected by your anxiety level. So relax, understand that this is a natural process that will improve over time, and do not tie yourself in emotional knots by trying to do it perfectly.

Recommended reading for parents

Ferber, R. (1986). *Solve your child's sleep problems*. London: Dorling Kindersley.

Glovinsky, P. and Spielman, A. (2006). *The insomnia answer: Groundbreaking solutions for getting to sleep, staying asleep, broken sleep*. London: Penguin Books.

Jacobs, G. (1998). *Say good night to insomnia*. New York: Henry Holt Books.

Kent University Department of Psychology. Sleep problems in young children. www.kent.ac.uk/psychology/department/people/quinel/sleep-problems.html

Mindell, J. (1997). *Sleeping through the night: How infants, toddlers, and their parents can get a good night's sleep*. New York: HarperCollins.

Quine, L. (1997). *Solving children's sleep problems*. Huntingdon: Beckett Karlson Ltd.

Royal College of Psychiatrists. Factsheet from Mental Health and Growing Up (3rd edn). Sleep problems in childhood and adolescence. http://www.rcpsych.ac.uk/info/mhgu/newmhgu7.htm

Weissbluth, M. (1999). *Healthy sleep habits, happy child*. New York: Fawcett Books.

Recommended resources for paediatricians

Canadian Paediatric Society (2004). Recommendations for safe sleeping environments for infants and children. http://www.cps.ca/english/statements/CP/cp04-02.htm

Mindell, J. and Owens, J. (2003). *A clinical guide to paediatric sleep: Diagnosis and management of sleep problems*. London: Lippincott Williams & Wilkins.

Owens, J. (2004). Sleep in children: Cross-cultural perspectives. *Sleep and Biological Rhythms*, 2, 165–173.

Stores, G. (2001). *A clinical guide to sleep disorders in children and adolescents*. Cambridge: Cambridge University Press.

Breastfeeding vs. bottle – dilemmas in infant nutrition

Banks

Choosing the right nutrition for your baby can seem like an insurmountable challenge, yet babies become toddlers, and toddlers ultimately become teens, and teens – after creating havoc for all – ultimately become adults. Whether those adults become Members of Parliament is unlikely to rely solely on whether those individuals were breastfed or formula-fed as infants. However, choosing the proper form of nutrition for your child should include consideration of the benefits and shortcomings of each form, as well as consideration for what would work well within your lifestyle.

While feeding your baby ideally should be a time of joy and not a source of stress, reality sometimes has other plans. One of the authors (E.S.) tells the story of her first experience with breastfeeding, which drives home the point that a process that should come 'naturally' does not always come easily but requires patience and practice. Esther relates:

> I vividly remember the first night back at home after the birth of my first child. Laura was a healthy baby, things had gone OK in the hospital, I was familiar with the scientific literature on breastfeeding, and I expected things to go fairly well. We lived in an old house and, in accordance with Murphy's Law, the furnace stopped working during that first cold October night home with the baby. So I sat in a freezing room on a rocking chair which suddenly seemed *so* much more uncomfortable to

sit on than it had pre-baby, not sure if I was feeding this baby properly, groggy from sleep, worried about whether my husband would be able to get the heat on again, tense and in pain. Fortunately, things improved from that point and my babies did well with breastfeeding, but that night gave me real compassion for parents who decide that breastfeeding is too difficult. I have since come to believe that breastfeeding is one of the most important parenting decisions that you can make.

Infant nutrition

Breast milk

It is well established that breast milk is the best form of nutrition for young infants. Even before the baby is born, the mother's body is busy preparing the important, nutrient-rich precursor of breast milk, called *colostrum*, which is released from the breasts and which can sustain an infant until the mother begins producing adequate amounts of breast milk. This colostrum has a high concentration of protein (especially antibodies for fighting infection) and a milk sugar called 'lactose', which gives the baby much of its early calories. As the breast milk 'comes in' two to four days after delivery, the colostrum is replaced with larger volumes of more mature breast milk.

Breast milk is essentially nature's perfect food source and contains nearly every nutrient to keep an infant healthy. While breast milk appears thinner than commercial formula, it is packed with nutrients. Like colostrum, breast milk contains antimicrobial products such as antibodies and white blood cells to help the infant fight off infection; it takes about six years for a child to develop a mature immune system, so the antibodies supplied in breast milk provide important protection against infection during the most vulnerable period of infancy. There are higher concentrations of lipids, or fats, in mature breast milk compared to colostrum; these lipids serve as the main energy source for growing infants.

Many new mothers spend the early postpartum days trying to lose the weight that pregnancy bestowed upon them. This is certainly understandable. However, it is not always necessary, or desirable, for those mothers to indulge in extreme dieting programmes. In fact, breastfeeding results in additional modest weight loss for many women. It is important for the mother to maintain her own nutrition when she is breastfeeding. While moderate amounts of dieting or weight loss (approximately 0.5 kilogram per week) after delivery have little effect on lactation, mothers must consume adequate numbers of calories daily to sustain sufficient milk production, and mothers should increase the intake of certain vitamins and minerals, such as vitamin D, folic acid, calcium, phosphorus and magnesium while breastfeeding. Prenatal vitamins are a good source of these nutrients and should be taken until the mother is ready to wean the infant from breast milk, although the need for vitamin D supplementation in some women may exceed the amounts found in prenatal vitamins. Since vitamin D in the body is 'activated' by sunlight, darker skinned infants – or other infants growing up in climates with limited sunlight exposure – may develop deficiencies of that vitamin, resulting in soft bones (rickets); these infants are likely to need vitamin D supplements while breastfeeding. It is also important for breastfeeding mothers to drink plenty of fluids (on average about a litre of extra fluid daily) in order to produce adequate amounts of breast milk.

The quality of breastfeeding depends in large part on the hormones that trigger the release of breast milk. Tactile triggers, such as nipple stimulation, are important, as are certain visual cues (such as the sight of your infant), sounds (such as the cry of your baby), or even particular aromas that are associated with breastfeeding time. Each of these stimuli can cause a surge of hormones which signal the breasts to release milk in preparation for feeding. This makes the initiation of breastfeeding quite simple for both mother and infant, although hearing another infant cry may trigger 'false alarms' that result in milk release at inopportune times.

By the same token, stressors or other unpleasant experiences can have a negative impact on breastfeeding. Fatigue, pain or anxiety can diminish milk release and interfere with successful feeding. Lack of support from family members can also greatly affect the success of breastfeeding attempts; if the spouse or significant other is not supportive, the mother is more likely to abandon the process altogether. Several studies done in the UK have looked at attitudes toward breastfeeding. It is clear in these studies that much of the negative opinion toward breast-feeding centres on misconceptions or lack of knowledge regarding breastfeeding. However, a significant factor in determining whether a mother will breastfeed successfully is the influence of family attitudes. Fathers seem consist-ently concerned about the implications of breastfeeding in public as well as concerned about how much milk the infant actually receives while nursing. Programmes directed at educating family members regarding the benefits and mech-anics of breastfeeding, as well as ways to provide maternal support for breastfeeding, have made an impact on the likelihood that a mother will breastfeed her baby success-fully for a longer duration.

To improve the success of breastfeeding, it is important to begin the process as soon after delivery as possible, preferably while still in the delivery room. Infants who begin breastfeeding within thirty minutes of birth are more alert and have stronger suckling reflexes and are more likely to continue breastfeeding successfully beyond two to four months postpartum. The early feeding ritual is an important part of the bonding process, and infants are more likely to benefit by having higher core body temperatures and better temperature stability after delivery.

The early hours after delivery are important for maternal bonding and for establishing good breastfeeding practices. A mother who chooses to breastfeed should request that her infant be permitted to stay in the hospital room with her, if the child is doing well medically. This will give the mother an opportunity to observe the infant and begin to learn the baby's signals that indicate when he or she is hungry, and it will enable the mother to nurse on demand. Having the liberty to nurse frequently will aid the mother in becoming comfortable with different nursing positions, finding the position that works best for the baby, and avoiding breast engorgement and reducing nipple soreness. It is most helpful to take advantage of resources such as lactation consultants, if they are available; these individuals are useful in evaluating the mother and infant as breastfeeding occurs and in making recommendations to address breastfeeding difficulties.

Infants who are breastfeeding must master a specific way of coordinating tongue and sucking actions in order to feed efficiently. These tongue and sucking mechanics are different from the techniques required for feeding from a bottle. Because newborns can develop 'nipple confusion' if presented with too many options, breastfed infants should feed exclusively from the breast for at least three to four weeks before being introduced to a 'dummy' pacifier or bottle; this will allow adequate time for the infant to perfect the nursing technique and prevent the infant from preferring the bottle over the breast. Early use of a dummy or pacifier has been shown to reduce the frequency and overall duration of breastfeeding, which reduces the benefits of long-term breastfeeding.

Because the amount of breast milk the infant receives cannot be directly measured, a common concern of mothers is whether their babies are receiving enough nutrition. This is especially true with young infants who are just learning to nurse. Breastfed infants should nurse eight to ten times per day. While most of the milk is obtained within the first five minutes on each breast, the more calorie-rich 'hind milk' is delivered to the baby after the first five minutes. Mothers can feel reassured if the infant makes gulping sounds while feeding, or if the breast is being drawn into the infant's mouth while feeding, and if the infant can be heard to breathe through the nose between swallows. The mother may also be able to detect throat movement after each swallow, which indicates that the breast milk is passing into the infant's mouth and stomach. Adequate hydration is reflected in the number of wet nappies an infant produces each day. As a general rule, a well hydrated infant should have at least one wet nappy for each day of life, up to six days. For example, a 3-day-old infant should have three wet nappies; after six days, infants should have six or more wet nappies. And while newborn infants typically lose weight for the first few days of life, breastfed infants should be back to their birth weights within two weeks. Infants not meeting these targets should be evaluated by their physicians.

While contending with these uncertainties and lifestyle challenges may seem overwhelming to some new parents, the benefits of breastfeeding to both infant and mother far exceed the nuisances. Infants who breastfeed are less likely to develop eczema and allergies, diabetes, or inflammatory bowel disease, or die from sudden infant death syndrome (SIDS) than are formula-fed infants. These infants also experience fewer ear infections, urinary tract infections, or respiratory infections such as pneumonia or respiratory syncitial virus (RSV), and they are less likely to require hospitalization. Some studies suggest that breastfed infants may experience greater cognitive development and higher IQs, although some larger-scale studies and meta-analyses do not confirm a significant effect on IQ.

Mothers also derive benefits from breastfeeding. Early breastfeeding reduces postpartum blood loss and anaemia. There is less likelihood of premenopausal breast or ovarian cancer among mothers who breastfeed, as well as a lower incidence of osteoporosis and subsequent hip fractures after menopause. Women who breastfeed also tend to lose more weight following delivery. Because frequent, regularly scheduled breastfeeding (eight or more times daily) maintains higher levels of certain pregnancy hormones, ovulation is delayed in women who exclusively breastfeed and there is less likelihood of unintended pregnancy, although this is an unreliable method of contraception and should not be used alone for the prevention of pregnancy.

In all fairness, there are also some little-recognized benefits for the father and the family as a whole. Because of the cost of commercial infant formulas, there are considerable cost savings with breastfeeding. There is also less demand for fathers to stumble blindly into the kitchen late at night to warm a bottle, although I recommend – based on no clinical evidence but merely on personal experience and the fact that I am still happily married – it is important for the father to remain a part of the breastfeeding process, whether it be assisting in mealtime nappy changes, burping the baby, or giving mummy a nice massage while the baby feeds.

Breastfeeding is not without its drawbacks, however. In addition to the initial social awkwardness (whether real or imagined) that may accompany breastfeeding in public venues, some mothers have extreme difficulty with the process of breastfeeding. While one might expect breast-feeding to be a natural process that mothers instinctively master, it can be a technical challenge that drives some mothers and infants to despair. Even for those who perse-vere and succeed, setbacks can occur. A significant number of breastfeeding mothers can develop a condition known as mastitis, a painful inflammatory condition of the breast characterized by localized tenderness and redness, fever, fatigue, body aches and headaches. A number of factors can contribute to this condition, including improper attach-ment, cracks in the nipples, the use of manual breast pumps, and blocked milk ducts. While the mother's first inclination may be to stop nursing on the affected breast, it is usually best to continue the feedings regularly and frequently, to prevent milk from pooling in the breast and leading to the development of an abscess. Warm com-presses and massage are also helpful, although in many cases antibiotics are necessary. It is safe for the infant to continue feeding from the affected breast, because the infant is likely to be already colonized with the same organisms that are infecting the breast. In addition, Buescher and Hair (2001) have demonstrated that milk from mastitis-stricken breasts contains anti-inflammatory agents that can help protect the infant further.

Commercial formula

Obviously, breastfeeding is not for everyone. Some breasts are just not very amenable to nursing effectively or efficiently, despite the number of gadgets and tricks that are available to assist, and breastfeeding becomes more of a struggle for some mothers than it is a bonding or nurturing experience. In fact, some infants do not seem to have the temperament for breastfeeding. Some parents may decide that breastfeeding cannot be accommodated by their lifestyles, or they may experience difficulties with breast-feeding that make them uncomfortable continuing the process. In some cases, lack of family support or lack of public awareness can steer mothers away from the breast-feeding option. In rare cases, breastfeeding failure can result in significant health hazards for the infant, if the infant is not gaining sufficient weight. For all of these reasons, commercial infant formula remains a viable and appropriate option.

Most commercial infant formulas use pasteurized cow's milk as the basic ingredient, although some have a soy-based substrate. Other nutrients such as vitamins, miner-als, whey proteins, carbohydrates and fats are added. Vegetable oils are typically added to provide the formula with its creamy consistency as well as providing a source of nutritional fat that more closely resembles the fats in human milk. For infants with feeding difficulties such as severe reflux, formulas can be thickened with substances such as cornstarch or cereal to reduce episodes of vomiting.

While the nutritional content of formulas can be mani-pulated to mimic breast milk, commercial formula cannot yet replicate the immunity factors that are found in human breast milk and which confer protection against some infections in young infants. Studies also suggest that formula-fed infants are more likely to develop adult obesity, diabetes, heart disease and high blood pressure, compared to infants who are breastfed. Some of this may be more related to the rate of weight gain that infants experience early in life, rather than to the use of formula itself. For example, a recent study by Singhal and colleagues com-pared the use of standard formula and nutrient-enriched formula (high-calorie formula) in infants born 'small for gestational age'. Infants fed the nutrient-enriched formula had more rapid weight gain during the first nine months of life and were more likely to have higher blood pressure (a risk factor for heart disease) at 6 to 8 years of age, compared to children who received the standard formula and had slower weight gain. Interestingly – and very importantly – similar findings were noted in a group of breastfed infants in the same study: breastfed infants with rapid early weight gain were more likely to have higher blood pressure later in childhood, compared to breastfed infants with slower weight gain. Thus, the rate of weight gain may be just as important as the nutritional source when we examine long-term risks of chronic illnesses such as hypertension and heart disease.

Colic

Since some theories suggest infantile colic is related to diet or intolerance to diet, it is appropriate to mention this subject now, although – in truth – little is still known about the causes of colic. There is general agreement, however, that colic is extremely unpleasant and offers additional challenges to parents who may already be overwhelmed by the challenges of caring for their new infant. Colic occurs in up to 30 per cent of newborns. While many parents attribute fussiness to colic, there is a standard definition that determines whether an infant truly has colic. Infants who have unexplained paroxysms of crying lasting three or more hours per day, for three or more days per week for a minimum of three weeks, would qualify as suffering from colic. These symptoms usually begin around the second week of life and usually resolve spontaneously by the third month, although some will persist until 5 months of age. Infants with colic will typically have prolonged episodes of crying that are difficult to console, along with facial flushing, and they will frequently draw up their legs and pass gas. To make matters more frustrating, these episodes usually occur in the late afternoon or evening when the parents are already fatigued.

Some have proposed that colic is related to lactose intolerance or allergies to certain food products such as cow's milk protein or substances in breast milk that are related to the mother's diet. Others have postulated that

re gut motility plays a role by causing abdominal
normal levels of normal gut bacteria may also play
a ... by interfering with proper digestion and creating
more gas, leading to abdominal distension and pain.
Another school of thought is that colic is more prevalent
among infants with difficult temperaments or in house-
holds where parenting skills are less than optimal and
maternal–infant bonding may be impaired.

Given all of these theories, it is unlikely that there is a
single cause for all cases of colic, and finding the correct
treatment may rely more on intuition or guesswork rather
than on clear, scientific foundation. However, a substantial
amount of research has been directed toward the treatment
of colic, and some methods have been validated while
others have fallen by the wayside as ineffective or even
potentially harmful.

Simethicone is found in a number of anti-gas products
and has been used widely to combat the symptoms of colic;
however, most studies show that simethicone has little or
no effect on crying episodes or 'gassy' symptoms and that
giving the baby a placebo works just as well. One medication, dicyclomine, has been effective for the symptoms of
colic, but because of its side-effect profile and the potential
harm to infants, it is no longer recommended for use in
young infants. Studies on the use of lactase, an enzyme
that can be added to milk products to aid in digestion of
milk sugars for lactose-intolerant individuals, have had
mixed results; while most studies show lactase-treated
formula has little effect on the symptoms of colic, limited
studies have suggested that symptoms can be reduced in
infants with true lactose intolerance.

For breastfed infants with colic, altering the maternal
diet can improve (but not eliminate) symptoms for some
infants, especially if dairy products, soy, wheat, eggs, nuts
and fish are withheld from the mother's diet. The use of
hypoallergenic formulas may have similar effects for bottle-
fed infants, and some infants with colic may improve with
soy-based formulas, as well. The use of herbal teas containing camomile, vervain, licorice, fennel and balm-mint
has been effective in reducing the symptoms of colic;

however, it is conceivable that these remedies could negatively impact the nutrition of infants by reducing the
calorie intake from breast milk or formula, and they
probably should not be used on a frequent basis.

Behavioural interventions such as carrying the infant
more regularly probably have little effect on the frequency
or duration of colic symptoms, although it is certainly not
harmful to the infant or the parent. On the other hand,
reducing infant stimulation may be helpful, although
design flaws in the relevant studies may overestimate the
effectiveness of this intervention. Gimmicks such as 'car
ride simulators' have been no more effective than placebo
on the symptoms of colic, as pointed out in an excellent
systematic review of colic treatments by Garrison and
Christakis.

Given the lack of a single identifiable source for colic,
and a variety of treatment options that are of variable
effectiveness, colic remains a frustrating problem for
parents – and often for any other humans within earshot.
It is not uncommon for the parents' distress to rise to levels
equalling the distress of the infant, and it is amazing that
those poor parents can function at all. During these times
of distress, it is important that the parents have a 'back-up
plan' on how to manage their infant and themselves. It is
helpful for the parent to be able to call a relative or trusted
friend to watch the frenzied child while the parent escapes
the fray for a short time, in order to engage in a little
parental self-soothing. While challenging, it is important to
remember that most parents have been in similar situations, and that children eventually outgrow this distressing phase.

Transitioning to solid foods

As with many issues in medicine, there has been dis-
agreement about when to introduce solid foods to infants
and for how long to continue exclusive breastfeeding. Much
of the debate has focused on the health effects of breastfeeding exclusively for six months versus introducing solid
foods at 4 months of age while continuing breastfeeding.

According to some well designed meta-analyses (the highest level of evidence which is based on careful analysis of existing research), infants who breastfeed exclusively for six months grow just as well as infants who begin eating solid foods at 4 months of age while breastfeeding, and they maintain better immunity against certain infections such as viral diarrhoea. In addition, mothers of the exclusively breastfed infants continue to benefit from faster weight loss. However, there is some evidence that infants in developing countries who exclusively breastfeed for six months may be more prone to developing anaemia (low red blood cell counts), so that iron supplements may be helpful. Nevertheless, both the World Health Organization and the UK Department of Health recommend exclusive breastfeeding for six months before introducing solid foods.

Infants will typically achieve the motor skills and coordination necessary to eat solid foods between 4 and 6 months of age, although many paediatricians recommend waiting until 6 months of age to introduce the first solid foods, even if the infant is formula-fed. In the past, much of the driving force behind this recommendation was to reduce the potential for developing food allergies or other allergy-related conditions such as eczema or asthma. However, these beliefs were based on inconsistent evidence, and more recent studies suggest that there is minimal risk in introducing solid foods after 4 months of age (with the exceptions of soya beans, nuts and cocoa, which should be introduced after 6 months of age, and with the exception of honey, which should not be introduced until 12 months due to the risk of botulism contamination). Infants whose close relatives suffer from significant allergies may be at higher risk of developing allergies themselves; for these infants, exclusive breastfeeding for six months may offer some protective benefit. It should be mentioned that introducing cow's milk before 12 months of age may be harmful to the infant by triggering inflammation and slow bleeding in the intestinal tract, which can lead to anaemia. Breast milk or commercial formula should be used until the infant has reached 12 months of age, regardless of when solid foods are introduced. The Department of Health in the UK has an excellent publication on weaning infants to solid foods; while the publication continues to advocate waiting until 6 months to introduce solid foods, it provides an excellent discussion on how to introduce new foods and maintain a nutritious balance of solid foods and breast milk or formula.

Breastfeeding mothers should realize that as solid foods become a more prevalent part of the infant's diet, there will be less demand for breast milk. As the infant drinks less breast milk, the mother's breasts will produce less. However, it is important that the infant continues to receive a significant portion of his or her calorie intake from breast milk (or formula, if the infant is formula-fed), even after the introduction of solid foods.

Poor appetites

Parents frequently worry when their child's appetite changes, particularly if there is a sudden decline in appetite. However, this is a naturally occurring phenomenon that reflects the nutritional needs of the child as the metabolism changes. The most rapid growth occurs during the first year of life. After the age of 1, growth and metabolism slow for a period of time, so that young children do not require as many calories. These children will require less food intake; forcing the child to eat when he or she is truly not hungry will only lead to frustration for the parent and child and could possibly lead to health problems or eating disorders later in life. A good rule of thumb for parents is to control the timing and content of meals, but allow the young child to determine the amount that is eaten. Provide small portion sizes and allow your child to ask for more, rather than piling the plate high with food and expecting her to eat everything. To ensure that the child will eat appropriately, nutritious snacks should be limited between meals and water should be provided if the child becomes thirsty. Juice should be limited, since it typically has a high sugar and caloric content and can interfere with appetite.

Refusing to eat may be something completely different. While refusal to eat is sometimes caused by an underlying medical condition such as gastric reflux, cystic fibrosis, or a psychological disorder, it is often related to 'sensory food aversions', in which a child finds particular foods distasteful (on the basis of taste, aroma, appearance or texture). We can certainly all relate to having certain foods we would prefer to avoid; I, for one, have always had an aversion to glands and organs, and it would probably require the efforts of three large men and a crowbar (or powerful sedation) to force a food from those categories down my gullet. However, children with widespread food aversions can develop significant nutritional deficiencies. Perhaps the best way to avoid this situation is to introduce new foods gradually to infants. Physicians typically suggest that only one new food be introduced at a time to infants, once they reach the age of 4 to 6 months. Small amounts of the new food should be repeatedly offered at each meal until the infant becomes accustomed to it and demonstrates that he or she can tolerate it. Older children, such as toddlers, are more prone to suggestion and are more likely to try a new food if they see the parent eating it.

Nutrition for toddlers

The toddler years can be quite challenging as these children attempt to develop independent eating behaviours. The dietary patterns they develop during these formative years can have a significant impact on their overall health as adults. It is during this period that children master the dexterity to feed themselves (although they will inevitably end up wearing a portion of their meals on their clothing), and it is also during this period that the children learn appropriate behaviour at mealtimes. While toddlers can be choosy eaters, they will continue to experience new foods – some of which will only be accepted after repeated exposure. Good meal 'hygiene' is important during this period: meals should be eaten at the table with the family, and the television should be turned off. The toddler will then be able to observe and sample the foods that the parents eat and will be able to participate in mealtime discussions.

Most dietary recommendations for young children are based on expert opinion or consensus panel reports, rather than on consistent, solid, well designed scientific studies. However, certain recommendations seem prudent. After the age of 12 months, cow's milk becomes an important dietary staple. Two or three servings daily are necessary to provide adequate amounts of calcium, vitamin D and vitamin A in the diet. On the other hand, juice should be limited and sweetened beverages such as fizzy drinks should be avoided altogether, as a number of studies suggest that excessive weight gain, dental problems and poor nutrition are related to the consumption of those beverages.

Allen and Myers report that while adults need to be aware of the fat content of their own meals, the American Academy of Pediatrics recommends *no* restrictions on fat or cholesterol for children younger than 2 years, since these provide a good source of calories and nutrients for growth and brain development. However, after the age of 2 years, only about 30 per cent of total calories should come from fats, and polyunsaturated fats should be the most prevalent form. Vegetables and fruits should be a mainstay of the toddler diet, as these will provide critical vitamins as well as important sources of fibre.

Vitamin supplements for children

Infants who are breastfed typically receive adequate supplies of most vitamins and minerals, with the possible exception of vitamin D. While vitamin D can be synthesized in the skin after exposure to sunlight, infants with darker skin filter out much of the ultraviolet light and therefore cannot produce adequate vitamin D from sunlight; infants living in climates or cultures where there is limited sunlight exposure have similar deficiencies. This deficiency can result in rickets, which is still a problem in the United Kingdom, especially among immigrant communities. It is therefore advisable that at-risk infants receive vitamin D supplements until they begin receiving adequate doses in fortified dairy products. In fact, some older children do not receive adequate vitamin D in their diets, and supplementation may be necessary until their diets provide at least five micrograms (200 IU) daily.

Older children who are healthy and eat a varied diet are likely to receive adequate nutrition without requiring special supplements. However, children with chronic diseases, children in impoverished communities where adequate nutrition may be limited, or children who are vegetarians may benefit from multivitamin supplements. It is nevertheless important to *avoid* exceeding the recommended daily amounts of certain vitamins and minerals, such as vitamin A and iron, since they can accumulate to toxic levels and lead to significant health problems.

It is clear that feeding one's infant or toddler does not require a doctoral degree or a team of spiritual advisers in order to be successful. Much of what we do has changed little over the course of thousands of years. However, making informed choices regarding breastfeeding versus formula-feeding, and when to introduce solid foods (as well as which foods to avoid), can impact on the health of the infant. It is also important for the parents to consider how their lifestyles and values can accommodate the choices they make, to ensure that the baby receives the best care with the least strain on the parents' relationship.

The Bottom Line

- **What are the key dilemmas parents have to struggle with on this topic?**
  - What are the benefits and drawbacks to breast-feeding?
  - What are the benefits and drawbacks to using commercial formula?
  - When is the best time to transition infants to solid foods?
- **What does the science say about this topic?**
  - Breast milk is superior in providing immunologic agents that help infants fight infections early in life, while providing all of the nutrients necessary for growth and development. Breastfed infants are less likely to develop eczema, diabetes, and some common childhood illnesses. For mothers, breastfeeding can

reduce postpartum bleeding, as well as premenopausal breast or ovarian cancers. Mastitis is sometimes a complication in breastfeeding mothers, but
the evidence supports the safety of continued breastfeeding throughout the infectious process.

- Commercial formula is a safe and viable alternative to
breast milk, although it cannot confer the immunity
factors present in breast milk. Formula provides
complete nutrition for the infant until solid foods are
introduced, and it should be continued until 12
months of age. While some studies suggest higher
risk of obesity, diabetes and hypertension in children
who feed exclusively on formula, some of that risk
may be related to how quickly the infant gains weight
during early infancy.

- Most medical organizations recommend waiting until
the infant is 6 months of age before weaning to solid
foods. However, studies indicate that after 4 months
of age, most infants can tolerate the gradual addition
of solid foods without increasing the risk of food
allergies. Certain foods, such as nuts and soya beans,
should be delayed until 6 months. Infants with relatives who have allergies should wait until 6 months
before weaning to solid foods. Infants should not
receive honey or cow's milk until 12 months.

- **What do the authors advise?**
  - Mothers who choose to breastfeed should do so as long
  as possible, so that the baby can get the greatest
  health benefits. Breastfeeding can be challenging and
  frustrating, especially for a first-time mother, but a
  lactation consultant may be able to help the new
  mother overcome difficulties with the process, and the
  support of loved ones is important.
  - Mothers who choose to use commercial formula should
  never feel embarrassed about their decision. Infant
  formulas are an excellent source of nutrition, although
  they can be pricey. Never dilute formula more than
  the manufacturer recommends, as this will reduce the
  nutrients that the infant receives. It is wise to talk
  to the baby's healthcare provider to determine the

optimum amount to feed your infant, and to monitor the baby's weight gain carefully.

- Although most babies can begin taking solid foods in small quantities after 4 months of age, it is not necessary to begin introducing solids until 6 months. Breast milk or formula should remain a principal source of calories and nutrition throughout the first year of life.

Diet dilemmas and childhood obesity

Strahan

In Chapter 2, we reviewed the intense passions that arise when parents discuss whether their children should co-sleep or whether they need to sleep separately from their parents. The only other topic that I have found that sparks a similar level of passion among parents is the question of what to feed children and when to feed it to them. Again, the emphasis in this chapter is going to be on what the best available scientific evidence says, and not on what the authors of this book believe because it worked for us.

In Chapter 3, Dr Banks discussed the science of infant nutrition, looking at breastfeeding and how that compares to formula feeding of your infant. The current chapter focuses on the decisions that begin once parents are able to give their children solid foods.

Remember that we are all prone to make errors when we reason anecdotally, based on an individual experience, rather than reasoning from well collected and well analysed evidence. No matter what bizarre nutritional practice you can imagine, you can be sure that parents somewhere will have raised a child successfully using that scheme, and they will be ready to promote their 'Gummi Bears Diet' or their 'Cabbage and Anchovy Diet'. Let us listen in for a moment on some of the internet-based parent chat rooms to see what parents are saying about how we should be feeding our babies (the excerpts have been edited for clarity).

My personal theory is – as soon as the child is eating solids, you should be giving her easy to eat versions of whatever you are eating. Cut it up really small, mash it, puree it, whatever it takes to make it safe. We did that for my son from the time he started eating, and he's a great eater now. He has an adventurous palate, and eats all his veggies (lima beans and spinach are two of his fav's). . . . He eats food that is Indian, Mexican, Chinese, Japanese, and my own bizarre home cooking! And this has been his diet from the beginning. It's taken some getting used to, because he has a lot of food allergies, so we've had to adjust a lot of recipes, but he eats just about anything. He's 3.5 now . . .

My daughter has had trouble gaining weight since birth, so we now see a paediatric specialist. At her appointment today, they told me her weight has dropped 10 percentile (from the 15th to the 5th, again) since we were there 6 weeks ago, which apparently isn't very good. . . . Today, the doctor told me I need to give her more food that is high in fat. Her examples were to melt real butter and put it in all her food or add heavy cream to all her bottles. We also need to change how we prepare her formula so it provides more calories per ounce. My question is, does anyone have any ideas other than butter or heavy cream to give an 8 month old? I just can't seem to grasp feeding my child butter; that seems like asking for a heart attack or something. She is also allergic to rice, of all things, so anything that contains it is 100 per cent off limits. Any thought or suggestions will help a TON!

Why is it on this board that when ANYONE disagrees with starting solids early someone else pops up and talks about how judgmental the people are being? If you are so insecure with the decision you made to start your baby early on solids – DON'T READ THE POSTS THAT DISAGREE!!!!. . . This is an open forum – for pete's sake – people are allowed to disagree. Quit taking everything so personally! If you're so right about your decision to start solids early then quit getting your panties up in a bunch about those who disagree with you! None of us are saying what's right or wrong. It's a DISCUSSION board, remember? You need to examine why you are so defensive about your own feeding decisions.

I selected these examples because of common themes that they illustrate. Current controversies have to do with when to start solid foods for babies, how to encourage children to enjoy a wide range of foods, how to reduce the risk of childhood obesity, and to what degree vegetarian and vegan diets are harmful, acceptable, or superior to diets containing animal products. The last post also illustrates the degree of negativity that can arise when others challenge our deeply held beliefs about nutrition.

I am particularly saddened by the second example above, from the mother who fears giving her 8-month-old baby cream or butter – this child is far more at risk from failure to gain weight than from a possible heart attack due to ingestion of dairy-based fats. This mother's post illustrates how deeply rooted a parent's nutritional biases can be. She apparently decided long ago that cream and butter are bad for everyone (the psychological term for this is 'forbidden foods'), and she is missing the point about her daughter's desperate need for concentrated kilocalories in her feeds. She also illustrates another common theme, which has to do with mistrust of the medical community on matters of nutrition. Historically, physicians have not focused much on nutrition in their training, and perhaps this is why other avenues for dietary information have flourished. This mother finds it more acceptable to ask her internet support community for advice on infant nutrition than she does a paediatric specialist in a major medical centre.

Food is an emotionally laden topic. Think of your favourite memories of your grandmother or perhaps your extended family gatherings. Chances are these memories will include foods that were always served. Food choices can also be laden with guilt. Think of how you would feel if you were asked to list everything you ate for a week. Women, in particular, tend to feel guilty about eating foods that they consider 'bad'. Usually these 'forbidden foods' are high in caloric density and they are seen as junk food. Crisps, chocolate, ice-cream, croissants . . . the guilt associated with eating these foods may make you want to leave them off the list. Additionally, parents are told not to use food as a reward or punishment, and not to tell their children to eat less, for fear of making their child obsessive about eating. Food choices can also be associated with guilt because of awareness of famines and hunger in other areas of the world. Parents in those areas struggle to find enough food to stay alive, while for those of us in developed nations, we struggle to keep our food consumption under control.

So parents are in a difficult situation. They are bombarded on the one hand with information about 'the obesity epidemic' that is sweeping industrialized nations, but they are also encouraged to beware of the possibility of instilling eating disorders in their children if they take a heavy-handed approach to what their child eats. They are told by their own parents that they should just raise their children the way they themselves were raised, but the television and the internet are full of conflicting advice on what to eat. Additionally, there is great debate about which foods are safe to eat. For example, scientific estimates of the actual prevalence of coeliac disease (this is characterized by intolerance to wheat gluten) are about 0.5 per cent of the total population. This is in stark contrast to statements posted on some websites. Some of these inform the reader that up to a third of all people suffer from a 'wheat allergy', and suggest that wheat is hard to digest and may poison our bodies.

Examining your own attitudes toward food

This step is perhaps the most important and most difficult step to take in deciding how you want to handle parenting food decisions. Questions you should be asking yourself include:

- Am I significantly overweight or underweight, based on the opinion of my physician?

- To what degree have I struggled with dissatisfaction with my body?
- What is my level of general physical fitness?
- Am I able to enjoy food without guilt or anxiety?
- Do I tend to be a perfectionist or compulsive (about eating, or fitness, or what others think of me)? This dimension is one that you should ask a trusted friend to evaluate you on, as very few people recognize their own level of compulsiveness or obsessions about eating

All of these dimensions can operate independently. For example, Mike is a very fit, moderately overweight man who is relatively content with his body and is relaxed about his food choices. Tina is a very thin woman who is extremely dissatisfied with her body, exercises and chooses foods compulsively and with guilt, and is very fit. Eleanor is very sedentary, very overweight, feels guilty about her eating habits, and is very dissatisfied with her appearance.

One of the first questions you need to ask yourself, as a parent, is what you value most in your children. If an honest self-appraisal tells you that you will be embarrassed or ashamed if your children are overweight, you may be in for some difficulties. If you would like to have healthy children but being overweight runs in your family and you feel it is hopeless to do much to change it, you are settling for too little too soon. If your heartfelt goal is to raise children who are physically healthy and enjoy a wide range of food choices, the road will be smoother for you and your children.

There are a number of online questionnaires that you can use to assess your own attitudes toward eating. David Garner's Eating Attitudes Test (EAT) is available at a number of websites. It screens for anorexia and bulimia.

Finding a healthy role model

There are many times in life when we benefit from recognizing our limitations and 'calling in the troops'. Think about people in your life who are generally fit and of a reasonable weight, who enjoy their food, and who are relaxed about their relationships with food. If you have a close friend or family member who fits that description, consider yourself fortunate. If you yourself fit that description, consider yourself doubly fortunate. What I am advocating is using the 'buddy system' to help parents raise children with good food attitudes.

For example, if Tina knows that she has an unhealthy attitude toward food, but her sister Nita has a good balance in her life between enjoyment of food and fitness, Tina will do well to use Nita as a support in raising her children. The children could cook with their aunt, go shopping with her, and generally spend enough time eating and cooking with her to provide them with a good exposure to healthy attitudes. Tina should also be monitoring her reactions and her children's reactions. If her daughter starts talking about fears of being fat and choosing foods that Mummy will like, that is a warning sign that Tina needs to check her attitudes and take action. Perhaps she needs to invite Nita over for a couple of meals and take note of how Nita deals with serving portions to the children, or how to react when they ask for additional servings. When the children are old enough, perhaps 9 or 10 years of age, it would be good for Tina to admit to them that their mother has not been very good at enjoying food as much as she should, and to put forward Nita as a better role model.

Similarly, Eleanor might have a neighbour, Sami, who is an excellent role model in relation to eating and exercise habits. Very early her children will begin to notice that their mother is overweight. If Eleanor can have the courage to discuss this problem with her children and take action by using Sami as a coach, her children have a much better chance of developing a comfortable lifelong relationship with food and fitness.

It can be very difficult, and somewhat humiliating, to acknowledge this problem. But just as a parent who has trouble managing money needs to seek help from a financial adviser, credit counsellor, or trusted friend to avoid financial disaster, so should a parent who has eating problems seek help from others who will help their children lead a less neurotic and more satisfying life of the body.

Understanding and preventing obesity in children

As nearly everyone who has not been living in a cave for the past decade knows, there is an 'obesity epidemic' affecting nearly all industrialized and many developing nations. Many researchers have examined this topic, and we are developing a scientific consensus about some of the most useful steps that parents can take, and also what schools can do to help.

The basic problem has to do with a mismatch between our genetics and our environment. The physical and psychological skills that helped us survive in our calorie-deficient past are quite different from the skills that are now needed to keep us fit in an age of caloric abundance and limited physical activity requirements.

A 2004 study by Dr Bassett at the University of Tennessee in Knoxville in the USA highlights how our nutritional intake relates to our modern lifestyle. Bassett studied the Old Order Amish, whose diet is high in fat. He found that Amish men averaged over 18,000 steps daily and Amish women averaged 14,000 steps per day. This compares to US and Canadian adult averages of about 2,500 steps per day. The Amish have extremely low rates of obesity, cardiac problems, and diabetes, compared to mainstream US and Canada residents.

Few of us would be willing to abandon technology altogether, but there is clear evidence that the more technology pervades one's life, the greater the risks to physical and emotional health. One of the best predictors of childhood obesity is 'screen time', which includes exposure to all forms of screen media (computer use, computer games, television viewing, films, etc.). Amazingly, one can predict how overweight a child is with a fair degree of accuracy simply by determining how much time the child spends peering at an electronic screen. Additionally, some good studies have been finding that 'screen time' predicts depression in adults. The lesson seems to be that humans do best physically and mentally when we are physically active and involved in face-to-face interactions with other humans (and animals).

One very powerful way to promote health is to live in neighbourhoods that have 'high walkability'. Having shops and libraries and parks within easy walking distance is an extremely important factor in how much people are going to walk. Parks with lots of active play equipment are also important, and working with your neighbourhood to promote sports programmes and other such activities is another very useful approach. Recently my family stayed in Oxford for a few weeks. We lived close to the South Oxford Adventure Park, which is a wonderful example of creating a space that encourages child activity, and I took my children there every afternoon. They loved it, and I must confess that some of the equipment was so tantalizing that I took quite a few turns on it myself (but only when there were no children queuing up to use it!).

In addition to working for communities with high walkability, there is sound scientific evidence that parents should work to make changes in their local schools. Schools can be places where children learn healthy habits, both for eating and for remaining physically active. A number of studies have found that schools can help shape children's preferences towards enjoying a range of healthier foods. For example, Jamie Oliver's school food campaign is one example among many of efforts to improve children's food choices.

Most importantly, schools should incorporate more physical activity into their daily routine. Particularly important to keep in mind, when administrators complain that there is no time for increasing physical activity, are studies which have found improved academic performance in more active children. One study found that increasing physical activity by thirty minutes per day, which meant there was less time for academic subjects, nevertheless resulted in an increase in children's scores in mathematics, and did not affect their test scores in reading and writing. Additionally, the teachers reported having fewer behaviour problems with students once they were more active.

It is best if the kinds of activities that schools plan during those thirty minutes each day are aerobic, and preferably things that can easily be transferred to daily life outside of school. For example, some schools have 'Walk Clubs' and similar programmes, where the children are encouraged to walk fast around a track or a trail. This takes away the anxiety of requiring that all activity be focused around competitive sports or games. Those are fine for the children who love them, but not for those who are less athletically gifted, or who hate competition. Additionally, we all need fitness strategies that we can use on our own and that do not require special equipment or a team of willing young athletes.

The other factor we need to remember is that our bodies evolved to prefer kilocalorie-dense foods such as sweets and crisps. This was an important survival strategy for our ancestors in the distant past when food was scarce and those who ate the fatty fish were more likely to survive than those who ate the lean fish, but it does not work well for us in our present environment. These preferences will remain, but focusing on the delights of eating fresh and well prepared healthy foods will result in heightened enjoyment of those foods.

How about children who refuse to eat whole categories of foods? Many vegetables, such as broccoli, have tastes that can be aversive to children, because of the sensitivity and preferences of their taste buds. Dr Elizabeth Capaldi (1996) has done considerable research on taste aversions. She has found that exposing people to a food they dislike *ten* times is usually sufficient for them to develop a liking for it. I used this approach with my son Isaac, who initially did not like broccoli. I simply required that he eat a bite or two every time I served it, using whatever bribe I found useful (despite common advice not to use bribes, quite often it works!). He came to love broccoli and often requests it now.

What about vegetarian and vegan diets?

The research is quite clear that well planned vegetarian diets can be quite healthy for children. In fact, adults in the general population who are vegetarian tend to be healthier than adults who are non-vegetarians. The trick is that 'well planned' vegetarian diets for children means that the parents need to be educated, conscientious, and collaborative in planning their children's vegetarian diets.

It is important that the parents, in this case, give thoughtful consideration to combining protein sources appropriately. The more restrictive the diet, the more the parent needs to rely on supplements in order to meet growth requirements. Thus, children raised on a vegan diet (no animal products of any kind) are at risk for nutritional deficiencies such as lack of B-12 and calcium. All vegetarian children, even those who consume some eggs or dairy products, need to have attention paid to their iron, zinc, and B-12 and vitamin D needs, as these are more likely to be too low in the diets of vegetarian children. Some children, because of small stomach capacity, will need to add high-energy sources such as nut oils to ensure adequate caloric intake.

The key seems to be in the planning, and in paying consideration to the child's growth. If that is handled properly, vegetarian children will demonstrate normal growth. The one exception is children raised on a macrobiotic or other highly restrictive diet. One Dutch study found that these children were smaller than the comparison groups on a variety of measures, including height and arm circumference. They did show a 'catch-up' spurt of growth when dairy products were added to their diets, but this growth spurt was not adequate for them to match their counterparts who were eating a broader range of foods.

I would suggest that, whatever diet you choose for yourself and your child, you should make sure the child's physician knows what it is. Periodically reminding the paediatrician that your child is being raised on a vegetarian diet, and asking for occasional testing for nutritional deficiencies, would be useful. This same advice applies to children whose parents are not intentionally restricting food categories, but the children are 'fussy eaters' who are refusing whole categories of food on their own (such as often occurs during the toddler years).

Dealing with fears of eating disorders in children

Anorexia nervosa is the psychological disorder with the highest mortality rate, and once it takes hold it is very difficult to treat. Thus, parents who have some acquaintance with eating disorders or have a family history of eating disorders often have great concern about passing on these disorders to their children. While anorexia nervosa is about ten times more prevalent in girls than in boys, it is a dangerous disorder in anyone. How does a family develop a focus on healthy eating without fostering pathological attitudes toward food? First, I want to emphasize that you will do best if you and your children do not go on diets. There is ample evidence that diets are often counter-productive for children and adults alike. Moving toward a healthy lifestyle and a 'health at any size' approach are more productive for most of us.

Families with the highest risk for eating disorders tend to be those in which parents are middle-class and upper middle-class, and where the parents are concerned with their own appearance and view thinness as important to being attractive. Another risk factor for anorexia is the extent to which the child is involved in pursuits that emphasize thinness (ballet, gymnastics, modelling). A family history of anxiety disorders and obsessive-compulsive disorders also heightens the risk of children developing eating problems. So if your family tends to have a lot of members with obsessive characteristics, you should be more aware of the potential for your child to develop eating disorders. Finally, family conflict, enmeshment (where the parents are very intrusive in the child's life), and perfectionism also make it more likely that a child will develop an eating disorder.

One of the things that is so difficult about anorexia is that, in the early stages, the child's behaviour is so universally praised. It may be triggered by a physician's comment that the child needs to lose some weight, by taunting by peers, or by a parent's offhand remark. The child then embarks on a diet and exercise regimen, and initially everyone around responds positively to the change in appearance as the child slims. Eventually the child's choice of foods can become more and more restrictive. One young woman I knew was trying to complete her university degree. She was down to eating one apple, half a bagel, and lettuce and carrots each day. Eating researchers have known since World War II that near-starvation causes permanent changes in the brain structures that regulate eating. This is in part what makes treatment of anorexia so difficult.

If you believe that your child may have an eating disorder, be very assertive about taking your child for a medical examination, and be willing to advocate for the child until she or he is assessed by a competent mental health professional. Getting the proper level of treatment early is very important. I have seen one clinical case where a girl of 16 had dwindled to just 69 pounds (31 kg) before she was treated for her eating disorder. In that case, the parents were still denying that there was anything wrong with their daughter, and the child's physician had to be extremely forceful in mandating treatment. By this stage in the course of the disease, the risk of death is considerable and the prospects for successful treatment are much diminished. By the time a child is 15 per cent below ideal body weight, he or she meets the criteria for anorexia (provided the weight loss is intentional and not related to a severe medical illness such as recovery from surgery).

Sometimes children mask an eating disorder from others and from themselves by couching it in terms of food sensitivities or allergies, which are quite trendy. These children may believe that they cannot tolerate eating dairy products, gluten, sucrose, meat, and so on. Eventually they are left with an extremely limited diet that results in severe weight loss. The difficult part of assessing these food sensitivities is that psychological factors play a huge role in how our digestive tracts respond. For example, learning relaxation techniques and self-hypnosis, even without any change in diet, can virtually eradicate 'irritable bowel syndrome' for many people. Conversely, becoming tense and anxious can cause any food to upset one's digestive system. You have only to think of people who are so nervous prior to giving public addresses that they vomit or develop diarrhoea, to gain an understanding of how closely linked are one's moods and digestive function.

Given all these considerations, what should parents do, and avoid doing, in order to maximize the odds that our children become happy and healthy, and develop good attitudes toward eating?

What *not* to do

- Do not focus on 'forbidden foods'. It is quite common for parents to treat some foods as 'forbidden foods', that should not ever be in the house. I am not referring here to poisonous mushrooms, or to mould-covered leftovers in the back of the refrigerator, which I quite agree should be banished from the house! This term refers, rather, to foods generally described in popular magazines as 'sinful'. Chocolate truffles, ice-cream, fried foods, and so on tend to appear in this category. The trouble with having such a concept is that telling your children they can never eat such foods tends to make them seem more appealing. Conversely, other children can take these lessons too much to heart and become highly anxious if they are in situations such as birthday parties where these foods are in abundance.
- Do not speak moralistically about your food choices (e.g. 'I was sooooo bad last night! I ate two chocolate croissants! Now I need to be good for a week!'). This confuses food choices with ethics. It also confuses food choices with one's worth as a human being.
- Do not eat at fast-food outlets more than perhaps once a week. Families who eat at home spend less money and time, and eat healthier food, than do those who get fast food on a regular basis.
- Do not put your children on a diet (unless a trusted health professional insists that it is necessary – in most cases, if you follow these recommendations, it will not be necessary).
- Do not take a heavy hand toward requiring healthy eating and exercise. The more tyrannical you are about your child's exercise or eating programme, the more

likely your child is either to rebel or to become obsessive. I have one client who struggles with morbid obesity. She describes having grown up dominated by a thinness-obsessed, intrusive mother who required her to go on two-hour-long bicycle rides every evening as punishment for not being thin enough, and who still telephones her almost daily and pleads with her to have stomach-banding surgery for weight loss.

- Do not complain about having to be physically active. If your child sees you circling the car-park at a Tesco, looking for the closest spot to the door, and complaining loudly if none is to be found, that is a strong message. The same shopping expedition would convey quite a different message if you said, 'Parking back here will give us a chance to stretch our legs after sitting so much at work and school today.'
- Do not present a martyred appearance when buying healthy foods or passing up the crisps and puddings in the supermarket.
- Do not rate your own, your child's, and others' worth based on their appearance. 'That Jenna is such a lovely girl. It's a shame her sister Lisa is a bit on the chubby side' is not a comment that ever needs to be made to a child (or an adult, for that matter).
- Do not use 'health' as a synonym for thinness.
- Do not show your children that you use food or alcohol as a reward for yourself or as a way to calm yourself when you are upset. 'I've had a rough day at work. I deserve this!' is conveying entirely the wrong approach to food.
- Do not talk about your own weight. *No one*, least of all your children, is interested in this topic. If you are pre-occupied with your weight, discuss it with your physician or with your best friend (who will also be bored with the topic but will be kind enough not to tell you!).

Instilling a healthy attitude toward food and fitness

- One of the most productive approaches is simply to encourage more physical activity. Some parents have good success by giving each member of the family a pedometer and setting a weekly family goal. This must be done in a light spirit and without descending into compulsiveness.

- Take a walk with your children every evening when the weather is fine.
- Get involved in more family outings that include walking, or in family games of volleyball, Frisbee, or other fun activities that give a cardiovascular workout.
- View all foods (within reason, and in keeping with your budget and your belief system) as acceptable. There is nothing wrong with your child eating an occasional chocolate truffle. Your child will learn this lesson best if you learn it first. Eating the entire box of truffles once the children are in bed will not hide your behaviour, as children have an uncanny ability to keep track of such goodies and you will be found out!
- Talk with your child about your food decisions, but only when they raise the topic. 'Why is it that the Desai family eats so many sweets and you hardly ever buy any?' is a great opener to such a topic.
- Emphasize health and vitality over appearance when you describe reasons for making food choices.
- If your child does decide to diet, do not praise her or him for looking better. Ask them if they have good energy and focus on whether they are taking in sufficient food and a wide enough variety of foods.
- If you yourself have a serious problem with over-eating or restrictive eating that has resulted in health problems or has absorbed too much of your own energy, talk that over honestly with your children once they are old enough to understand it.
- Re-think your own attitudes toward eating. Get some honest feedback from a perceptive family member or friend about whether you are unintentionally conveying unhealthy attitudes toward food.
- Demonstrate to your children that you enjoy walking instead of driving whenever possible. You might be faking this at first, but once you get the hang of it, you will truly enjoy it and you won't want to give it up.

- Make decisions about your lifestyle that promote health. For example, if you are in the market for a new house or flat, discuss with your family how some locations that have lovely homes are not going to be as healthy for you because they have low walkability.
- Demonstrate the enjoyment of fruits and vegetables rather than dutiful purchasing of them. Aim for 'Aren't these berries lovely! Let's have them tonight!' rather than 'Oh, what a bother! I know we need to eat more vegs, but I'm just too tired to go to all that trouble!'
- Allow yourself the occasional food 'splurge' without guilt or judgement.
- Encourage an open mind toward new foods. Remember that if you want your child to enjoy something new, that will usually happen if the child tastes that food ten different times. Keep this process low-key and avoid lecturing (which will sour the taste of even the most delectable treat).
- Focus your energies, whenever possible, on interests that transcend your own waist measurements. If you volunteer for worthy causes, get involved in civic affairs, take a university course, etc., you will learn that these activities are more enriching and life-sustaining than a focus on appearance.

The Bottom Line

- **What are the key dilemmas parents have to struggle with on this topic?**
  - How do we raise children who are open to a variety of healthy foods, who enjoy physical activity, and who are neither rigid nor compulsive in their eating behaviours?
- **What does the science say about this topic?**
  - It is clear from the literature that parents who take a 'forbidden foods' approach are not serving their children well. This makes those foods doubly attractive.
  - Putting children on a diet is not nearly as helpful as a broader lifestyle change that the whole family adopts.

- The most effective interventions in this area have less to do with techniques you use on your children and more to do with re-shaping your own attitudes and behaviours.
- Vegetarian diets are generally quite healthy, but require attention to protein combinations, and to adequate intake of several key nutrients.
- **What do the authors advise?**
  - Work first on your own attitudes toward food and health, and you will have a fairly easy time of it with your children.
  - Being too controlling with your children's food intake is likely to backfire.
  - Focus your energies instead on enjoying healthy food, on encouraging physical activity, and on minimizing electronic 'screen time' for your children.
  - If you have problems with eating too much or too little, or obsessing too much about food, you may need to help your child by ensuring that they spend time preparing and eating meals with a trusted friend who is a better role model for the child's attitudes toward food.

Recommended reading for parents

Beck, J. (2007). *The Beck diet solution: Train your brain to think like a thin person*. Birmingham, AL: Oxmoor House.

Brownell, K. (2004). *Food fight: The inside story of the food industry, America's obesity crisis, and what we can do about it*. New York: McGraw-Hill.

Capaldi, E.D. (1996). *Why we eat what we eat: The psychology of eating*. Washington, DC: American Psychological Association.

Dewey, K. (2004). Guiding principles for feeding non-breastfed children 6–24 months of age. Department of Child and Adolescent Health and Development. World Health Organization. Retrieved January 2008 from www.who.int/child-adolescent-health

Ellis, A., Abrams, M. and Dengelegi, L. (1992). *The art and science of rational eating*. Fort Lee, NJ: Barricade Books.

National Institute for Clinical Excellence (2006). Preventing obesity and staying a healthy weight. Retrieved March 2008 from www.nice.org.uk

Wilhelm, S. (2006). *Feeling good about the way you look: A program for overcoming body image problems*. London: Guilford Press.

The 'Mozart Effect', baby Einsteins, and other media-related mythinformation

Dixon

It goes without saying that most parents want what is best for their children. Definitions of *best* may vary from parent to parent, even from generation to generation, but by and large we parents do what we can to mobilize our resources to prepare our children for long and happy lives. Usually this means that we strive for the most relevant, most important, and most useful experiences within our reach, and to allocate as many of our disposable resources as we can toward achieving this end. Of course, resources are limited, and so we are incentivized to look for bargains that will provide our children with desirable experiences at little or no cost.

And lots of low-cost, high-yield experiences do indeed abound. Going for a walk or a hike provides great physical exercise. Going to a neighbourhood playground provides great social experiences. Spending time with grandparents can provide great personal history, and for many of us, exposure to a novel language. And visiting zoos, aquariums and museums produces great intellectual experiences, often for little more than a small donation.

But gaining access to exceptional experiences usually costs extra – sometimes *lots* extra. We agonize over whether to invest in experience-rich, but also tuition- and fee-rich, private schools, or to settle for cheaper, but we hope *good enough* state ones. Matters are further compounded by social pressures to achieve, and by capitalistic, market-based economies that reward us for achieving more and performing better than our peers. Accordingly, we fear that making a wrong choice will deprive our children of opportunities to gain success and fortune. We worry that no matter what we do, the result will be costly. In England, the average termly fee for boarding schools within the Independent Schools Council during the 2006/2007 school year was £3,717 per term, exclusive of the boarding fee. The *Sydney Morning Herald* reports that attending an independent school in Western Australia (as of January 2008) could set you back AU$14,201 per year.

Obviously, the cost of experience-rich private education escapes the grasp of most of us, leaving state schooling as the only alternative. Any exceptional educational experiences we chance upon will be fortuitously acquired. So who can blame us when we keep an eye out for experiential opportunities with the potential to deliver disproportionate gains at minimal cost?

Enter the 'Mozart Effect'. Nothing short of an international phenomenon, the Mozart Effect first appeared on the international scene in the early 1990s, and carried with it the promise of exceptional intellectual growth for the cost of an ordinary music CD. In the modern competitive market economy, the Mozart Effect was ripe for the picking, and promised to open intellectual horizons for children in a way never before thought possible.

The Mozart phenomenon started with an article published in the prestigious British journal *Nature* in October 1993. Now, as far as scientific journals go, some are considered good, some are considered very good, and some are considered excellent. But *Nature* has such a strong reputation and international acclaim that describing it as merely 'excellent' seems somehow inadequate. Scientists who publish in *Nature* often go on to have illustrious careers.

Hence, it is no surprise that when Frances Rauscher, Gordon Shaw and Katherine Ky published their article 'Music and spatial task performance' in *Nature*, they fired a shot a heard around the world. In their now famous and highly controversial one-page-long article, the authors describe how they conducted a very simple experiment. They had college students listen to ten minutes of (1)

Mozart's sonata for two pianos in D major, K448, (2) a relaxation tape, or (3) silence. Immediately afterwards, they tested those students' spatial reasoning using the Stanford-Binet Scale of Intelligence, which is a typical test used by psychologists to measure intelligence. The ground-breaking results showed that when students listened to the Mozart piece, they gained 8–9 IQ points; but students showed no IQ change in the other two conditions. This effect, which according to Rauscher was dubbed 'the Mozart Effect' by the *Los Angeles Times*, was considered a monumental step forward in our understanding of music's effect on the brain. Many believed it was proof positive that listening to music increased IQ, and it carried with it a landslide of cheap, no-frills ramifications. For example, if listening to Mozart for only ten minutes resulted in a gain of 8–9 IQ points, then maybe listening daily would turn an average Joe into a genius, or at least someone whose intelligence was above average. But consider further. Maybe governments could save millions of dollars if instead of investing in complex and costly remedial curricula, they just distributed some Mozart CDs to needy children in their communities. For that matter, maybe a small investment in music could cut down on the need for formal schooling altogether.

Exaggeration? Maybe. But these notions did take root. In 1998, American governor Zell Miller of Georgia proposed a state budget which included a line item of US$105,000 so that every Georgian newborn could be granted a personal cache of prerecorded classical music. Governor Don Sundquist of Tennessee followed suit shortly after. These were surely thoughtful gestures, but they prevented much-needed money from being spent on more legitimate educational expenses elsewhere. It wasn't such a problem *per se* that state monies were being spent on classical music for children. Rather, the problem was that the Mozart Effect was illusory; hence, spending any money toward achieving such an end was barking at the moon.

We have learned since that time that the reported IQ enhancements were not so much the product of college students listening to Mozart, as they were a product of more mundane, motivational factors. What is more, the effects were only temporary, and were limited to a relatively small set of highly specific spatial tasks. So how can we account for the Mozart Effect if not for the effects of Mozart? Canadian researchers Kristin Nantais and Glenn Schellenberg believe they have come up with the most rational alternative explanation, and this one is of a decidedly non-Mozartian strain. Nantais and Schellenberg argued that college students who performed better on tests of spatial reasoning after listening to Mozart did so not because Mozart was particularly special, but because listening to Mozart simply increased their overall levels of arousal.

In reviewing the Mozart Effect literature published since the original 1993 article, Nantais and Schellenberg discovered that all the research which supported the existence of the Mozart Effect (almost exclusively the work of Rauscher and her colleagues) always compared spatial reasoning performance after listening to Mozart, to spatial reasoning performance after (a) listening to nothing, (b) listening to a relaxation tape, or (c) listening to repetitive dance music. Nantais and Schellenberg reasoned that compared with doing nothing, or compared with listening to relaxing or repetitive music, listening to Mozart would probably increase general levels of pleasant arousal. They argued that it was this heightened level of arousal, and not Mozart proper, that enhanced spatial reasoning performance. This explanation also accounted for why the effects on IQ scores were always temporary.

To prove their point, Nantais and Schellenberg conducted an experiment in which half of their subjects listened to Mozart, and half just listened to a story. The subjects were asked to rate whether they preferred listening to Mozart or to the story. Then, after listening to either the Mozart piece or the story, the subjects were given tests of spatial reasoning, just as was done in the original study. The results were telling. First, they found that listening to Mozart actually did improve spatial reasoning performance. But they found that listening to the story *also* improved spatial reasoning performance. So what does this tell us? As it turns out, the thing that most affected performance on the spatial reasoning tasks was whether the participants *preferred* listening to Mozart, or to the story. Participants who preferred Mozart performed better after listening to Mozart. Participants who preferred the story performed better after listening to the story. In other words, both types of exposure enhanced spatial performance. But which type of exposure was most effective for a given individual depended on that individual's preference.

Based on this study, along with many others published by scientists such as Kenneth Steele and Christopher Chabris, the most reasonable conclusion we can draw is that there simply is no Mozart Effect. Because far more parsimonious and plausible alternative explanations for the Mozart Effect have been proposed, given a choice between a simple, straightforward explanation and a more complex, somewhat magical one, Occam's razor dictates that scientists must choose in favour of parsimony. ('Occam's razor' is a guide to careful thinking, in which we give preference to the simpler of two competing theories.) So in the absence of any stronger or more compelling data, I am afraid we have no other option than to ring the death knell for the Mozart Effect. Of course, none of this is to suggest that listening to Mozart, or any other classical music, should be avoided by our children. There are a number of scientifically valid reasons why parents should facilitate children's exposure to Mozart and other classical composers, but getting an IQ boost is not one of them.

The post-Mozart-Effect effect

Unfortunately, the demise of the Mozart Effect in the scientific community has not been met by a corresponding demise of the Mozart Effect among the lay population. Quite the contrary has taken place. In the public market, the Mozart Effect is alive and well, and can be found at the core of a particularly cunning marketing ploy designed to capitalize on parents' compulsion to provide the best possible experiential opportunities for their children. In its revised role, the Mozart Effect has catalysed an entire industry aimed at making our children smarter. This isn't entirely unexpected. Just because scientists have revealed the illusion of the Mozart Effect doesn't mean that either (1) parents are not still seeking cheap, cost-effective ways to boost their children's IQs, or (2) toy-makers can't act as if the Mozart Effect really does exist. Consequently, authors, toy companies, and television producers who have aimed their products toward increasing the intelligence of children have learned that the baby IQ industry is a profitable one, and that parents are willing to shell out big money to buy a piece of the Mozart Effect. It isn't necessarily a bad thing when an industry wraps itself around the common good of facilitating children's development. It is only bad insofar as these institutions make claims that aren't supported by the scientific literature for the sake of maximizing their profits. Notably, even Frances Rauscher describes her research team as being 'horrified' at how their Mozart Effect findings have been pillaged and commandeered by the nascent baby IQ industry.

The baby IQ industry appears densely packed. Baby IQ enhancing products abound and are prominently displayed in department stores worldwide. Harrods, John Lewis, Sears, Target, Walmart and Zellers are all on board. There is even a dedicated toy retailer hailing from New Zealand called IQToys. Among the most popular suppliers are such cutely named brand lines as Amazing Baby, Baby Bumblebee, Baby College, Baby Einstein, Baby IQ, Baby Prodigy, Brainquest, Brainy Baby, Cranium, Genius Babies, Infantino and So Smart – not to mention the well established senior citizen of the toddler market, *Sesame Street*. One of the most popular media formats for these companies – what seems to be the bread and butter for many of them – is the DVD. This is interesting considering that the original Mozart study was based on audio recordings. It is also interesting that the industry has sprung up in the service of infants and toddlers, when the original findings were derived from college students.

But these many companies differ in terms of the inferences they wish consumers to draw regarding the nature of their products' impacts. On the one hand are companies who claim outright that their products directly *cause* babies to get smarter. Consider the following claims taken from company websites:

- Baby Bumblebee 'has a number of titles designed to boost language development. These are great for an infant or toddler, or for parents concerned about their child's language development.'
- Baby Prodigy: 'We are dedicated to helping parents, grandparents, and caregivers all over the world raise **SMARTER, HAPPIER** young children in **NEW** and **FUN** ways' (emphasis in original).
- Baby College: 'Accelerates and maximizes learning. Your child will speak and understand language quicker.'

On the other hand are companies who appear more sensitive to the political consequences of making scientifically unsupported claims, and who focus instead on how their products can facilitate parent–child interaction. Consider the following:

- Baby IQ: 'our DVDs encourage you and your baby to explore a world of learning together; a world that is fun and spectacular.'
- Baby Einstein: 'the entire Baby Einstein collection is specifically designed to promote discovery and inspire new ways for parents and babies to interact in age and developmentally appropriate ways.'
- Brainy Baby: '[our] products always work best when adults use them interactively with their child. When using a DVD, for example, watch it with your child, talk about what you see, and repeat the names of new things, just as you do when reading a book together.'

Clearly, the latter companies appear much more cognizant of the scientific literature, which really does suggest that parent–child interaction is the foundation upon which successful child development rests. But despite their care in avoiding overstatements, these companies cannot prevent parents from buying their products for the wrong reasons. A recent study commissioned by the Henry J. Kaiser Foundation revealed that 88 per cent of parents of children aged 6 months to 6 years rated watching educational videos or DVDs as either 'very important' or 'somewhat important' in helping the intellectual development of their children. With so many parents believing that video-recordings promote the intellectual growth of children, it is hard to believe that they wouldn't buy them for that purpose.

Perhaps the best known of the smart-baby products is the Baby Einstein line. The Baby Einstein worldwide sensation began in 1997, when Julie Aigner-Clark and her husband produced a video in their basement, bankrolled by their own savings, implicitly designed to stimulate the intelligence of babies. This first video, 'Language Nursery', helped the Baby Einstein product line generate US$20 million in sales by 2001, which eventually led to their acquisition by the Walt Disney Company that year. By 2007, the Baby Einstein brand was a US$200 million business. Aigner-Clark's rise to the top was even showcased as a model of entrepreneurial success by President Bush in his 2007 'State of the Union' address.

Because the Baby Einstein people are careful not to attribute IQ-boosting properties to their products, other than those resulting from parent–child interaction, they are in the highly desirable marketing position of being able to send two messages to their target audience while paying for only one. Some parents may only hear the implicit claims of, 'Buy from us, and we'll boost your children's IQ.' The very fact that the products employ the 'Baby Einstein' moniker, coupled with perhaps a vague recollection of something called a Mozart Effect, may be sufficient for these parents to conclude that Baby Einstein products do promote IQ development. On the other hand, scientifically knowledgeable parents can appeal to the company's explicit marketing claims and use Baby Einstein products to jump-start interactions with their children.

But even this more relaxed claim doesn't hold up well to scientific scrutiny. In an effort to find research that showed whether Baby Einstein products facilitated parent–child interaction, I searched through all the international peer-reviewed child development journals I could find. Using electronic databases, I looked through the abstracts of articles published in *Child Development*, *Developmental Psychology*, *Infancy*, *Infant Behavior and Development*, *Infant and Child Development*, *British Journal of Developmental Psychology*, *European Journal of Developmental Psychology*, *Merrill-Palmer Quarterly*, *Cognitive Development*, *Journal of Cognition and Development*, *Journal of Experimental Child Psychology*, *Child Psychiatry and Human Development*, and many, many others. Not a single published study evaluated whether Baby Einstein's, or any other company's, baby products, DVDs or otherwise, boosted parent–child interaction.

The only study I found which addressed the issue at all was a very recent 2008 unpublished doctoral dissertation by Tiffany Pempek of the University of Massachusetts Amherst. In this study, Pempek tested whether baby-oriented videos from either Baby Einstein or Sesame Beginnings (an infant-oriented offshoot of Sesame Street) could impact the quality of interaction between parents and children. Pempek had parents and children co-view videos from either one or the other company over a two-week period. Parents and children were then invited to the lab where Pempek analysed their interactions with one other, both while watching the video they had been assigned during the previous two weeks, and while the TV was turned off. A full review of her experiment is beyond the scope of this chapter, but three interesting findings are germane to the discussion. First, she found that parents and children interacted significantly less frequently in the lab when the TV was on than when it was off, regardless of which video they had been watching the previous two weeks. This is not particularly surprising because co-viewing a video requires periods of non-interaction.

What might be more surprising, however, especially for antagonists of the baby video movement, was that she also found that parents interacted a great deal with their children when co-viewing the videos. Active parent–child involvement occurred *more than half of the time* during video co-viewing. A third finding of interest was that for parents and children who watched the Sesame Beginnings videos, there was a correlation between the time spent co-viewing at home, and the amount of high-quality interaction in the laboratory. In other words, more co-viewing of Sesame Beginnings videos in the home predicted higher-quality parent–child interactions in the lab. A similar result was not found for families who watched Baby Einstein videos.

What might account for this last result? Pempek believes it stems from the fact that Sesame Beginnings videos provide parents with normative information about child development and child rearing, and actually portray parents and children engaging in high-quality interactions. By showing parents how to promote high-quality interactions, parents can then incorporate that information into their own repertoires. Baby Einstein videos have a different goal, which is to capture and maintain children's attention *per se*, rather than to demonstrate desirable parenting behaviours.

Summary

So let us review what we know up to this point. A study by Rauscher and colleagues was published in 1993 which suggested that listening to a Mozart sonata for ten minutes would increase the IQs of college students by 8 or 9 points. The term 'Mozart Effect' was used as a label for these findings. The baby product market got hold of these findings and began producing DVDs of Mozart and other classical composers, purportedly to boost the intellectual functioning of infants and toddlers. Other forms of media were developed to boost children's IQ, and these didn't necessarily even include the works of classical music composers. Meanwhile, further scientific efforts to replicate the Mozart Effect consistently failed, except when Rauscher herself attempted them. The scientific credibility of the Mozart Effect has since faded, but it has achieved considerable public credibility. The baby product industry is as strong as ever, and most companies claim that their products will boost the intellectual functioning of babies. But companies differ in what they emphasize. Some companies claim their products will boost the intellectual functioning of infants and toddlers directly. Others claim their products will enhance parent–child interaction quality, and through this means boost IQ. To date, only one scientific experiment has investigated either type of claim, and even this study is an unpublished doctoral dissertation (although it appears to be a good one). Prospects look better for the future, as some researchers at the University of California Riverside have begun experimental investigations of the topic.

On the shortcomings of baby-science and correlational research

It is tempting to tie off this chapter by simply concluding that there is no Mozart Effect, and consequently that Mozart Effect-type products will not improve the intellectual functioning of infants and toddlers. And I would hope that a corollary conclusion would be that science is our best means to evaluate magic bullet claims of this sort. But relatively recently, a chain of events has transpired that should serve as a parable for why the process of scientific enquiry must itself be held up to scientific scrutiny from time to time. The story has to do with the so-called 'scientific recommendations of experts' (yes, people like the authors of this book) about whether and to what extent parents should let their children watch television and be exposed to other forms of visual media. The story also strikes at the heart of the scientific enterprise. It underscores that despite its monumental achievements and successes, science remains a human endeavour, and is subject to the same shortcomings and pitfalls as any endeavour that relies on human reasoning for its decision-making. Unlike other human endeavours, however, science is also *self-correcting*. So when rogue scientists get off the beaten path and start making claims in the absence of evidence, other scientists can take up the charge and hold them to their professional code of conduct (which we hope we are doing by sharing this story).

The story has three scenes. The setting for Scene 1 is 1999, some six years after publication of the first Mozart Effect findings. Perhaps in response to the rapid growth of the baby IQ industry that took place in the wake of the Mozart Effect, but yet in a complete evidentiary vacuum, the American Academy of Pediatrics (AAP) Committee on Public Education releases its recommendation that 'Pediatricians should urge parents to avoid television viewing for children under the age of 2 years.' The rationale the AAP cites for this baseless, and hence rather bizarre, proscription is simply that 'research on early brain development shows that babies and toddlers have a critical need for direct interactions with parents and other significant caregivers . . . for healthy brain growth and the development of appropriate social, emotional, and cognitive skills'. In the United States, AAP policy statements carry a great deal of weight, and the sheer statement of a thing by the AAP is sometimes enough to bring the thing into existence. And indeed, consumers ought to feel confident when the organization responsible for overseeing the actions of baby doctors takes a position on a contemporary issue.

It is unfortunate, therefore, when an organizational lobby as powerful as the AAP throws its weight around in support of arbitrary and capricious positions. A review of the scientific literature reveals that in suggesting a ban on TV for the under-twos, the AAP really had no evidence to back up its claim. Accordingly, the AAP jumped off the credibility train. Quite simply, the fact that interaction with primary caregivers enhances brain growth has nothing to do with whether or not children under 2 should watch television. To conclude otherwise is tantamount to what philosophers would call a *non sequitur*, or a conclusion that doesn't follow from the premises. I doubt anyone would deny that healthy human brain development requires direct, social interaction with loving, caring people. But this does not mean that brain development will cease in the context of passive, non-social stimulation sources (of which programmes like *Teletubbies* and Baby Einstein videos are an example). The evidence simply does not lead to the conclusion drawn by the AAP. Still the AAP seemed to have no difficulty leaping to this illogical, panic-inducing, fear-peddling conclusion.

Obviously, watching TV reduces opportunities for babies to directly interact with mum and dad. But preventing TV-watching does not entail that the void left by not watching TV will be filled by *more* parent–child interaction. Surely, it is not reasonable to expect that all waking moments of children's lives will be filled with active parent–child interaction. There will be times when children watch dad cook dinner, watch mum weed the garden, or simply go for a passive walk in a pushchair. Yet, we find no indication that the AAP recommends against any of these activities, which are just as non-direct and non-social as watching TV. In any case, Pempek's dissertation reveals that co-viewing videos may actually be relatively social, at least compared with some of the other passive activities one can think of. Even if we were to assume momentarily that passive stimulation *could* inhibit normal brain development, TV- or video-watching being the case in point, wouldn't it make sense for the AAP to also recommend against driving toddlers to the grocery store? Sitting in an infant seat in the rear of an automobile is replete with non-interactive sources of stimulation: smelling the vinyl seats, hearing the engines of passing cars, and looking through the windows at telephone poles whooshing by.

From a scientific point of view, the scariest prospect of the AAP's recommendation is that parents and consumers, both in the US and abroad, might actually believe that the AAP did have scientific evidence that watching TV or videos before the age of 2 is harmful to brain growth or function. But the proposition simply has no scientific merit, because no studies to date have been undertaken to test it. It seems to me that scientists should avoid expending priceless credibility on bandwagon TV- and video-bashing when they can invest it instead in establishing a research agenda to substantiate the real effects of TV-viewing.

As if the 1999 AAP policy statement didn't misinform parents and consumers enough, TV- and video-viewing took a couple more hits, first in 2004 and then in 2007, when two highly publicized research articles appeared on the scene. These articles were interpreted by many readers as providing further proof of the hazards of TV- and video-viewing. Both of these articles were surely useful contributions to the scientific literature. But both also received international acclaim for making proclamations that were untrue, unjustifiable, and ultimately scientifically impermissible. Both articles were founded on observed correlations between (1) the amount of time children spent watching TV or videos in infancy or toddlerhood, and (2) some bad developmental outcome that nobody wants their children to have. These articles represent Scenes 2 and 3 of the unfortunate parable. I review each of these briefly, and then explain why their authors overstepped their bounds and delivered a public proclamation which the science did not permit.

The damage of Christakis, Zimmerman *et al.*, 2004

Scene 2. Fade forward to 2004. An article is published by Christakis, Zimmerman, DiGiuseppe and McCarty, and is titled 'Early television exposure and subsequent attentional problems in children'. The article reports that parents' recollections of children's TV-viewing habits at age 1 and 3 years are negatively correlated with parents' judgements of their children's attention spans at age 7 years. The article receives international attention. The authors embark on an international lecture tour and submit to radio, television and print media interviews. Misunderstanding, misinterpretation and misinformation are propagated, and follow in the wake of the authors' appearances. The take-home message in the wake of all appearances is that TV- and video-viewing causes attention problems in children.

For researchers who are biased against television programming, I can imagine it is a very small leap to conclude that correlations between TV-watching in toddlerhood and attentional problems in childhood underscore a true causal relationship. That is to say, it is easy for some people to imagine that TV-watching *causes* attentional problems. But in the absence of causal data, truly sceptical scientists have an obligation to their profession to remain neutral and avoid making policy claims. The fact of the matter is that correlations can *never* be interpreted causally.

Unfortunately, although Christakis and his colleagues are careful not to draw causal conclusions in their article *per se*, in their public appearances they take liberties and promote a causal interpretation of the data. For example, in the video located at http://www.msnbc.msn.com/id/21134540/vp/ 4671115#4671115, Christakis implicates a causal relationship. His quoted claims in print media can also be found on websites such as http://www.medicinenet.com/script/main/ art.asp?articlekey=31871, where he is quoted as saying: 'We found that watching television before the age of 3 increases the chances that children will develop attentional problems at age 7.' Similarly, at http://research.seattlechildrens.org/ about/feat_research/harnessing_technology_for_the_benefit _of_children.asp, Christakis is quoted as saying: 'Childhood obesity, excessive aggression and attention problems all have roots in excessive or inappropriate television viewing.'

These kinds of claims inflame respectable scientists. Causal conclusions from correlational data simply cannot be drawn, no matter how much you want it to be true. Now, to be clear, I am not challenging the validity of the correlations themselves. I trust that the authors conducted their analyses accurately. I am also not especially concerned with the fact that the authors' definition of attentional problems is their own concoction and would not pass muster as real diagnostic indicators of attentional disorders under any rubric. I am even willing to let it go that the size of their effects is pretty small. No, my problem is that the authors fail to consider any alternative explanations of the data.

At least two alternative explanations can be made to account for the correlation between TV-viewing in infancy and attention-related disorders at age 7. First, it is possible, maybe even probable, that children with attention-span problems are more likely to find TV and video programmes interesting than children without attention-related problems. Children's television programmes are made exceptionally attention-grabbing by virtue of their fast-paced, musical, exciting, and frequent-scene-changing styles.

Although this kind of action-packed format is appealing to all children, and maybe even many adults, it is not surprising that the format is also appealing to attention-disordered children. Attention-disordered children may find the normal world boring. TV may provide the most stimulating of any environmental stimuli that attention-disordered children can find. Unlike attention-disordered children, children without such disorders may be able to find solace in lots of other stimuli besides child-directed TV; but for attention-disordered infants and toddlers, fast-paced TV may be the best there is. This is roughly the position of internationally acclaimed ADHD researcher Russell Barkley.

Yet the authors dismiss this possibility because, according to them, most 'experts' believe that attention-related disorders don't emerge until later childhood. But the beliefs of experts have nothing to do with reality, unless those beliefs are grounded in data. The truth is that researchers have rarely studied attention disorders in infants. It is true that attention-related problems may not be diagnosed until middle childhood, as opposed to infancy, because it is not until then that children's attention-related problems crash head-on into the structured school setting; and school settings tend not to give children with attention-related disorders much latitude. But there is no reason to believe that attention-related disorders cannot be traced to infancy. There is considerable evidence from large-sample twin-studies that attention-related problems are highly heritable (i.e. traceable to genetic sources) throughout childhood, even before school age. If a child has an attention-related problem in childhood, it is very likely that they had it in infancy, and will continue to have it into adolescence. It is at least reasonable, then, that toddlers with attention problems are drawn to television programming precisely *because* of their attention problems.

This leads to a second alternative interpretation of the data reported in the article that the authors failed to consider. That is that parents of infants who have attention-related disorders may turn to TV as a last resort for dealing with their temperamentally difficult children.

The literature on infant and toddler temperament is replete with data linking temperamental difficulty to parenting practices. Children with difficult temperaments tend to have weary, tired, hapless and frustrated parents. Is this a coincidence? Probably not. It makes sense that children with difficult temperaments would produce parents who develop parenting tactics to deal with their children's difficult temperaments. TV-viewing might be one of the parenting tactics they use. If this explanation were true, then TV-viewing would not be responsible for attention-related disorders; rather, attention-related disorders would be responsible for parenting tactics that result in TV-viewing. But alas, this possibility is not even considered by the authors. The fact is that infants and toddlers with difficult temperaments also tend to have short attention spans. Consequently, parents who have found a means to successfully maintain the attention of their temperamentally difficult infants and toddlers may have also found a means to attenuate their infants' and toddlers' temperamental difficulty.

The received and, it seems to me, extremely destructive result of this article may be that when children have ADHD, their parents will be blamed for letting them watch too much TV, when in fact watching TV may have been the only solace for infants and toddlers with exceptionally short attention spans. Meanwhile, publicly funded research aimed at identifying the real cause of ADHD may be reduced because communities have been misled by 'experts' about the origins of children's attention problems.

The damage of Zimmerman, Christakis *et al.*, 2007

Scene 3. Three years later. Zimmerman, Christakis and Meltzoff publish a new article in the *Journal of Pediatrics*, titled 'Associations between media viewing and language development in children under age 2 years'. In this article, Zimmerman and colleagues report a correlation between the vocabulary size of babies, and the amount of time their parents said their babies watched Baby Einstein-type DVDs.

The correlation is *negative*, which means that greater DVD-watching predicted smaller vocabulary size.

As before, there is little problem in the content of the article *per se*. In fact, the authors actually come out and say that their 'study's correlational nature precludes drawing causal inferences'. This is an important recognition that they should be lauded for making, in light of the 2004 debacle. However, as with the 2004 article, it seems their precautionary statement amounts to little more than hand-waving. Bafflingly, as they did in the wake of their 2004 article, the authors throw credibility to the wind, and make appearances in a variety of public venues where they make precisely the kinds of causal claims they cautioned against in their article. For example, in an August 2007 appearance on the US National Public Radio, archived at http://www.npr.org/templates/story/story.php?storyId=12560124, Christakis actually comes out and says that Baby Einstein-type videos inhibit language development. This is plain and simply an overstatement of the data, and an attribution of a causal relationship where none may exist.

As in the previous study, it is easy to generate alternative interpretations for the correlations reported in the article. Ironically, one good candidate explanation can be found in the authors' own article. Because baby video products are advertised as promoting intellectual and language development, parents of language-delayed infants would presumably be the ones most likely to buy development-promoting videos. We know that state school systems spend disproportionately more money on children who are in need of remedial academic help, relative to their peers who don't, so why would we be surprised to find that parents do the same thing? Yet this sensible explanation is not given the same weight as their preferred, yet no more valid, pet hypothesis, that watching baby videos is the source of developmental delay.

Summary

In this section, we observed that we are obliged to hold even scientists' feet to the fire. We saw first how the prestigious American Academy of Pediatrics got away with making recommendations about TV-watching; both in the absence of evidence, and apparently in the absence of accountability. We next briefly reviewed two studies in which highly publicized scientists such as Christakis and Zimmerman published correlational data on the relationships between infant TV/video-watching and developmental outcomes, warned against the dangers of drawing causal conclusions based on correlational data, and then in multiple public venues hypocritically drew precisely the kinds of causal conclusions they admonished. I believe it is fair to describe such fallaciously drawn causal conclusions as 'myths'. Unfortunately, Christakis and Zimmerman continue to perpetuate two fundamental myths in their 2006 book, *The elephant in the living room: Make television work for your kids*:

Myth 1. Rehashing their 2004 study, Christakis and Zimmerman write in their book that,

> What we found was that for each additional hour per day of television (including videos) that children watched during the first three years of their lives, the chance of having a level of attention problems consistent with ADHD was increased by 9 percent. Put another way, a child who watched 2 hours of television a day before age 3 would be almost 20 percent more likely to have attention problems at age 7 than a child who watched none.
>
> (p. 34)

This claim is false if you read it as implying that watching television in infancy contributes to ADHD in childhood. As noted repeatedly, such an interpretation is scientifically invalid. An equally valid, more reasonable, and probably more likely explanation of these findings is that infants and toddlers with short attention spans are simply more likely to watch TV for extended periods of time.

Myth 2. 'In fact, even shows like *Sesame Street* are good for 3- and 5-year-old children's cognitive development yet harmful to their cognitive and linguistic development when viewed prior to age 2½' (p. 29). Although the first part of this claim is correct, the second part is factually wrong. No scientific studies ever conducted have found that shows like *Sesame Street* are harmful to children's cognitive and linguistic development when viewed prior to age 2½. Christakis and Zimmerman cite two studies to support this false claim; one is their own and one is a study conducted by Linebarger and Walker, but both studies incorporated a correlational design.

If you believe these kinds of claims, then you might as well believe that the more lung cancer you have, the more you are at risk for smoking. Or you can believe that the more robberies you commit, the more your educational level will decrease. There is just no way around the fact that correlational data alone do not permit an unambiguous conclusion that one direction of effect is any more valid, correct, or accurate than its complement. Normally, this isn't a problem because scientists almost never draw causal conclusions with correlational data, and almost certainly never make policy recommendations based on correlational data. But when it comes down to the effects of an omnipresent media on the mental health of our babies, policy recommendations based on mythology can not only interfere with our regular, everyday functioning, they can contribute to excessive anxiety within society as a whole.

Conclusions

Perhaps it is a bit ironic that this chapter began by challenging assertions that various forms of media enhance infant development, only to end by challenging assertions that media inhibit infant development. It is interesting that such polar opposite claims could both build up such heads of steam within a culture. Clearly, there are a myriad of ways that media might impact our children, and with them are a myriad of ways that we can develop anxieties about those effects. We hope it is at least reassuring to know that as of this writing neither of the propositions we have evaluated carries much scientific weight. It is well within the scope of modern-day science to investigate these claims, and eventually science may provide us with solid, relatively airtight data that would permit us to draw legitimate causal conclusions. But these experiments simply haven't been conducted yet, and so it is premature to act as if they have.

Taking these duelling considerations into account, we may be best served by a middle-of-the-road guiding principle, coupled with a dash of good sense, in which we recognize that infant-targeted media are neither necessarily good nor necessarily bad, unless we make it so. Obviously, I am in no better a position to make recommendations about whether, or how, to expose our children to media than those who have been the subject of the previous criticism. But I propose the following for your reasoned consideration, with the caveat that under no circumstances should you ever leave your baby insecurely attended while watching TV or videos:

1 It is perfectly OK if your baby does not view TV or Baby Einstein-type products. Your child will not be any the worse for it.
2 It is probably OK if your baby does view certain (non-violent, non-vulgar, etc.) TV programmes or Baby Einstein-type products. Contrary to the claims of some alarmists, there is no evidence to date that viewing such products causes brain damage, or developmental delays. On the other hand, don't expect IQ gains either.
3 It is a really good idea to interact with your baby as much as possible, even, or especially, when your baby is viewing TV or Baby Einstein-type products. But limited episodes of non-interaction will not cause harm, and cannot be avoided during the normal course of infants' and toddlers' daily lives.
4 For some babies, such as those with difficult temperaments or short attention spans, viewing TV or Baby Einstein-type products may be one of the few experiences that attracts and maintains their attention, and may be a primary source of pleasure – both for you and your child. But this isn't meant to be a *carte blanche* approval

for all television-watching. There are many, many more important activities that you should be engaging in with your baby, and TV-watching should be curbed within reasonable limits.

The Bottom Line

- **What are the key dilemmas parents have to struggle with on this topic?**
  - Should parents let their infants and toddlers watch television or other forms of media, or should media-viewing be avoided altogether?
  - Can certain kinds of media, such as Mozart's music, accelerate development?
  - Can certain kinds of media exposure, such as the Baby Einstein video series, retard development?
  - Is there any merit to the American Academy of Pediatrics' position that no child under 2 years should ever watch television?
- **What does the science say about this topic?**
  - There is very little experimental science on this topic one way or the other, at least as it relates to children.
  - The general findings, as they pertain to the 'Mozart Effect' in adults, are that:
    - There is no Mozart Effect.
    - The effects on intelligence that have been attributed to Mozart's music are not unique to Mozart's music, and do not apply to overall intelligence.
    - Any effects that have been found are short-lived.
- The published science on media exposure in infants and children has been almost exclusively correlational. Correlational findings can never be used to prove a causal influence. Thus, no study has ever shown that television or other forms of media have accelerated or retarded development in children.
- Nevertheless, some 'scientists' have sold books that intentionally mislead their audiences, and that inappropriately draw causal conclusions from correlational data.

- Early evidence from preliminary experimental science points to the possibility of potentially *positive* benefits of media exposure.
- **What do the authors advise?**
  - Media exposure in limited amounts is OK.
  - Certain types of media exposure may occupy the attention of temperamentally difficult children, and provide a respite for parents.
  - Infants and children should never be left unsupervised, even when watching interesting media programming.
  - Media exposure should never be used as a substitute for parent–child interaction. But some forms of media exposure may actually facilitate parent–child interaction.

Understanding and dealing
with temperament
Dixon

In the field of psychology, we psychological scientists often
have a hard time communicating with lay people because
the 'big-ticket' words we use can be interpreted by them in
dramatically different ways from those we intend. 'Temperament' is one of those words, and it has the potential to
cause lots of confusion. Of course, everyone is entitled to
use the word *temperament*, both psychologists and non-
psychologists alike, but unless we are careful about laying
out our common understanding, it can be quite difficult for
the average person to try to talk to psychologists or any
child healthcare provider about children's temperament.
The communication gap goes something like this:

> *Parent*: My Niall is so temperamental that some days I
>   just want to pull my hair out!
> *Child healthcare professional*: Is that so? What does he
>   do?
> *Parent*: He's just temperamental. At night when I'm
>   trying to get him to go to bed, I could just scream!
> *Child healthcare professional*: Yes, but what does he do?
> *Parent*: He's just temperamental. Hey, what kind of a
>   _____ are you? Haven't you ever heard the word
>   *temperamental*?

The miscommunication here comes from the fact that
parents use the common, everyday meaning of temperament, which can translate into anything from 'picky' to

'throws temper tantrums all the time'. But since parents don't have a clearly specified meaning for the term, they may use it to mean different things on different occasions. One time it may mean *fussy*, another time it may mean *lethargic*, and yet another time it may mean *aggressive*. The child healthcare professional, on the other hand, may use the word *temperament* quite differently.

To the child healthcare professional, *temperament* is actually a collection of several characteristics that can be used to describe a child. Depending on the theory of temperament employed, there could be anywhere from a couple to more than a dozen characteristics that are bundled up in the word 'temperament'. So even among professionals there are differences in opinion as to the meaning of *temperament*, or more specifically, the range of behaviours under the umbrella of temperament. Fortunately, there are a few aspects of temperament that seem to be typical among most theories of temperament, so we can get a sense of the scientific definition of temperament by reviewing these aspects here. They include:

- *Activity level* – which reflects how much a child sits still versus fidgets and runs around.
- *Positive / negative mood* – which reflects how happy versus how sad or angry a child seems to be on a day-to-day basis.
- *Attention span / distractibility* – which reflects how well the child can pay attention and stay on task.
- *Fearfulness of new places, people, or things* – which reflects how bold a child can be in the face of new situations or whether she views new situations as threats that require hiding behind mummy's leg.
- *Soothability* – which reflects how easily or quickly a child can be calmed down after some arousing event.
- *Sensitivity to the surroundings* – which reflects how much stimulation it takes before a child acknowledges it through some sort of response. Some kids can sleep through the whistle of a freight train, while others can be wakened by the rustling of their own nappies.

Because these dimensions of temperament are more or less incorporated into most major theories of temperament, there is a good chance that when you refer to these specific behaviours, your child healthcare professional will recognize what you are talking about as temperament. But even if she isn't up to speed on the latest scientific achievements in the field, if the purpose of your visit is to talk about potentially troublesome child behaviours, you should still make sure you describe as specifically as possible the behaviours in question on as many aspects of temperament as you can. That way, you will identify any suspect behaviours, and your healthcare professional will appreciate the level of detail you have provided to help her troubleshoot and isolate any problems.

For their part, when parents haven't kept good notes, healthcare professionals should make efforts to probe parents about their children's temperament by asking questions like: (1) Is it hard for you to keep after Jenny – is she always running ahead of you (activity level)? (2) Is Jenny pretty happy-go-lucky all the time (positive/negative mood)? (3) Does she spend a lot of time in focused concentration when she plays (attentiveness)? (4) Does she hide behind your leg when you visit other people (fearfulness of new people and places)? (5) Is she easy to calm down when she gets upset (soothability)? And (6) Does she notice the tiniest of changes in her surroundings (sensitivity to the environment)? Answers to each of these questions can help the child healthcare professional piece together the temperamental profiles of children, which they can use, in turn, to better guide parents toward effective management and coping with the troubling behaviours.

So now that we have briefly defined the notion of temperament, you might be wondering why temperament should matter to you or your healthcare professional in the first place. As it turns out, for some children, the temperamental profile matters a lot. In fact, an infant's temperamental disposition may be a key indicator of the disposition yet to come – in later childhood, adolescence, or even adulthood. In some ways, a child's temperament can be a magnifying glass on her future. In the next section we take a look at how these early temperamental indicators are related to later developments in life.

Basic notions

Temperament scientists around the world (not to be confused with scientists who are temperamental) think of temperament as something inborn and relatively enduring. Although temperament is not immutable, most scientists assume temperament is highly resistant to change. Changing a child's temperament, if it is to happen at all, would happen very slowly and over extended periods of time. However, to my knowledge there have been no scientific attempts aimed directly at changing children's temperament.

Most scientists even believe that temperament is genetically based. Because children inherit their temperaments, it is important for all of us to realize that children in large part cannot help being who they are and doing what they do. Children's temperamental characteristics are evident in all aspects of their lives – at home, at school, in the supermarket, and in the doctor's office. On the other hand, because temperament represents a behavioural profile that is biologically rooted and longstanding, it should not be confused with behaviour that is temporary, perhaps linked to a unique condition or situation. When Niall throws a temper tantrum at not getting an attractive chocolate bar in the grocery store, or when he screams out piercingly when getting his vaccinations in the county health clinic, he isn't necessarily revealing his difficult temperament. His behaviours in these conditions are primarily just reflexive responses to the immediate environment, the kind of responses most children would exhibit under similar circumstances (except, perhaps, for temperamentally *low-key* children).

The scientific definition of temperament extends beyond the temporary type of temper tantrums. True temperamental types are attached to children like a shadow, and underpin much of what they will do throughout almost all aspects of their lives. Because of the enduring character of temperament, scientists have developed theories and conducted investigations designed to find out how far- and wide-reaching the effects of temperament extend. We report on some of these studies below. However, before we consider the scientific findings, we should clarify a couple of points.

First, we need to point out that all of the scientific knowledge that has been accumulated on children's temperament has been based on *correlational research*. When two factors are correlated, it means that changes in one thing 'go with' changes in the other thing. But a correlation *doesn't* mean that changes in one thing *cause* changes in the other thing. So, for example, although it is true that a person's weight is pretty well correlated with his height, since taller people tend to weigh more than shorter people, it is not true that changes in a person's weight can *cause* him to become taller or shorter. The fact that height and weight are correlated simply means that a person's weight *is predictive* of his height. A 50 kg (110 lb) person tends to be taller than a 15 kg person (i.e. a child), and a 100 kg person tends to be taller than a 50 kg person. So, when we talk about the correlational research linking temperament to other aspects of children's lives, we are not saying that temperament *causes* them to have those other aspects. We are only saying that temperament is *predictive* of those other aspects.

We also need to point out that psychologists tend to think about temperament in two ways. Do you remember your high school physics class where you learned that light has characteristics of both waves and particles? The same kind of thing is true with temperament. On the one hand, psychologists think of temperament as comprising multiple *dimensions*. We have talked about six of these dimensions already: activity level, mood, attention span/distractibility, fearfulness of new people and places, soothability, and sensitivity. From the *dimensional* point of view, children are described in terms of where they fall on each dimension simultaneously; in this case, their overall activity level, their degree of positive or negative mood, their ability to focus their attention, their fearfulness, their ease of being soothed during times of distress, and their sensitivity to environmental goings-on. Differences between children are a matter of degree, depending on where they fall on each of these dimensions. So, for example, Niall might be extremely active, somewhat positive in mood, generally not afraid of new things, not easily soothable, and highly sensitive to the surrounding environment; but sister Jenny might be rather inactive, happy-go-lucky, afraid of new things, but easily soothable, and insensitive about changes in the environment.

However, psychologists also have a tendency to group children into 'either/or' categories, or temperamental *types*. Just as doctors might classify children as sick or well, some temperament researchers might classify children as *difficult* or *easy*. The labels 'difficult and easy' are commonly used in the scientific literature of temperament, and again we will talk about them in more detail in a moment, but these two temperament categories are really just shorthand for describing clusters of dimensional characteristics that seem to go together in some children.

The bottom line is that even though healthcare professionals may occasionally lapse into dichotomous, either–or thinking when they talk about temperament, such as when they refer to kids as easy or difficult, what we are really doing is calling children who score high on many dimensions simultaneously one thing, and calling children who score low on those same dimensions something else.

Now, let us consider the most popular dichotomy discussed in the scientific temperament literature: that of *difficult* versus *easy*. If we were to adopt the theoretical formulation of husband and wife psychiatric research team Stella Chess and Alexander Thomas, who began their research on this topic in the 1950s (and whose work, incidentally, fell on deaf ears at the time), we would describe difficult children as those who are negative in mood, not easily soothed, and afraid of new things. Easy children, in contrast, could be described as positive in mood, easily soothed, and not afraid of new things. Technically, Chess and Thomas characterized the easy–difficult distinction using five temperament dimensions instead of three; I have narrowed it here for simplicity. In any case, the easy–difficult distinction is by far the most popular one made by child healthcare providers and lay people alike. And the distinction has a tight hold on the professional and lay nomenclature, probably because embedded in the terms are the value judgements we place on children with one or the other profile.

Easy temperament → good.

Difficult temperament → bad.

If you have ever been around a difficult child, you understand why many people would not wish a difficult child on their own worst enemy . . . or maybe they would. Dealing with children who are difficult requires incredible levels of energy to accomplish even the most mundane of daily activities. Bathing becomes a show of brute strength and courage for parents, not only in catching the beelining child and restraining her in the bath, but in overcoming the ear-splitting wails that paradoxically result from the direct contact of child flesh with otherwise pleasantly warm water. And feeding becomes an exercise in blind faith – faith that some of the peas that started out on the dinner plate actually ended up in the child's tummy, rather than in her intended destination of the floor or the wall. Yet, despite the sheer exhaustion caused by parenting difficult children, most parents seem to have no shortage of love, caring and affection for their high-intensity offspring. In fact, a parent's care and concern for their difficult child might even be greater than for a *non-difficult* child, because life seems so much harder for children with a difficult profile, and no one enjoys seeing their child struggle through life.

A good side of being temperamentally difficult?

So what is the prognosis for difficult children? Well, good and bad. Consider the following. In 1974, the Masai people of East Africa were struggling to survive through the peak of a ten-year drought. Dependent on their cattle for sustenance, life became cruelly unforgiving for these nomadic families when many lost nearly their entire herds to the excessively parched conditions of the sub-Saharan region. Difficult as it was for the hardiest of adults to survive these extreme conditions, life was even harder for babies born into Masai families during the time, their inexperienced little immune systems often having been rampaged by tuberculosis and parasitic infestations.

Enter researcher Marten deVries. With the goal of exploring whether temperament impacts infant survival rate under such harsh conditions, deVries wanted to find out whether babies born into these conditions were capable of survival. Confirming our worst fears, deVries found that seven of the thirteen babies died between the time he first visited the Masai families, when the babies were about 4 months old, and when he returned only three months later. At first glance, this mortality rate would seem to confirm deVries's initial expectations that difficult babies would be particularly at risk. After all, difficult babies are a great deal of trouble for mothers under the most normal conditions. Under extremely harsh, life-threatening conditions, doesn't it stand to reason that temperamentally difficult babies would be even more troublesome, perhaps even unwelcome? Wouldn't these be the most sacrificial babies? As it turns out, no.

In what is now a classic study, deVries found that the temperamentally difficult babies actually had a survival advantage during that sub-Saharan drought. That is, the difficult babies were actually less likely to die under those environmentally extreme conditions. Only one of the six difficult babies died, whereas six of the seven easy babies died. Contrary to what we might have expected, the easy babies were the ones at risk. Why? Probably because when they got hungry or thirsty, the easy babies didn't fuss or wail a lot, and generally did a poor job of expressing and getting their needs met. As a result, they may have been overlooked or neglected when it came to distributing food rations. Parents of easy babies may have lapsed into a false sense of security about the well-being of their children. The difficult babies, in contrast, were probably very likely to get their caregivers' attention, and to let them know, in no uncertain terms, about their nourishment needs.

Clearly, a difficult temperament can have its advantages under some conditions – such as in extremely harsh climates. But what about under less difficult circumstances? Are difficult children advantaged in any way during times of plenty? Maybe so, but here the evidence is murkier. A review of the scientific literature doesn't reveal much longitudinal research focused on the positive outcomes of babies with difficult temperaments. One study found that babies who had difficult temperaments between 4 and 8 months of age tended to have higher IQ scores at 4 years of age, at least among middle and upper status families. In a study I conducted, I found that 5-month-old babies who got bored faster while looking at pictures, and who would therefore seem to be at risk for becoming fussy as a result of such boredom, also had aspects of a difficult temperament at age 1 year. These latter findings are significant because we know from other research that babies who get bored fast while looking at pictures tend to become children who have relatively high IQs. In sum, at least two studies have shown a slight IQ advantage among children with difficult temperaments; but this is the kind of preliminary evidence that really needs to be confirmed by additional research.

Now, it makes sense that a difficult baby might have an advantage over an easy baby under harsh environmental conditions, primarily because difficult babies might be better prepared to broadcast their biological needs; but why would difficult babies tend to have higher IQs? To be honest, your guess is as good as mine. At this point, we don't have the scientific backing to support any conclusions. But we can hazard a speculation or two.

If you think about what it means to be difficult, with all the fussiness, and crying, and discontentment that it entails, it is easy to imagine that difficult babies draw a lot of attention to themselves. In some cases the attention could be the bad kind, such as when a parent spanks a baby to get the baby to stop crying (which is utterly foolish since spanking a crying baby is not likely to get the baby to stop crying) (see Chapter 9). But in many cases, the attention brought about by fussiness and crying might be the kind of attention that leads to higher survival rates, such as in the deVries study described above, or that leads to a greater range of experiences under more normal conditions.

Think about it this way. When your child is discontented, you pick her up to cuddle her and make her feel more comfortable, you talk to her, and you may even walk around and do your household chores with her on your hip to prevent another crying spell. In this case, your child is clearly gaining world exposure. She gets to go with you to see other rooms in the house, she gets to look around at the stuff in the kitchen when you make dinner, she gets to check out the living room when you do your vacuuming (vacuum in one hand, child in the other), and she may even accompany you to hang the washing out in the garden. Certainly these kinds of opportunities provide the difficult baby with considerably more experience than that of the easy baby, who might be perfectly content just lying around in her cot marvelling at the ceiling texture throughout the day.

Of course this is all speculation on our part, aimed at explaining how it could be possible that temperamentally difficult babies would have an IQ edge over easygoing babies in later childhood; and until we do more scientific research to find out how parents interact with difficult versus easy babies, we won't really know for sure. We simply wanted to give hope to parents of difficult children, to suggest that all is not lost when they discover they are the proud new parents of a temperamentally difficult child. Considering the enormous body of evidence suggesting that temperamental difficulty presents parents with some serious long-term challenges to overcome, we thought a slice of positive news was in order. But the fact of the matter is that in the scientific literature, temperamental difficulty has been associated with far more numerous negative outcomes in later childhood than positive ones. So, at best, temperamental difficulty in infancy is an indication that parents should be on the watch for possible future cognitive and social-behavioural problems.

The other side of difficult temperament

Temperament and language

So what is the down side of having a difficult child? Are there any risks confronted by temperamentally difficult children? Unfortunately, it turns out there are quite a few, which for present purposes we can break down into three types. First, temperamentally difficult children seem to express some language milestones a little later than normal. Despite the evidence giving temperamentally difficult babies a slight IQ advantage over easygoing babies, other studies have shown that difficult temperament is predictive of slower language development, particularly in terms of vocabulary size. In a series of studies, for example, I found that babies who wade in the difficult end of the temperament pool consistently showed slower language progress throughout childhood.

Although the precise reason for this correlation is unknown, research is underway to explore two possible reasons why temperamental difficulty could be related to slower language development. On the one hand, because temperamentally difficult children often have shorter attention spans, it makes sense that these children would be at a disadvantage in paying attention to the mother when she points out and names things in the world. Difficult children may simply miss out on a lot of the naming that is going on in their surroundings. On the other hand, because temperamentally difficult children are socially challenging, they may simply gain little exposure to language to the extent that many of their potential conversational partners may not find it enjoyable to talk with them. (And who would? Don't forget, these kids are fussy, whiny, and cranky!)

Risks for abusive parenting

A second concern for temperamentally difficult children is that they seem to be at increased risk for maltreatment or abuse by parents. Of course, parents have control over whether they choose to mistreat or abuse their children. But all things being equal, temperamentally difficult children, perhaps because they are so demanding, finicky, and fussy, are at risk for pushing their parents over the edge when it comes to disciplinary efforts. At the end of the day, when parents are exhausted from dealing with the trials and tribulations of their jobs, even the most well-meaning parent can be at his wits' end in dealing with his difficult children. Under these trying conditions, even pacifistic parents can occasionally lose control, and engage in disciplinary practices they don't endorse. Many a parent has washed herself in guilt and self-doubt after implementing an undesirable behavioural control strategy such as excessive yelling or spanking. It needn't be the case that parents who yell or spank when their children push them over the edge are bad parents; rather, temperamentally difficult children have a way of getting to their parents. Difficult children can push their parents' buttons to the point where they can *pull* extreme forms of disciplinary tactics right out of their otherwise well controlled parents. Easygoing children do not share this risk of pushing their parents 'over the edge'.

Having said this, we must also point out that the scientific evidence on this issue, at least at this point, is somewhat inconsistent. Some studies have found a correlation between temperamental difficulty and abusive disciplinary tactics, but other studies have not. How could some scientific studies fail to replicate what other studies have found? Well, there could be lots of reasons. The reason that seems most likely here is that the relationship between temperamental difficulty and abusive parenting is complex, involving what we scientists sometimes call a *moderating* variable. When a complex relationship involves a moderating variable, it means that one condition is present when one set of findings is obtained, but that another condition is present when another set of findings is obtained. Such a complex relationship could explain why some studies report a temperament–abuse relationship while others do not. That is, the different outcomes could result from the presence or absence of certain conditions in the different studies.

The most likely candidates for the role of moderating variables in the abuse research, as suggested by German researcher Anette Engfer in a 1992 review of the scientific literature, are: (1) the expectations of the parent, and (2) the characteristics of the child-rearing environment. With respect to the first variable, it seems that when parents have false expectations about the capabilities of their children, such as when they believe children ought to behave more maturely than their years permit or that children should never fuss or cry, then temperamental difficulty is predictive of harsh, abusive disciplinary techniques. However, when parents have reasonable expectations for their children's behaviour, or are aware that children may exhibit problem behaviours through no fault of their own, they seem not to be particularly put off by temperamental difficulty, and seem less inclined to employ harsh, punitive discipline. In this scenario, the moderating variable is *parental expectation*. Difficult children who have parents with inaccurate parenting beliefs are more at risk for abuse and maltreatment than difficult children with knowledgeable, understanding parents.

Environmental conditions also seem to play a moderating role. In this case, it seems that parents who attempt to raise their difficult children in the absence of much help, in the form of either financial or social support, are also at risk for occasionally 'exploding' or 'going over the edge' when it comes to their disciplinary tactics. Parents who are given the chance to let off some steam or get away from it all every now and then, either because they have a spouse or relative who can take over, or because they can afford to pay for child care, seem less inclined to take out their anger and frustration on their difficult children. In this scenario, the moderating variable is *environmental support*, and the evidence suggests that temperamental difficulty is a risk factor for abusive parenting under conditions of an unsupportive environment.

Emotional and behavioural disorders

A third negative outcome associated with temperamental difficulty, and the most extensively studied, is that difficult children are in danger of developing a host of emotional and behavioural problems and conduct disorders in later childhood. Let us first make a quick definitional distinction between two types of general disorders talked about in the literature: *internalizing* and *externalizing* disorders. Externalizing disorders are probably the most well known, since they are easy to see when children exhibit them. Externalizing behaviour disorders include such behavioural problems as attention deficit hyperactivity disorder, impulsivity, aggressiveness, acting-out, or oppositional-defiant disorder (when children consistently defy the authority of their parents). These behavioural problems are called 'external' because their existence depends on the child's interactions with the external environment. Internalizing disorders, in contrast, are more internal to the child, and are harder to spot by the casual observer. These disorders are linked to imbalances in mood, and are linked primarily to depression and anxiety disorders.

It turns out that difficult children are at risk for both internalizing and externalizing disorders. A number of scientists have taken measures of temperament in early infancy and childhood and, after following the same children for a number of years, taken measures of behaviour disorders in later childhood, adolescence, and even adulthood. Almost without exception, researchers report that children with higher scores on dimensions of temperamental difficulty also tend to be rated as having more serious disorders in later childhood, both internalizing and externalizing. And the researchers who have investigated these temperament–behaviour disorder relationships have observed correlations over impressively long periods of time. For example, Professor Avshalom Caspi and his colleagues at the Institute of Psychiatry at King's College London found difficult temperament at age 3 to be correlated with internalizing and externalizing disorders as late as 9, 11, 13 and even 15 years of age. In another study with the same group of children, Caspi still found relationships between difficult temperament at age 3 and behaviour disorders at age 18. In other words, what your toddler does now may tell you something about what your young adult may be engaging in fifteen years later.

And these kinds of findings are not restricted to Britain. In perhaps the largest temperament-based, longitudinal study anywhere in the world, the Australian Temperament Project (ATP) has produced some of the most impressive long-term findings to date. Headed up by researchers Margot Prior, Ann Sanson, Frank Oberklaid and Diana Smart, with the help of many others, the ATP began following more than 2,400 children from the time the children were born in 1982. Among the ATP's more recent findings is that children who were rated as shy by their parents during infancy and toddlerhood developed risk factors for anxiety disorders in their later childhood and early teen years. And, importantly, it appears that toddler girls high in negative mood as 3- and 4-year-olds may be especially vulnerable for becoming at risk for developing eating disorders as pre-teens.

What is a parent to do?

For parents of difficult children, these scientific findings seem to paint a fairly bleak picture. But as the old adage goes, biology is not destiny. Just because you have a temperamentally difficult baby, you are not destined to have a child with a behaviour disorder, a teen with an eating disorder, or a young adult with an aggression problem. Remember, all studies on the long-term outcomes of temperamental difficulty are still only correlational – they do not prove that temperamental difficulty *causes* the problems we have just described. And don't forget about the possible moderating variables, such as parental expectation and environmental support, which are known to influence the statistical relationship between temperamental difficulty and negative outcomes in later life. Still temperamental difficulty is predictive of later problems, so it is probably best to assume that difficult children are *at risk* for a number of later problems, and it is probably wise for the parent of a difficult child to recognize their child's difficulty as a potential problem, and to begin crafting strategies to deal with it. So what is a parent to do?

We must admit that as good as science has been at isolating relationships between temperamental difficulty and negative outcomes in later life, the evidence is not so clear on what recommendations parents of difficult children should follow. One of the obstacles science has faced in finding the intervention answers it wants is that we are not exactly sure *why* difficult temperament is linked to later behaviour disorders. There are a couple of plausible explanations being bandied about, and both of them are being investigated by a number of ongoing research efforts. But at the moment, we simply don't know.

One explanation, perhaps the less optimistic of the two, is that difficult temperament and behaviour disorders are both outward expressions of some sort of underlying central nervous system functioning. It is easy to understand this perspective, since measures of temperament and measures of behaviour disorders have a number of features in common. For example, remember that one dimension of temperament is attention span/distractibility. Then is it a coincidence that a common symptom of externalizing behaviour disorder is attention deficit disorder? Both the temperament dimension and the behaviour disorder reflect children's abilities to maintain attention for long periods of time. So it could be that when children have extremely short attention spans as infants, they are demonstrating a very primitive version of a behaviour disorder, which might not be recognized and/or come into full bloom until several years down the road when the child enters school. This biologically oriented approach has led to the development of a number of drug treatments which have enjoyed a great deal of popularity and a modest degree of success in alleviating some of the symptoms of severe disorders of behaviour in later childhood. In particular, stimulants have been successful in treating symptoms of externalizing behaviour disorders, whereas anti-depressants have been used in the treatment of internalizing behaviour disorders. This is *not* to say that you should be thinking about medicating your temperamentally difficult toddler, this is only to point out that there is some evidence pointing toward biological underpinnings of both difficult temperament and later behaviour problems.

A second, perhaps more optimistic, explanation is that temperamental difficulty is linked to negative outcomes through a negatively spiralling temperament–environment feedback loop. What I mean to suggest here is that negative outcomes in later childhood may be the end result of a complex, protracted series of interactions between the difficult child and a relatively unsympathetic, unforgiving, or at least unknowing environment. From the moment difficult babies are catapulted into the world, they place extraordinary demands on the patience and socialization skills of their parents and other socially significant people. For their part, parents may not have the skills or knowledge, or may not have the environmental resources, to cope effectively with their difficult infants. Their dealings with their babies may then be suboptimal, causing parents to lapse into negative, maladaptive and ineffectual tactics of child-rearing. Then, because the parents were ineffective in dealing with the baby's needs at earlier points in time, the baby's difficult temperament becomes even further exaggerated, further exceeding parents' abilities to cope. This cycle may continue endlessly, from child to parent to child to parent and so on, eventually spiralling out of control, and perhaps eventually resulting in the forms of maltreatment and abuse we described earlier, and/or leading to externalizing and internalizing behaviour disorders.

Despite the dark cloud hanging over this assessment, the reason we would describe this second explanation as more optimistic is that it at least suggests that if parents are part of the feedback loop contributing to the problem, they can also be an integral part of contributing to the solution. They can develop intervention techniques to keep the loop from spiralling out of control, for example. Rather than responding negatively to their difficult child's extraordinary demands, the parents can generate and implement alternative strategies to help address their child's needs.

Redressing the two moderating variables we have already visited would seem to be a good place for parents of difficult children to begin when attempting to pre-empt that negatively spiralling feedback loop. Self-education about what *is* normal for children in terms of developmental milestones ought to go a long way in preventing at-risk parents from having false expectations about the developmental progress of their children. Indeed, simply letting parents know that some children are temperamentally difficult in the first place may be the single most important step in reversing any negative direction that so many temperamentally difficult children are biologically pointed toward.

Similarly, finding ways to encourage the growth of social support networks among at-risk parents may help provide them with the means to let off some steam every now and again. Although there may be little that parents with low or no income can do to remedy their weakened financial situation, there truly is power in groups. It would take very little beyond the formation of something like a stress-reduction co-op, formed among parents in similar circumstances, to allow parents with otherwise very little social support to find some much needed time for themselves. Indeed, the very act of looking forward to time away from their difficult children may provide a kernel of strength; it may give parents the fortitude to withstand the perceived torments of their difficult offspring long enough to resist temptations to resort to disciplinary tactics they would otherwise find unimaginable. And again, it may benefit parents of difficult children simply to know that it is OK to want to be away from their difficult children.

Importantly, there is scientific evidence to show that what parents do has an effect on the continued development of temperamental difficulty. In a study of the techniques mothers use to teach their children, for example, American researcher Eleanor Maccoby and her colleagues found that from age 12 months to 18 months, the more effort mothers put into teaching their difficult boys at 12 months, the less difficult their children were at 18 months. Consequently, mothers of difficult boys expended considerably less energy in teaching their children at 18 months than they did at 12 months. In this case, parenting behaviours were associated with changes in temperamental difficulty, at least among boys, and at the surface level, it appears to suggest that mothers who forge ahead and go the extra mile in dealing with their children are rewarded with a decrease in temperamentally difficult behaviours.

And Dutch researcher Dymphna van den Boom seemed to find proof positive for the potential for success of using parent-training classes to help parents cope with their irritable babies. In a fairly well known study, Dr van den Boom trained parents in how to deal with temperamentally irritable babies when the babies were 6 months old. By 9 months of age, after three months of training, parents who were given the special training were not only more closely attached to their babies, but the babies themselves were more likely to explore their surroundings. So the very act of teaching parents how to cope with their irritable babies changed not only their own behaviours, but also the exploratory behaviour of their babies.

Recommendations

To the concerned parent who may not have access to specialized training or parenting classes, we can offer the following advice.

- Recognize that your child's difficult temperament is real, is probably genetic, and that there was probably very little you could have done to prevent it.
- Recognize that the difficult temperament will probably not go away on its own, and one way or another, sooner or later, it is something you will have to reckon with.
- The way that you deal with difficult temperament may make all the difference in the world. Treating difficult temperament harshly, with strict, inflexible disciplinary limits, is not likely to be very productive, and may even result in a negatively spiralling feedback loop, which itself results in outcomes both you and your difficult child may regret.
- Difficult temperament requires a different tack altogether, one that involves trying harder, while being patient and tolerant of the difficult child's unique but demanding personality. This is not to suggest that limits should not be placed on the behaviours of difficult

children, just that it is important to understand that sometimes limits which are easily met by your easygoing children will be next to impossible for your difficult ones to achieve.

- Advertise in the local paper to find other parents of difficult children. Parents in the same boat as you may be interested in developing a 'difficult-child' support group. Just getting together and being able to talk with someone else who shares your experiences can often ease the distress you are undergoing.

- Finally, some parents of temperamentally difficult infants and toddlers have reported some relief by having their children watch certain episodes of infant-directed media such as those produced by the Baby Einstein people. But this is a highly controversial practice, as are Baby Einstein videos more generally (see Chapter 5 on Baby Einstein). But in no case should infants and toddlers be left unattended.

The Bottom Line

- **What are the key dilemmas parents have to struggle with on this topic?**
  - Some parents may be worried that their child's difficult temperament is a result of their parenting style.
  - When confronted by a temperamentally difficult child, who by definition makes excessive demands, should parents respond with strictness and firm resolve? Or should they approach the situation with flexibility?
- **What does the science say about this topic?**
  - There is little debate in science that children differ from one another from birth onward, and that some babies possess a cluster of biologically based predispositions that make them harder to manage than other babies.
  - There is very little experimental science that tests the effectiveness of different parenting strategies for dealing with difficult temperament.

- But what little research there is suggests that parents would do well to manage temperamentally difficult babies sensitively, patiently, and flexibly.
- **What do the authors advise?**
  - If you are the parent of a relatively easy baby, you are in the majority; but you should still consider yourself fortunate.
  - Parents of difficult babies should avoid the temptation to 'fight fire with fire', and should instead develop compassionate, flexible strategies for managing temperamental difficulty.
  - Parents of difficult babies might consider scouring their communities for other similarly situated parents, and setting up a 'temperamental difficulty' support group.

Medical decisions for the faint of heart

Banks

From the day our children are conceived, we are challenged to make important decisions that could affect them for the rest of their lives. Sometimes the answers come easily, as if we have foreseen all outcomes and can choose the proper course with confidence. At other times, the options have significant implications and weigh heavily on our hearts. How can we, as mere mortals without specialized training, make choices for these tiny, gurgling, squirming masses of flesh, drool and stool which we hold bundled in our arms, or which we support as they toddle on unsteady legs? It is challenging enough to make decisions for ourselves, at times (how many times have we kicked ourselves for the poor choices we have made?). And yet, as our children utter their first cries in the delivery room, we become the Decision Makers, and we take on the responsibility without the benefit of an owner's manual.

While it is important that we, as parents, make decisions that are in the best interests of our children, it is equally important to recognize – at the risk of feeling paranoid – that many of these decisions can have lasting positive or negative effects. Otherwise, parents would be content to just make snap decisions based on what 'felt right'. In many cases there are no clear right or wrong answers, and we make our choices to the best of our abilities, reflecting our values. We see this with a number of medical issues, ranging from circumcision to treating the common cold, and we often do not give these matters a second thought, despite the impact on our children's lives.

Immunizations

One of the greatest advances for the prevention of debili-
tating disease has been the development of childhood
immunizations. Unfortunately, nothing creates a greater
sense of dread among children than a visit to the physician
to await a series of injections that are less than pleasant. I
still have vivid memories of the Nurse With Blue Hair
wielding a giant syringe, the shiny foot-long needle catching
the glint of light as it followed a rapid, unerring path down-
ward toward one of my exposed fleshy parts, and I remember
the sound of my screams reaching operatic proportions in
the tiny room pungent with the aroma of rubbing alcohol.

While my memories of those childhood moments may
be slight distortions of reality, I have certainly come to
appreciate the value of those immunizations. Some diseases,
such as naturally occurring polio, have been completely
eradicated from Western society, and other diseases, such as
certain types of meningitis and severe respiratory illnesses,
are much less common than before the vaccinations were
developed. Nevertheless, there are critics of the vaccination
policies, and some have expressed concern about the safety
of vaccines.

Vaccinations are designed to stimulate immunity to
certain potentially devastating viral or bacterial infections,
with the goal of preventing those infections from developing, even if the child is exposed to someone who has the
infection. Some vaccines contain the actual infectious agent
in a killed form, while others contain live but weakened
forms of the disease. Other vaccines contain genetic copies
of the protein coats typically found on the virus or bacteria,
so that the body can later recognize the actual infection and
fight it off before it becomes invasive. In some countries,
such as the US, it is felt that vaccinations have such a
profound effect on public health that children are required
by law to receive certain immunizations at various times
during their development, unless there are medical or
religious reasons for not receiving those vaccinations. While
no immunization is 100 per cent effective, each of the
required vaccines has a proven track record.

For example, in the early 1980s, there were 200,000 to 300,000 cases of hepatitis B in the United States; however, after routine vaccination for hepatitis B began, the number of infections dropped to less than 80,000 cases in 2001. Since hepatitis B can lead to cirrhosis, liver failure, and even liver cancer, this reduction in the number of hepatitis B infections will play a significant role in improving the health of children as well as adults.

Even greater improvement has been noted in the number of potentially fatal diphtheria cases. In the 1920s, prior to the vaccination, there were more than 200,000 cases of diphtheria in the United States and more than 70,000 cases reported in England and Wales each year. Now, with routine immunization, there are only about five cases each year in these countries.

In developed countries where the measles, mumps and rubella vaccine (MMR) is given, there has been a dramatic decrease in the number of infections. While there are still 750,000 worldwide childhood deaths from measles each year, there are now less than a hundred cases of measles in the United States annually, and most of those cases come from unvaccinated individuals entering the country. Before the introduction of the MMR vaccine in the United Kingdom, the incidence of measles infections peaked at nearly 800,000 cases; now the number of acute infections is almost undetectable.

Prior to 1990, one in 200 children in the US were affected by a bacterial infection known as Haemophilus influenza type b (H. flu), a potentially deadly infection that could lead to epiglottitis, where the upper airway would swell up and restrict the ability to breathe, as well as meningitis and pneumonia. After a routine vaccination programme was started in the US, the number of serious infections in young children was reduced by 99 per cent. Similar effectiveness was seen in the UK after routine vaccinations for H. flu began in 1992; while one in 600 children developed invasive H. flu disease before age 5 prior to the vaccination initiative, a rapid and dramatic drop in the number of serious cases occurred. In 1998, only twenty-one cases of invasive H. flu were identified in the UK.

The 'poster child' for childhood illnesses, however, is polio. This crippling and potentially fatal disease was extremely common into the mid-twentieth century, and one can still see the effects of it lingering in today's society. Even adults who were once infected but later became symptom-free can experience a recurrence of many of the symptoms, in a condition known as post-polio syndrome, which is characterized by a recurrence of muscle weakness, fatigue, and even joint deterioration. Fortunately, polio has been completely eradicated in its 'wild' form from the Western hemisphere, although with the earlier oral vaccine a few cases of vaccine-related polio infections would occur each year. However, in recent years, clinics have begun using an inactivated injectable vaccine which eliminates this problem.

One of the newest vaccinations to create a stir in the media is the human papillomavirus vaccine. This series of three injections was developed to prevent the most serious strains of the human papillomavirus (HPV), an organism responsible for causing nearly all cases of cervical cancer, as well as many other genital cancers and genital warts. According to recommendations by the Centers for Disease Control in the United States, the vaccine should target girls and women between the ages of 9 and 26 years, with routine vaccination for girls at age 11–12 years. Routine immunization of 12–13-year-old girls has begun in the UK. The importance of immunizing young adolescent women prior to the onset of sexual activity is further emphasized by studies that suggest nearly half of women will have cervical HPV infection within three years of becoming sexually active.

This is not a perfect world, and just as no vaccine works all of the time, no vaccine is completely without possible side-effects. However, most side-effects are minor and include redness, warmth or discomfort at the injection site, as well as possible fever and virus-like symptoms. Some vaccinations, such as the MMR, may slightly increase the risk of febrile seizures (seizures resulting from a high fever) for a brief period after the vaccination, but this risk is small and does not increase the likelihood of developing epilepsy

or other neurological problems. More serious reactions, s
as anaphylaxis (a severe allergic reaction), are extremely
rare – about one reaction for every million doses given,
which is much less than the risk of complications from
disease in an unvaccinated child. Even recent reports in the
media that suggested a link between the MMR and other
vaccines and autism have not been supported by numerous
carefully designed scientific studies, and merely reflect the
theories of a handful of scientists.

For example, in the late 1990s a team of researchers led
by A.J. Wakefield published a paper suggesting that the
onset of behavioural symptoms from autism was associated
with inflammatory bowel conditions and receiving the
MMR vaccine. However, this study was completed on only a
small number of children referred to a gastroenterology
department and did not represent a random selection of
children from the general population who had received the
MMR vaccine. Although this study did not show a 'cause
and effect' relation between the MMR vaccine and autism,
it was enough to trigger a media frenzy that led to a
number of inaccurate assumptions and panic about the
safety of immunizations. Later studies done in Britain have
shown that the incidence of autism spectrum disorder has
not increased since the introduction of the MMR vaccine to
Great Britain in 1988, and that the rates of vaccination in
children with autism are similar to the rates of vaccination
in children without autism. Studies done in other countries
such as Sweden have also failed to show an increase in the
rates of autism after introducing the MMR vaccine.

It is therefore appropriate to state that immunizations
are a safe and effective means of preventing serious
childhood illness, and parents are strongly encouraged to
follow the medical recommendations to have their children
vaccinated in a timely fashion.

The sick child

Few things are as unsettling as a sick child. It is a terrible
feeling for parents to watch their children suffer, and
taking care of a sick child is also disruptive to the parents'

and obligations. Perhaps most disturbing is
elplessness and uncertainty that the parent
hild is racked by paroxysms of coughing,
re throat, blanketed in fever or bombarded
tinal symptoms too unpleasant to mention.
However, some of the parental anxiety can be relieved
by knowing what to do before braving the physician's
waiting room.

Fevers, colds and respiratory infections

Children with cold symptoms (cough, sneezing, runny nose
and fever less than 38.3 degrees centigrade (101 degrees
Fahrenheit)) usually do not need to see a physician unless
the symptoms last more than a week. Treating the symptoms with over-the-counter medications is usually adequate, unless the child has a medical condition in which
those medications would be inappropriate. Fever and pain
will usually respond to paracetamol (known as acetamino-
phen in the US) or children's ibuprofen, although care
should be used in providing the correct dosing of these
medications. Fevers running higher than 39.4 degrees
(103 F) that are difficult to control with medication may
need to be treated with tepid sponge baths for at least
thirty minutes. A child with a high fever will often shiver
and complain of feeling cold. However, the child should
never be overdressed or covered in heavy blankets during
these episodes, or heat will be retained and the fever could
rise to dangerously high levels. Once the fever improves,
the child will feel more comfortable.

Although paracetamol/acetaminophen and ibuprofen
will help fever and pain, these medications do nothing for
the other symptoms associated with a cold. Antihistamines
are the medications of choice for runny noses, drainage and
sneezing, and decongestants are ideal for nasal or sinus
congestion (although not always appropriate for young
children). Saline (a fancy name for salt water) nose spray
can help nasal discomfort caused by congestion or drainage.
Coughs can sometimes be helped by suppressants such as
dextromethorphan, and guaifenasin can loosen thick

secretions. Many cold remedies for children contain a combination of these medications; however, to minimize the chances of side-effects, one should use only the combination that is appropriate for the child's symptoms. Special care should be given when using these medications in younger children (under 2 years of age); there are significant risks of side-effects or serious complications when medications are used inappropriately in younger children, and you should probably ask the child's physician for advice before starting their use. While all medications can be dangerous when given in large or frequent doses, paracetamol/acetaminophen in particular can have serious effects if the recommended dosage is exceeded. Aspirin, and any medications containing aspirin, should probably never be used in children during an acute illness unless recommended by a physician, since Reye's syndrome may develop in children taking aspirin during some viral illnesses such as influenza or chicken pox. Reye's syndrome is a potentially fatal condition that attacks the liver, brain and other organ systems, primarily in children during a viral illness, especially if aspirin products have been used to control the symptoms. Symptoms of this condition include uncontrollable vomiting, listlessness, drowsiness, personality changes, confusion, combativeness, seizures or loss of consciousness.

The old adage 'Starve a cold and feed a fever' (or is it 'Feed a cold and starve a fever'?) does not make much sense medically, although grandmothers worldwide will swear to it. However, I am aware of no scientific studies conducted by grandmothers that would support this approach, and so I cannot recommend one over the other. It is best that the child receive proper hydration and nourishment during any illness.

'The scoop on poop'

Constipation

When 4-year old Priscilla starts prancing around in a corner, crossing her legs, rocking back and forth on her toes and turning red in the face, it is unlikely that she is conditioning herself for the lead ballerina role in 'Swan Lake'. However, there is an excellent chance that she is trying to avoid having a bowel movement. This behaviour is frequently seen in children with constipation. While many parents think these contortions are an effort to stimulate a bowel movement, the opposite is usually true. Children with chronic constipation typically have large, very firm stool, and they often resort to extreme measures to delay bowel movements in an effort to avoid the discomfort of 'giving birth' to the large stool. This, of course, makes matters worse.

Not all children will have a bowel movement on a daily basis; there is considerable variability in normal stool frequency, with some children having bowel movements several times daily while others have bowel movements on a weekly basis. As long as the child appears healthy and comfortable, this should not be a cause for concern.

Causes for constipation are also variable. While the occasional child will have a medical reason for prolonged constipation, most will have no physical cause. In these instances, an occasional flare of constipation may be related to changes in diet or activity level, or it may be related to a particular social situation. Children with longstanding constipation, however, may be anxious or have poor self-esteem, or their constipation may be a consequence of a physical illness, intolerance to cow milk protein, stress, fear of using public toilets, or a frightening event that is related to defecation.

This is a frustrating problem for both the parent and child. Many of these constipated children will soil their underwear when liquefied stool works its way past the hard stool, and it is easy for parents to think the child is being rebellious. However, this is not usually a form of rebellion, but rather a direct consequence of retaining stool.

Correcting this problem is often difficult, although the child with mild constipation will frequently improve with temporary use of laxatives or stool softeners. The first step in treating chronic constipation should be behaviour modification. This might involve scheduled time sitting on the toilet for five to ten minutes immediately following meals, reinforced by a calendar with stickers to record each stool passed in the toilet. Rewards can then be given after the child reaches a certain target. Similar tactics can be used to reward the child for each twenty-four-hour period in which the underclothing is not soiled.

Dietary changes may also be useful. Infants with constipation may improve after switching from a cow's milk formula to a soy formula; studies suggest that the iron content of infant formulas probably does not contribute significantly to the constipation. Fruits such as prunes and pears contain substances that help the stool absorb water and stimulate more frequent bowel movements. On the other hand, bananas and apples may have the opposite effect and worsen constipation. Increasing the fibre content of the child's diet is also likely to be helpful, since studies show that constipation is more likely in children whose diets do not meet the recommended daily intake of fibre. This can be accomplished by the use of whole grains, fruits and vegetables.

Refractory constipation may require the evaluation of a physician in order to rule out underlying medical causes for the constipation, or who may prescribe a prolonged course of a combination of therapies in order to address the problem.

Diarrhoea and vomiting

Gastroenteritis (diarrhoea with or without vomiting) is an extremely common and bothersome problem in children, and it is one of the primary reasons for hospitalization in younger children. For every thousand children under the age of 5 in the United States, thirteen will be hospitalized for gastroenteritis annually, while seven will be hospitalized in the United Kingdom. In developing countries the problem is even more severe and contributes to significant mortality in young children.

Fortunately, most cases of diarrhoea are viral and are self-limited, with the greatest concern being the prevention of dehydration. Thorough hand-washing and proper hygiene go a long way towards preventing the spread of diarrhoea, of course, but once the child has the infection, proper treatment can shorten the duration of the symptoms in most cases. Unfortunately, the traditional approaches to treatment were often based on little or no medical evidence and, while probably not harmful, were not very helpful either.

In the past, physicians have recommended at least twenty-four hours of a clear liquid diet (or sometimes nothing at all by mouth) for the child with vomiting and diarrhoea. While clear liquids are important in the initial treatment of gastroenteritis, it is now known that twenty-four hours of an exclusive clear liquid diet is unnecessary in most instances, and withholding food or fluids from a child not requiring hospitalization is needless torture.

The best choice for clear liquids would be one of the oral rehydrating solutions for infants or children, sold in many grocery stores and pharmacies. These solutions contain salt, sugar and other electrolytes in the proper balance to promote healing and prevent dehydration. Watered-down juice, sports drinks, tea or soda pop are *not* good choices for rehydration, since the sugar and salt concentrations of these substances are not balanced properly and may cause worsening of the diarrhoea.

Most studies show that these oral rehydrating solutions should be given for three or four hours; after that, an age-appropriate diet can be continued cautiously, with additional rehydrating solution given for each episode of diarrhoea or vomiting. 'BRAT diets' (bananas, rice, apple-sauce, toast), which are frequently recommended by healthcare providers, really provide no extra benefit to the child and may limit the amount of nutrition that a child receives. As long as the child is properly hydrated and able to keep food down without vomiting, an age-appropriate diet in reasonable quantities is best. Breastfeeding should not be discontinued during an episode of gastroenteritis, although supplementation with the rehydrating solution may be necessary. The child's family physician or paediatrician should be able to suggest a schedule for rehydration, if you are uncertain or feel uncomfortable about the child's condition. The child should be evaluated promptly by his physician any time the child appears lethargic or confused, if there is a significant reduction in urine output or tear production, if the skin loses its normal tone, or if the diarrhoea is bloody.

When to see the doctor

This chapter was not intended to overwhelm the parent, nor was it meant to be an exhaustive text on treating a child's illnesses or eliminating the need for obtaining medical care for the child. Physicians do not expect the typical parent to be able to diagnose and treat their child's illnesses or to make medical decisions without the input of a trained professional. After all, parenting is challenging enough without carrying that extra responsibility around. However, most minor medical problems can be managed at home for a short time. Once those problems persist or worsen, however, the child should be evaluated by a healthcare provider.

The child with an earache should probably always be evaluated, since many medical conditions can cause ear pain; many of those conditions will resolve on their own, but some will require treatment. Children with sore throats should be seen by their physician if the pain is severe or is associated with high fever, or if the symptoms last more than four days. Most sore throats are caused by viruses and do not require antibiotics; however, strep throat (caused by a certain strain of streptococcal bacteria) should always be treated to prevent the development of rheumatic heart disease or kidney problems. Cough is a common problem with children and will also usually go away spontaneously. However, any cough associated with high fever or other worrisome symptoms, or lasting more than two or three weeks, should be evaluated. In the meantime, parents can eliminate the child's exposure to tobacco smoke to see if symptoms improve, since smoke is a common cause for cough.

Even when the child is evaluated by a physician, there is no guarantee that the child will be treated with an antibiotic. In recent years there has been an increase in the number of antibiotic-resistant bacteria, which can lead to devastating infections that are difficult to treat. Most of these resistant bacteria result from the inappropriate use of antibiotics for infections that would ordinarily clear on their own. Children who harbour these resistant organisms can spread them to other children attending nursery/ daycare or school, which can lead to dangerous epidemics. Most physicians are very aware of this problem and are conscientious about using antibiotics only for infections that require aggressive treatment. However, many parents become perturbed when an antibiotic is not prescribed. Rest assured that if an antibiotic is not used, the physician has the best interest of the child (and the community) in mind.

As a general rule, sick infants should be seen by a physician promptly, while for older children who are otherwise healthy but have minor symptoms, medical evaluation can usually be delayed. There are exceptions to nearly every rule, of course, so the back-up rule (to which there are *no* exceptions) is this: if in doubt, ask. Asking the child's healthcare provider whether a child needs to be seen is not a sign of weakness, stupidity or desperation, but demonstrates the parent's concern for the child. It is always better to err on the side of being overly cautious than to ignore a potentially dangerous problem.

Circumcision

One of the first questions that parents face in some cultures (predominantly in the United States) is whether to have their baby son circumcised. Just when proud parents are adapting to feeding schedules and nappy changes, and marvelling at how the child has Grandpa's nose and Aunt Betty's large ears, the nurse or physician presents this option to the parents, often before the infant is a day old. It amazes me how often the parent has an answer, without first asking for more information. As a rule of thumb, couples prefer that the child look just like dad, even though the anatomical feature in question is rarely, if ever, displayed in public; if the father is circumcised, then the parents generally want their baby boy to follow suit.

The practice of circumcision has been recorded since the days of the ancient Egyptians. Artistic depictions of the ceremonial procedure, with all of its pomp and circumstance, have been engraved on the walls of tombs dating back 6,000 years. From these engravings, it appears the surgical procedure was performed on distressed young adults rather than infants, but the general premise of circumcision has been preserved over the course of history.

For many years it was thought that circumcision prevented and cured a number of maladies, including alcoholism, epilepsy, hernias and gout. Not until the 1940s did the medical community realize that it was bestowing powers on the foreskin that the appendage just didn't deserve, and that it was quite possible to be an alcoholic or have seizures *without* a foreskin. Of course, most physicians at that time were male, which might explain some of the grandiose misconceptions.

Since that era, circumcision has fallen in and out of favour a number of times, and various medical organizations, including the American Academy of Pediatrics, have changed their recommendations periodically to reflect the prevailing evidence regarding circumcision's potential health benefits – or lack of them.

In a review of the history of circumcision, Lerman and Liao (2001) point out that, while the rates of circumcision have declined somewhat in the United States in recent years, the rates are still much higher than in Canada and European and Asian countries, where circumcision is a rarity. Some of this decline in circumcision numbers may be due to the influence exerted by a number of vocal non-medical groups that make unproven claims about the effects of circumcision, including permanent psychological harm and sexual impairment.

Given the extraordinary amount of controversy that surrounds the removal of this tiny fragment of flesh, it is surprising that parents are able to make an informed choice regarding the fate of their son's foreskin at all. Most decisions are based on religious, ethnic, cultural or cosmetic preferences, rather than on a clear understanding of the medical risks and benefits. Reviewing evidence and myth regarding circumcision may help parents feel more comfortable with the decision they must make.

One time, circumcision was touted as an effective means of preventing penile cancer. However, penile cancer is rare, and the risk varies in different regions of the world. Rather than being related exclusively to the presence of foreskin, the risks of developing penile cancer seem more related to issues of hygiene, clean water supplies, multiple sexual partners, genital infections and, in some studies, tobacco abuse. Studies estimate that nearly a thousand circumcisions would need to be done in order to prevent one case of penile cancer.

On the other hand, there is fairly strong evidence that circumcision can help prevent urinary tract infections (UTIs) in male infants. While the overall risk is low, uncircumcised infants under the age of 1 year are ten times more likely to develop UTIs and four times more likely to be hospitalized because of the infections, compared to male infants who are circumcised. Based on these data, only a hundred circumcisions need to be performed to prevent one urinary tract infection in a young infant.

In some populations, circumcision may help prevent certain sexually transmitted diseases, although lifestyle (such as limiting the number of sexual contacts and routine use of condoms) probably plays a larger role. However, there is budding evidence suggesting that circumcision may reduce the risk of HIV, the virus which causes AIDS. Microscopically, there are cells lining the inner surface of the foreskin which fuse with the HIV virus, allowing it to penetrate and multiply in the body. In developing countries, where routine condom use and proper hygiene are limited, a few studies suggest lower rates of HIV transmission among men who are circumcised. However, these studies are not always well designed, and their results may not be applicable to the general population. A number of large-scale, well designed trials are currently in progress to investigate this matter further.

Some boys and men who remain uncircumcised will develop a condition called phimosis, in which the foreskin becomes tight and cannot be retracted. While this does not always cause significant problems, phimosis can sometimes lead to difficulty urinating, and it has been linked to higher rates of penile cancer. The foreskin can also become inflamed and painful, in a condition known as balanitis; this is particularly common among men with diabetes. Good hygiene reduces the risk of phimosis and balanitis, but circumcision clearly prevents these problems.

Most medical organizations now take a fairly neutral stance regarding circumcision. There are clearly some medical benefits to circumcision, although these benefits may be small in the general population. There are also risks associated with the procedure, especially bleeding and infection, which are usually minor; however, serious complications can occur, which in some cases may even result in amputation, although they are fortunately very rare. No clinical studies support the theories that circumcision interferes with sexual sensation or satisfaction, or that there is psychological harm from the procedure. Parents should weigh the benefits and risks of circumcision and discuss them with the baby's physician before making a final decision.

The Bottom Line

- **What are the key dilemmas parents have to struggle with on this topic?**
  - To immunize or not to immunize?
  - What are the keys to managing vomiting and diarrhoea?
  - To circumcise or not to circumcise?
- **What does the science say about this topic?**
  - Immunizations have effectively reduced the incidence of many dangerous childhood illnesses and have made a significant positive impact on public health in communities in which immunizations are done routinely. The likelihood of severe adverse reactions is extremely small compared to the health benefits received. Well designed, large-scale studies do not support the link between certain vaccines and autism.
  - Oral rehydrating solutions are useful in the treatment of vomiting and diarrhoea. Most evidence supports resuming a normal diet as soon as possible after the

initial treatment with oral rehydrating solutions, rather than adhering to a strict 'clear liquid' diet for at least twenty-four hours.

- While circumcision has been shown to reduce the chances of urinary tract infections and long-term complications related to inflammation, such as phimosis, proper hygiene of the foreskin may also be able to reduce the risk of those problems. The risks of the procedure may therefore not be worth the benefits derived from circumcision. On the other hand, there are no compelling studies which support the claims that circumcision results in emotional harm or sexual dysfunction.

- **What do the authors advise?**
  - Unless there is an overwhelming contraindication to having a child immunized (for example, a previous severe reaction to a vaccine, or a religious belief), children should receive immunizations. This may prevent serious medical complications from illness and reduce the incidence of illness within the community.
  - For children with vomiting and diarrhoea, the first line of treatment is an oral rehydrating solution. One should avoid using juices, soda or sports drinks in children, because the imbalance of sugars and salts may make diarrhoea worse. As soon as the child is tolerating liquids well, resume feeding a healthy, well balanced diet.
  - Since the medical benefits of circumcision are minimal, but the risks of complications from the procedure are also small, the choice regarding circumcision becomes one of personal preference, largely driven by one's culture. If parents elect to have their sons circumcised, the procedure should be done by someone who has had extensive training and experience in performing the procedure.

Recommended reading for parents

The Green Book, Department of Health, www.doh.gov.uk

What goes in must come out: medical perspectives on toilet training

Banks

Parents are frequently mystified by the process of elimination. By this, I am not referring to the sleuthing skills of Sherlock Holmes as he tracks his elusive nemesis Professor Moriarty, but to the child's controlled release of waste products. Unfortunately, for parents who are looking for easy answers on the most effective methods of toilet training, they must realize that the issue is still fairly controversial within the medical science community. Much of what physicians recommend regarding toilet training is based on theory, and not necessarily on facts that are demonstrated in carefully controlled studies. The outcomes are clear: we want our children to be functional members of society, capable of making it through the day without soiling themselves or others, and learning that process at an early age without developing neuroses related to bowel and bladder control. How we get to that point is not always so clear.

Common approaches to toilet training

Toilet training methods have varied considerably throughout history, and still vary to some extent depending on culture, race, or even socioeconomic status. In a manuscript by a respected nineteenth-century paediatrician, a strict, regimented training approach was advocated:

> *How may a child be trained to be regular in the action of its bowels?*

By endeavoring to have them move at exactly the same time every day.

At what age may an infant be trained in this way?
Usually by the second month if training is begun early.
What is the best method for such training?

A small chamber . . . is placed between the nurse's knees, and upon this the infant is held, its back being against the nurse's chest and its body fully supported. This should be done twice a day, after the morning and afternoon feedings, and always at the same hour. At first there may be necessary some local irritation, like that produced by tickling the anus or introducing just inside the rectum a small cone of oiled paper or a piece of soap, as a suggestion of the purpose for which the baby is placed upon the chamber; but in a surprisingly short time the position is all that is required. With most infants, after a few weeks the bowels will move as soon as the infant is placed on the chamber.

What advantage has such training?

It forms the habit of having the bowels move regularly at the same hours, which is a matter of great importance in infancy and makes regularity in childhood much easier. It also saves the nurse much trouble and labour.

(Luther Emmett Holt, The Care and
Feeding of Children (1894))

Not all clinicians endorse such a rigorous toileting experience. While some societies approach toilet training in a similar manner, most modern-day recommendations utilize some version of 'child-oriented readiness' to influence the onset of training. In fact, some have theorized that – since infants do not develop the neurological capacity to control bowel and bladder function until at least 9 months of age – efforts to attempt training prior to that period would most likely result in frustrations for both parents and child.

In the 1960s, T. Berry Brazelton defined the *child-oriented* training method. In this approach, both child and parents must be willing to participate actively. To be successful, the child must be physiologically and emotionally ready, meaning that the child needs ample neurological control of bladder and bowels, as well as maturity to cooperate and follow instructions. Basic signs of readiness include the child's ability to imitate behaviours, the ability to demonstrate independence by saying 'no', having an interest in toilet training (for example, by following the parent into the bathroom and watching the parent closely), having the ability to walk, and having the skills to pull clothing on and off. Most children do not reach all of these milestones until around age 18 months, and for this reason it is believed that most attempts to train the child should wait until after the age of 18 months.

The Brazelton training process itself involves a stepwise approach, first allowing the child to become familiar and comfortable with the 'potty chair'. This may require allowing the child to sit fully clothed on the seat until comfortable with the process, before allowing her to sit on the seat without clothing. If the child exhibits significant fear of the seat, it is probably appropriate to delay toilet training for a short time in order to allow her to get used to the idea. Once the child is sitting comfortably on the seat, it may be helpful to place stool from the child's nappy into the potty chair so that the child learns the purpose of the basin.

While most physicians and parents tend to support the use of the Brazelton 'child-oriented method', more aggressive models – ideal for impatient parents desiring to complete toilet training over a shorter time-frame – have also been recommended. Perhaps the most widely studied of these methods is the 'structured-behavioural theory' of Azrin and Foxx, first touted in the 1970s as a method of toilet training institutionalized mentally disabled adults but later adapted for use in children. In this *parent-oriented* method, parents must first determine if the child is physically and emotionally ready for training. If the child is capable of having periods of dryness and able to perform tasks such as walking short distances, dressing, and sitting upright, then the child probably has the physical capabilities to be toilet trained. The child who can understand instructions, point to body parts and imitate tasks may possess the psychological readiness for toilet training.

Once readiness is determined in this approach, a young child must be taught a number of component skills that involve recognizing elimination stimuli. This is accomplished in four steps, each of which is designed to bring the child closer to bladder control. The first step is increasing the child's fluid intake, which effectively keeps the bladder full and poised to void at a moment's notice. This step should probably not be tried just before a long and relaxing Sunday drive in the country with the family, unless the parents are fond of pulling off the road and leading the child into the thickets. The second step is scheduling regular and frequent time for the child to sit on the toilet, to eliminate the opportunities for bladder mishaps. The third step is to provide positive reinforcement for successful voiding in the toilet – rewarding the child with verbal praise, small gifts (stickers are very effective), special privileges, or uninterrupted fun time with mum or dad. The final step in the Azrin and Foxx method is to provide negative consequences (or 'overcorrection') for toileting accidents; it is this phase of the training that is the most controversial, since frustrated parents might resort to providing consequences that are potentially abusive or inappropriate for the child's level of development.

While the Azrin and Foxx method can potentially result in more rapid training of the child, studies have shown that there is a more negative reaction from children, particularly with temper tantrums during the mandatory toilet time. This sometimes leads to parent frustration and causes them to abandon this method of toilet training, resulting in children who regress back to their untrained state. On the other hand, the Brazelton method probably involves a longer training period, but because it relies more on child readiness, there is generally less friction between the parent and child.

Factors affecting toilet training

Parents must recognize that there will be stumbling blocks and setbacks during toilet training, and they must also recognize that the successful choice of a toilet training method depends to some degree on the child's temperament and the parent's personality. Nevertheless, there are other factors that inherently affect the success or timing of toilet training.

Girls tend to start toilet training earlier than boys, and as a rule girls succeed at an earlier age. Studies suggest that children who begin toilet training at an earlier age typically complete training at an earlier age, although the duration of training is generally longer; however, the same studies show that there is really no advantage in beginning toilet training before the child reaches the age of 27 months, because the child has not developed sufficiently to complete the training successfully.

Interestingly, both race and family income may also play important roles. A US study showed that African Americans tend to begin toilet training at an earlier age than European Americans, perhaps due to cultural beliefs regarding the developmental levels of children. Age differences were also seen among family income levels, with lower income families initiating toilet training at an earlier age than in higher income families. Some of this effect may be due to the cost of disposable nappies; families who can afford the luxury of disposable nappies may rely on them longer because of the convenience factor and may therefore delay toilet training until the child is older.

Toileting success may also be affected by child temperament. In Chapter 6 on temperament, Dr Dixon discussed the significance of those traits and how they can influence parenting. Toilet training is yet another milestone that can be enhanced or foiled by temperament. Studies have shown that children with difficult temperaments – particularly those who are less adaptable, who do not adjust well to new situations, who are more likely to whine or cry, or who are more easily frustrated by challenges – are more likely to have difficulty with toilet training. These 'challenging' children are more likely to hide and defecate in their clothing, indicating that they have social awareness that stooling is a private event and that they have the ability to recognize the signs of an approaching bowel movement. These children are also quite likely to develop constipation se of their tendency to retain stool, which makes defecation more uncomfortable and therefore less likely to occur on a regular, controlled basis. Many of these children have full bowel control, despite their frustrating toileting behaviours. While parents of these children can become disconcerted, disillusioned and dyspeptic, it is important to step back, take a deep breath, and recognize that part of the work is already done – in many of these cases the children already possess the developmental skills needed to be toilet trained. However, these children need reassurance, and the parents must recognize that when the child disappears and becomes very quiet, this is a signal that the child may need gentle redirection to the toilet. For children with chronic constipation, treatment may be necessary (the reader is referred to Chapter 7 on medical decision making for helpful hints).

Other factors, such as physical and developmental disabilities, may also affect the initiation and completion of toilet training, but discussion of those factors – and how to best overcome them – is beyond the scope of this chapter. Nevertheless, it should be recognized that toileting difficulties related to disabilities (as well as the disabilities themselves) can be significant stressors to parents and can lead to disruptions in family interactions as well as depression or other internalizing disorders among parents. Fortunately, parental support groups can be instrumental in helping to deflect some of this distress and in developing appropriate coping mechanisms.

Toileting mishaps

After spending months training one's child to void or stool successfully in the toilet, it is understandably frustrating for the parent when the child relapses and begins having toileting 'accidents'. There are a number of possible explanations for these relapses. Children who undergo more intensive toilet training are more likely to have relapses once the parents become less attentive to supervising toileting. Children who are fatigued or suffering from an illness may also regress and begin losing control of the bladder or bowels. Some medications can lead to bladder or bowel mishaps. Stress is also a key factor. While toddlers and school-age children may not be able to voice levels of anxiety or frustration resulting from instability in their home lives, school-related anxiety, or even physical or sexual abuse, the response to stress may manifest itself by a sudden loss of bladder or bowel control. In instances related to stress, a number of other symptoms may also be present, including frequent headaches, abdominal pain, or even generalized aches and pains. Sorting out the causes is probably best accomplished by the child's physician.

One of the most emotionally traumatizing failures of toileting – especially among older children – is bed-wetting. When a child over the age of 5 years has been dry at night for at least six months and then develops bed-wetting, this condition is known as 'nocturnal enuresis'. While the parents can be frustrated by this condition, the child may feel devastated and embarrassed to the point of avoiding social interactions with friends. This social isolation is unfortunate, particularly because the condition of bed-wetting is surprisingly common, occurring in 2 to 15 per cent of children, depending on age. In fact, for children who suffer from nocturnal enuresis, there is a strong likelihood that one or both parents also experienced the same condition. While children eventually outgrow this pestilence, there is often an urgency that cannot wait on the normal processes of biology; children and their families often search desperately for quicker solutions, especially as the children approach the age where they start spending nights at the homes of friends.

Fortunately, there are a number of solutions for bed-wetting that have a substantial amount of medical evidence supporting their effectiveness. Bed-wetting alarms have been in vogue for some time. There is a large variety of alarm systems. One of the most common designs involves sensors that are placed in the underwear and detect moisture, triggering a bedside alarm when the child loses bladder control. Theoretically, by awakening the child each time he loses bladder control, the child becomes conditioned to recognize the sensation of a full bladder and is ultimately able to awaken himself in order to void appropriately. Studies show that bed-wetting alarms are effective at promoting dryness, although many families abandon this method because of the effort it entails. Some children who achieve dryness while using the alarm system relapse after the alarm is discontinued. I have often wondered with amusement, when prescribing a bed-wetting alarm, whether the alarm itself could make the *parents* lose control of their bodily functions as they are awakened abruptly from a sound slumber. That would truly be a nice touch of irony, I think.

'Dry bed training' is another method employed to achieve bladder control at night. This technique utilizes a combination of interventions, including the bed-wetting alarm, waking routines, involving the child in clean-up activities after bed-wetting, and providing rewards for dry nights. Dry bed training without the alarm system is *not* effective, according to well designed studies; dry bed training in conjunction with the bed-wetting alarm is an effective tool, although really no better than using the bed-wetting alarm alone. Thus, while dry bed training may teach the child a bit of responsibility, I cannot recommend it as a more effective mechanism for solving the bed-wetting problem.

Medications have been used successfully and safely in the treatment of bed-wetting. Desmopressin, a synthetic derivative of the body's natural antidiuretic hormone, works to suppress the production of urine when used before bedtime. Given in the form of a nasal spray or tablet, this medication is extremely effective at preventing bed-wetting; however, the effects are only temporary, and bed-wetting may resume once the medication is discontinued. Because of some extremely rare but potentially hazardous electrolyte abnormalities that may occur with desmopressin, it is no longer prescribed as an aid for bed-wetting in the United States.

Medications from the class known as tricyclic antidepressants have also been used effectively for bed-wetting. Imipramine is perhaps the most commonly used tricyclic for the purposes of bed-wetting; studies show that it is as effective as desmopressin in controlling night-time urination, but its effects are also likely to be temporary. Once the medication is discontinued, bed-wetting may occur again. Like all medications, there are potential side-effects that can produce problems for the child, including stomach upset, excessive drowsiness, confusion, agitation, or difficulty sleeping.

Most studies show that medications along with the bed-wetting alarm work better than either intervention alone, and the combination is more likely to have lasting effects after stopping the use of medications and alarm systems.

Toilet training is a sometimes stressful but ultimately rewarding period in raising your child. Not only does it require that the child is biologically and emotionally ready for the task, but it requires a strong level of commitment and patience on the part of the parent. Children do not always need to use the facilities at a time convenient for the parents, but it is important that the parent be willing to drop everything at a moment's notice – with minimal audible grumbling – in order to take their child to the WC. As the child becomes more enthused with toileting, the parent must be prepared to visit every public restroom in the community; the child will be looking at these opportunities as something akin to visiting an amusement park. So take a cautious deep breath and remember that this is a milestone in your parenting efforts; all too soon, your son or daughter will be asking to borrow the car keys.

The Bottom Line

- **What are the key dilemmas parents have to struggle with on this topic?**
  - What is the best method of toilet training?
  - What is the most effective way of dealing with bed-wetting?
- **What does the science say about this topic?**
  - While toilet training is one of the key accomplishments in raising a small child, there is surprisingly little evidence to support a 'single best method' for

toilet training. The most popular methods are largely based on observations and recommendations of the 'experts'. The Brazelton 'child-oriented' method is initiated after certain developmental milestones have been achieved by the child, and the stepwise approach can create a slower process; however, the child is less likely to rebel and there is less likelihood of back-sliding. On the other hand, the 'parent-oriented' method of Azrin and Foxx is initiated after certain physical and psychological milestones have been attained, and there is a more aggressive approach utilizing reinforcement techniques for successes and negative consequences for accidents. While this technique is likely to succeed more rapidly than the Brazelton method, studies suggest that the Azrin and Foxx method may result in more child distress and ultimately rebellion.

- Bed-wetting alarms are more effective for stopping bed-wetting than other methods, and when used in conjunction with prescribed medications their effectiveness is increased further and is more likely to be longer-lasting.

- **What do the authors advise?**
  - Whichever method of toilet training is chosen by the parent, it is crucial to avoid making toilet training a battle. This author prefers the Brazelton method because of its non-threatening approach. However, depending on the temperament of the child and the needs of the parents, a blend of approaches may work well.
  - Bed-wetting usually resolves on its own, and the timing is often dependent on the child's genetic factors. However, if the problem is significant enough to cause distress or embarrassment for that child, parents should seek the assistance of a health-care provider who can prescribe the bed-wetting alarm along with appropriate medications to achieve the desired period of dryness. The parents should be prepared for the return of bed-wetting in some children when the interventions are stopped.

How to discipline your child
Banks and Dixon

There are times when even the stoutest of parents is pushed to the edge of reason by a misbehaving child. The signs are unmistakable: the father, looking dazed, unshaven and wearing mismatched shoes, pushing the trolley aimlessly through the supermarket while little Edward screams at a decibel level previously unachieved by a mortal child. The father has long abandoned pleading with the child, and any effort to squelch the banshee screams with threatening looks only results in retaliation by the toddler. As beads of perspiration begin forming on the father's red face, in a final act of desperation, he directs the trolley to the confectionery aisle and reaches his quivering hand toward the box of chocolate-covered caramels. Father feels a wave of calm descend, and gulping hard – and nearly hating himself – he manages to croon the fateful words, 'If you quiet down, I'll give you a sweet.' Game, set and match to little Edward.

Who among us has not been in a similar position? A parent who has never been frustrated publicly by screaming offspring has either never left the home or is heavily medicated. If we are honest with ourselves, we all dread the disapproving looks from others, and we are all threatened by the anticipation of what others think of our parenting skills. In reality, there have never been perfect children, and there have certainly never been perfect parents.

Much of what we practise as parents we learn from our own observations of others – our parents, our friends, and sometimes strangers. Unfortunately, what we learn may not be the most appropriate parenting skills for our own children. This is a common problem when we are trying to develop good behaviour in our children, because everyone has an opinion about how children should behave, and how the parents can best accomplish that objective. Perhaps one of the most omnipresent hurdles in developing our own new identities as parents will be overcoming the parenting attitudes and beliefs handed down by our own parents. Although our parents may be fairly enlightened as to the most recent evidence-based trends in child-rearing, they may nevertheless look down their noses at us as we strive to implement approaches with which they have not yet become acquainted.

Our primary goal as parents is to successfully *socialize* our children. Technically, socialization can be defined as the process of inculcating in our children the beliefs, behaviours and values regarded as essential to becoming full participating members of our culture. Thus, socialization processes and outcomes can be expected to vary from country to country, from region to region, even from neighbourhood to neighbourhood. The process of moulding socialized behaviour in children is known as 'discipline'. While many people mistake discipline for punishment, the two are not the same. In the case of socializing children, discipline includes helping the child acquire socially acceptable behaviours while simultaneously reducing undesirable ones. As will be described in more detail below, punishment is only one of many forms of disciplinary tactics that parents may use to guide their children on the journey toward socialization. We believe the goal of the enlightened parent should be to modify the child's behaviour using as little punishment as possible, so that the child can achieve maximal self-control and self-direction. As the scientific literature shows more and more, this is a process that requires planning and persistence on the part of the parent.

Sources of misbehaviour

While parents are sometimes convinced that children misbehave merely to drive the parents to distraction, children rarely possess such sinister motives. Often the behaviours are merely age-appropriate playfulness or exploration. But in our adult world of high social standards, coupled with concerns for appearances, we may find many of those behaviours difficult to tolerate, even if they are 'normal'. However, true misbehaviour can be due to a number of factors.

In many cases, misbehaviour can actually result from our own poor parenting practices, especially when we fail to provide consistent guidance or limits. We might, for example, fall backwards in our chair laughing the first time our exceptionally cute toddler dumps a bowl of spaghetti on his head. Although we laugh because the act was hilarious, how is our child to know that our floor-rolling laughter should not be the gauge for choosing similar behaviours in the future? Similarly, a child may be getting different messages from different people about what is OK to do. Behaviour viewed as cute and endearing by one parent may not be so viewed by another. W.D. (the second author of this chapter) remembers his anguish when his wife helped their toddler daughter pull out all the plastic storage containers from the cabinet to use as high-volume, bangable, playthings. Clearly, mum thought this routine was just fine (and it was). But it still caused dad a great deal of anxiety, what with his obsessive-compulsive cleanliness tendencies and all. Tupperware® drumming was simply not the preferred mode of play when dad was in charge. Of course, there is plenty of room for differences of opinion between parents with regard to what is OK to do. But parents can only achieve maximal success in their disciplinary practices when they are consistent with one another, and when they are consistent with themselves across time. So parents would be well served to come to terms of agreement with respect to what will be allowed, and what will not – *before* their differences of opinion become manifested in their child's misbehaviour.

Inattentive parenting may also be the source of misbehaviour, such as when dad has been on the phone for a long period of time or when mum is trying to finalize closing arguments for an upcoming court case. Without close parental supervision, one ill-conceived misbehaviour on the child's part may beget another. So long as there are no unpleasant consequences coming from the inattentive parents, and so long as the transgressions are fun things to do, well, why not? But in this case, who is to blame for the misbehaviour? Is it the child's fault for doing what toddlers are wont to do? Or are mum and dad to blame for their lack of vigilant supervision? Clearly it is the latter.

Obviously, parents aren't always to blame for children's misbehaviour. Sometimes it can be as simple as children being tired, hungry or bored (and not coincidentally, when the parent is also tired, hungry or bored). Some misbehaviour may also result from children's biological predispositions, such as having a difficult temperament (see Chapter 6), or having syndromes such as attention deficit hyperactivity disorder. Certain personality disorders, which can have their origins in childhood and persist into adulthood, may also be responsible for misbehaviour, sometimes even extreme misbehaviour. Extreme misbehaviour, which by definition is more severe than typical childhood misbehaviour, may eventually require psychological and/or medical intervention. A compounding consequence of these serious or chronic conditions is that parents may not be emotionally or intellectually prepared to deal with the unique characteristics of their child, and so may select parenting tactics that, while appropriate for most children, may not be appropriate for their own.

Of course, there are times when misbehaviour is not directly anyone's fault, but reflects symptoms of unplanned, unwanted or undesirable changes in family circumstances. It is not uncommon, and in fact it is usually considered normal, for children to increase their misbehaviour when their parents are separating or divorcing, or when a parent or other close relation dies. Similarly, children living in profound poverty or in homes where there is parental substance abuse or mental illness may have more challenging behavioural extremes.

Key factors in effective discipline

Fortunately for dedicated parents, there is a great deal of scientific research showing that children's misbehaviours can be fixed, removed, changed or modified based on some very simple principles. And unlike some of the other scientific topics we have talked about in this book, where the science is still new or evolving, the science of behaviour change is based on exceptionally sound footing, with extremely well supported scientific evidence, and with almost zero controversy.

The major field of scientific study that addresses children's behaviour change is called *applied behaviour analysis*. As the name suggests, this approach focuses exclusively on children's behaviours. Most practitioners who use applied behaviour analysis don't really focus all that much on children's thoughts, beliefs, or feelings. What matters to them is how children are behaving, and whether that behaviour needs to be corrected. The overarching goal of this approach is to decrease the undesirable behaviours and increase the desirable ones. If the procedures work without taking children's thoughts, beliefs and feelings into account, all the more power to them. Applied behaviour analysis is based on the lab work of the famous Harvard psychologist B.F. Skinner; and the real-world application of Skinner's work has been made accessible by researchers Donald Baer, Montrose Wolf and Todd Risley.

Given how effective applied behaviour analysis has become, it is surprising that it is not more popular and widely known. But this may be changing, especially with the increasing popularity of reality TV programmes such as *Supernanny*, the protagonist of which uses applied behaviour analysis techniques in nearly every show. Still, one reason why applied behaviour analysis may not have achieved a greater foothold in the parenting market is because of the strange and confusing nomenclature that it comes with. A lot of terms used in applied behaviour analysis are odd-sounding, and if not explained clearly, they can be difficult to understand. Other behavioural terms are commonly used by lay people, but are used wrongly, and so only create confusion. We use this chapter to help acquaint parents with some of the foundations of applied behaviour analysis in order to create a flexible, effective framework for making parenting decisions about the child's behaviours.

Antecedents and consequences

A basic tenet of applied behaviour analysis is that target behaviours should be viewed in their temporal contexts. What this means is that to understand misbehaviours, it is important to understand the events that occur right before and right after them. Events that occur immediately prior to misbehaviours are called *antecedents*, while those that occur immediately afterwards are called *consequences*. Both antecedents and consequences are also called *controlling variables*, because if you change the antecedents and consequences of children's misbehaviours, you can control the misbehaviours themselves. Hence, in order to control the target behaviours, you must control the antecedents and/or the consequences.

Most of us are probably already aware of the importance of *consequences* for changing misbehaviours. When W.D. was 10, he thought it would be fun to stick his finger in an electric light bulb socket. Since the light bulb socket was switched on, the consequence of that behaviour, as you might imagine, resulted in W.D. never feeling the need to stick his finger in a light bulb socket again. Clearly, consequences play a very important role in influencing future behaviours. Accordingly, most of us probably assume we can effect change in our children's behaviours by managing the consequences of their actions. We expect, for example, that when we punish or praise our children for their behaviours, we are changing the likelihood of those behaviours happening again. By definition, behaviours that we *punish* effectively decrease in frequency, and behaviours that we *reinforce* effectively increase in frequency. Punishments and reinforcements, then, are two very broad classes of *consequences* of children's behaviours that influence the likelihood of those behaviours occurring in the future. (More on this below.)

But we tend not to think about behavioural *antecedents* too much. This is unfortunate because antecedents can also be very powerful determinants of behaviour change. They are powerful because they modify the effectiveness of the consequences. Consider one of the most important *antecedents* of children's behaviours: parental attention. If a child has gone a long time without parental attention, she may decide to engage in certain behaviours so as to produce parental attention. The antecedent of *not having parental attention* renders the consequence of *getting parental attention* very powerful, and thus renders children much more likely to engage in behaviours that will produce the desired outcome. On the other hand, if the child has already been getting *too much* parental attention, she will probably engage in behaviours designed to reduce the amount she is getting.

Consider a more concrete example of how two different antecedents can completely reverse the effectiveness of a consequence. Three-year-old Jenny is colouring quietly in the corner of the room, and decides to write on the wall with her markers. Jenny's father punishes her for that behaviour by scolding, and then Jenny doesn't write on the wall again in the near future. Here the scolding serves effectively as a punishment because there is a decrease in the misbehaviour. Now suppose that Jenny has gone quite some time without interacting with dad, and suppose further that because he is hard at work, dad has ignored several of Jenny's bids for attention. What is Jenny to do? From the behaviour analysis point of view, the antecedent conditions at this point have set up a situation where one possible option for Jenny is to write on the wall. By writing on the wall, Jenny may get the desired response from dad, namely some attention (unpleasant though it may be). Thus, even though she is likely to get the same response as before, a scolding, the antecedent to the behaviour relegates the consequence of the behaviour to more of a reinforcement, and not the punishment that it was the first time.

Note here that from dad's point of view, his choice of scolding as a consequence was the same on both occasions. But from Jenny's point of view, the two scolding consequences are completely opposite in terms of their effect: the first time it worked as a punishment, the second time it worked as a reinforcement. The difference between the two effects is owing entirely to the differing antecedent conditions across the two occasions.

More on reinforcements and punishments

Now let us consider reinforcements and punishments in a little more detail. First, it is important to point out that 'reinforcements' and 'punishments' are often confused in the popular press, and they are often used wrongly by the individuals we depend on for child-rearing advice, including our children's physicians and teachers. So before assuming that professionals in your life know the proper meanings of these terms, you should be sure you have a firm grasp of them yourself. It can be empowering to realize that you know as much about a parenting issue as the experts you rely upon. In any case, if you hold fast and firm to a few definitions in applied behaviour analysis, you can avoid a lot of the confusion that comes from inappropriate application of these terms. As mentioned above, a punishment is any consequence which *decreases* the occurrence of a behaviour. Likewise, a reinforcement is any consequence which *increases* the occurrence of a behaviour. But as we have seen with the Jenny example above, each of these consequences may function differently over time depending on the antecedent conditions. How a parent *intends* a consequence to function is not the same as how a consequence actually *does* function.

Second, punishments and reinforcements can both be administered in two ways: positively and negatively. This gives parents four types of consequences to choose from: positive punishments, negative punishments, positive reinforcements, and negative reinforcements. In the context of applied behaviour analysis the words positive and negative do not mean *good* or *bad*, or *desirable* or *undesirable*, which is what we usually expect them to mean. Rather, they are used in the mathematical sense, where 'positive' means *added* and 'negative' means *subtracted*. The mathematical meanings of *positive* and *negative* are precisely the meanings Skinner wanted these terms to have.

If you administer a positive punishment or a positive reinforcement, it means you are *adding* something to the situation (to decrease or increase a behaviour, respectively). But if you administer a negative punishment or a negative reinforcement, it means you are removing something from the situation (to decrease or increase a behaviour, respectively). As a handy quick reference, we can list and define the four different types and manners of consequence administration this way:

- *Positive punishment*: **decreases** the probability of a behaviour by **adding** something to the situation (typical parenting tactic: scolding).
- *Negative punishment*: **decreases** the probability of a behaviour by **removing** something from the situation (typical parenting tactic: time-out or grounding).
- *Positive reinforcement*: **increases** the probability of a behaviour by **adding** something to the situation (typical parenting tactic: praise, star, or weekly allowance).
- *Negative reinforcement*: **increases** the probability of a behaviour by **removing** something from the situation (typical parenting tactic: nagging).

The pair of consequences most frequently confused is probably 'negative reinforcement' and '(positive) punishment', perhaps because they both seem to imply something unpleasant. But if you read their definitions closely, you will see that negative reinforcement is exactly the opposite of positive punishment; the former increases behaviour by removing something from the situation, whereas the latter decreases behaviour by adding something to the situation. These two consequences are about as different as can be. Having provided a rough overview, we now turn to a more detailed discussion of punishments and reinforcements.

Punishment

Although we argue below that reinforcements are far superior for socializing children than are punishments, there are occasions when punishments are necessary. But there are several caveats to the effective use of punishments:

- Punishments are only effective to the extent that they are coupled with reinforcements for desirable behaviour.

- Punishments should *never* be used for revenge or to 'get back' at a child.
- Punishments must be carried out promptly and consistently in order for the child to appreciate the relationship between the specific misbehaviour and the consequence.
- The connection parents have in mind between the punishment and the misbehaviour may *not* be the same connection that forms in the mind of the child.

Consider, for example, the parent who spanks a toddler for crying too much (or too loud, or too long, or whatever). In this case, the parent seems to have the idea that the child will associate the pain from the spanking with the behaviour of crying, and will therefore stop crying so as to stop the spanking (and the pain that comes with it). But what the parent *thinks* will happen may not be what actually *does* happen. In fact, the toddler will probably *not* associate the pain with the crying. Rather, he will probably associate the pain with the parent. Surely this is not the outcome the parent had in mind when choosing spanking as the consequence to administer. More appropriate for a crying toddler would be to attempt to alleviate the child's anguish by redirecting the child to a more pleasurable activity, and praising her when the crying stops. Punishments are best directed at cases where children are wilfully disobedient or can otherwise control their behaviour. There is not much point in punishing a child when a behaviour, such as crying, is not entirely within the child's realm of control.

Punishments should also be reserved for contexts that are appropriate to a child's age or developmental level. It would be inappropriate to punish a toddler for not keeping his room clean, for example, although an older child would be expected to have that ability. At best, a toddler may be expected to help put away a few toys after playing with them; but keeping a room clean would far exceed reasonable expectations. It would also be inappropriate to punish for accidents or behaviours that are part of normal development, for which children may not yet have fully developed the necessary cognitive or behavioural skills.

For example, parents should not punish behaviours such as toilet-training accidents or thumb-sucking, at least when they occur in late toddlerhood. Nor should parents punish young children for crying when upset or talking to imaginary friends; nor for being afraid of the dark or of being alone in later childhood. The ability to regulate emotions under these circumstances requires skills that children are only in the process of attaining. Punishment should always be carried out respectfully and should avoid teasing, shaming, or intentionally humiliating the child.

Negative punishment and extinction. Most punishments that come to mind in our everyday experiences are of the positive variety. They are *added* to the situation. A parent gives a warning, a scolding, or even a spanking to a child. A police officer fines a speeding driver. A judge gives a jail term to a convicted felon. But in general, positive punishments leave a lot to be desired. Spankings, for example, cause physical pain, or even physiological damage, and risk damaging the parent–child relationship. Scoldings can cause humiliation and embarrassment. All things being equal, if punishments are to be used at all, negative forms of punishment are usually preferred because they can eliminate undesirable behaviour just as effectively as positive punishments, but often with less physical or psychological harm.

Perhaps the most famous disciplinary technique which uses negative punishment is the 'time-out' technique (sometimes called 'grounding' when applied to older children and adolescents). Although knowledge about time-out is nearly universal, it is so frequently mismanaged that when parents first attempt to use it they often become frustrated and abandon it prematurely. Negative punishment is defined as removing something from the child's environment (usually something of value to the child) so as to decrease the likelihood of an undesirable behaviour. Consequently, as a type of negative punishment, the proper use of the time-out technique involves immediately taking the child out of a problem situation, placing the child in the corner of a room, or in another room altogether, free of stimulation from toys, books, computer, and television, and withholding parental interaction for a brief period of time. During the time-out, the parent does not lecture or scold the child or have any other interactions, because in all likelihood parental attention is what the child was seeking in the first place. Providing parental attention, even in the form of lecturing or scolding, may undermine the utility of the time-out. Of course, time-outs must occur in an environment that is non-threatening and safe, but parents should strive as far as possible to ensure that the location is neutral and boring.

Time-out is most effective in children between the ages of 18 months and 5 or 6 years. While the technique may not resolve all misbehaviours, it is an extremely helpful form of discipline for the correction of tantrums, whining, yelling, fighting, and other forms of non-compliance. There has been a great deal of conflicting advice about how much time a time-out should take. The internationally acclaimed scientist Russell Barkley has recommended that children should remain in time-out for no longer than one minute per year of life. But to our knowledge there is no scientific evidence to support such a recommendation. For children younger than 3 years, a time-out of less than one minute may serve the purpose. For children of 5 or 6, it may take as many as seven or eight minutes, or as few as two or three minutes, before the time-out achieves maximum effectiveness. The 'one minute per one year of age' rule may be a good starting point, but parents should be willing to adjust as needed for the unique characteristics of their own children – perhaps a little less time for younger children and a little more for older children.

More important than time restrictions, however, the key to successful time-out is for the child to be fairly well ignored during that period. This is the most challenging element; it is extremely tempting for parents to respond when little Ivan is screaming at the top of his lungs and causing the window panes to rattle. By ignoring the behaviour and allowing Ivan out of time-out only when he has calmed himself, he learns that the behaviour is unacceptable. He also learns to develop self-calming skills. The child who attempts to escape prematurely from the confines of time-out should be picked up and gently placed back in the time-out location, without verbal interaction from the parent. If this becomes a frequent behaviour, the child should be informed in a few simple words that he will not be allowed out of time-out until he has cooperated and become still and quiet. For the most non-compliant children, having them sit on your lap and gently holding them in place may be necessary. But social interaction should still be minimized so that the child does not receive the attention the time-out was designed to eliminate.

Even when parents have incorporated time-outs into their repertoire of parenting tactics, they should still be regularly employing heavy doses of desirable attention when their children are behaving as expected. Some of the parenting websites describe this as a 'time-in', and it is probably a good idea to have at least as many 'time-ins' as time-outs, but the more the better. Exhibiting frequent displays of pleasant attention helps children develop an appreciation for the contrast between time-out inducing behaviours and praise-inducing behaviours, and it increases the likelihood that the time-out will have the desirable impact that negative punishment strategies were designed to have. Of course, children who live in homes where the parents are too preoccupied to spend quality time with them in the first place are not likely to respond well to time-outs. For them, living in a parentally preoccupied environment is very much like being in perpetual time-out.

Even in the best of circumstances, parents should realize that time-outs are unlikely to be effective immediately. Time-out is a technique which trains the child as to which behaviours are unacceptable, and results happen only with persistence, patience, and practice. Long-term effectiveness in modifying a child's behaviour is excellent, if the parent uses the technique properly.

Older children do not respond as well to time-out, and parents should therefore change their disciplinary tactics to match the developmental needs of the older child and adolescent. Negative punishment is still an effective disciplinary strategy for older children and adolescents, but it must occur in the context of depriving them of cherished items or withholding privileges, rather than having them sit quietly in corners. In the US, this practice is commonly called 'grounding'. It is far more agonizing for a teen to lose the use of her mobile phone than it is for her to sit in a quiet room and dream about her favourite rock star. Although effective in modifying behaviour, withholding privileges works best if it is used infrequently and is in some way a logical consequence of and connected to the nature of the transgression. For an older teenager, bringing the car home past curfew could result in the loss of access to the car for a specified period of time, for example. And like other forms of discipline, the privilege should be removed immediately after the misbehaviour, for an established and reasonable period of time, and the parent must be able to enforce the punishment consistently. This is no time for the mother to use the 'Wait till your father gets home' tactic (or vice versa).

A subtype of negative punishment is called 'extinction'. Contrary to what its name might imply, extinction in this case does not refer to the annihilation of an individual or species by an extreme form of punishment. Rather, it refers to a form of negative punishment that suspends (i.e. removes) the reinforcement for a targeted misbehaviour. This method of punishment is highly effective for dealing with tantrums and whining. Assuming that the reinforcer believed to be supporting a misbehaviour can be accurately identified, extinction simply involves removing the reinforcer.

Consider the child from the beginning of the chapter who gets sweets in the supermarket after throwing a temper tantrum. Of course, giving in to little Edward and buying him the sweets results in a quick resolution of the fit, but the resolution is only temporary because Edward is being conditioned to use the tantrum technique again, through reinforcement, making the misbehaviour more difficult to correct in the future. Extinction in this case would simply involve the parent ignoring the screaming, not buying the sweets, and thereby removing the positive reinforcement for that behaviour. It may be socially difficult for the parent to put up with a tantrumming child in the supermarket, but reinforcing that tantrum is not going to make little Edward's predilection for throwing tantrums any more socially palatable. The parent simply has to have confidence that after enough trials without the supporting reinforcement, the tantrums will eventually become extinguished.

There is one caveat to the extinction procedure, however. When a parent first attempts to extinguish misbehaviour by removing the reinforcement, there is usually a temporary intensification of the misbehaviour. It is as if the child thinks the parent isn't hearing the whining, and so decides to ramp it up to an even higher intensity so the parent can be sure to respond to it. This temporary increase in the misbehaviour is called an 'extinction burst'. Extinction bursts are normal, they almost always happen, and they are the first indication that the extinction procedure is on its way to becoming successful.

Verbal punishment. All parents have – at one time or other – resorted to scolding as a means of correcting their children. Those same parents – at one time or other – have recognized that scolding rarely has any long-term impact on a child's behaviour. In fact, studies suggest that while verbal expressions of disapproval may work for short periods of time if used sparingly, frequent use of scolding may lead to anxiety in the child and encourage the child to ignore the parent. In some cases scolding, which most parents probably assume is a form of positive punishment, may reinforce misbehaviour inadvertently because the antecedent conditions may prejudice the child toward perceiving the verbal correction as parental attention. This is especially true when the parent is trying to enforce time-out.

For these reasons, when used without other forms of discipline, verbal disapproval may have the unfortunate side-effect of increasing child non-compliance. This leads to frustration for the poor parents. Frustrated parents tend to escalate their futile scolding and begin shouting, and this in turn can have an excitatory effect on young children. In addition to resulting in greater misbehaviour, shouting may lead to unhealthy spikes in the parent's blood pressure and stabbing pains behind his or her eyes. That is certainly less than desirable, as parents should strive to survive the discipline effort with no adverse health outcomes.

Corporal punishment. Corporal or physical punishment is the most controversial form of discipline, although its use is quite common. Studies suggest that 75 per cent of Canadians and more than 90 per cent of Americans use physical punishment at least occasionally. The definition of physical punishment encompasses all extremes of punishment strategies, including spanking, slapping, grabbing, shoving, or even more violent methods of behaviour control, but the common theme is that some degree of pain is inflicted on the child. Traditionally, acceptable spanking has been limited to the use of an open hand on the buttocks or extremity without causing injury, in order to modify behaviour. However, because of the tendency for physical punishment to escalate and become more severe as its effectiveness declines (potentially to the point of inflicting serious injury), even this degree of punishment remains passionately challenged by many.

Most medical and psychological societies discourage physical punishment because there is no clear benefit, and the risks to the child usually outweigh any positive outcomes. Unfortunately, most of the research that examines the benefits and negative outcomes of spanking can only demonstrate correlations; it is difficult – and surely inhumane – to design studies that show cause-and-effect outcomes from a specific form of physical punishment. It is also difficult to compare studies on corporal punishment, since the investigators frequently include families who use varying extremes of corporal punishment. Studies in which the parents use harsh forms of punishment cannot conclude that *all* forms of spanking are harmful, since most families use milder forms of spanking as well. On the other hand, for the same reason, studies that involve only parents who use mild forms of corporal punishment cannot claim that *all* spanking is helpful. Arguments either in support of spanking or which condemn spanking often centre on moral and religious beliefs, rather than firm science.

Without question, spanking is inappropriate for children younger than 18 months. These children are too young to appreciate the connection between the behaviour and the punishment, so spanking is unlikely to successfully change behaviour in this age group. Perhaps more importantly, however, corporal punishment in young children is more likely to result in physical injury.

Some scientists theorize that the frequent use of physical punishment interferes with the teaching of non-violent modes of conflict resolution. Recall that the principal goal of parenting is successful socialization. But if our view of socialization includes benevolence and non-violence, how can we expect our children to be non-violent toward others if we are modelling aggressive behaviour toward our own children? Perhaps scrappy little Brian spends so much time in the headteacher's office because his parents inflict pain so frequently at home.

There certainly seems to be an association between receiving corporal punishment as a child and using physical punishment as an adult. In fact, there is a correlation between corporal punishment and domestic violence, as well, since children who are spanked are more likely to physically assault their partners as adults. When parents use physical punishment on their older children, there is a greater likelihood that the child will be physically aggressive and participate in criminal or violent activities, and the child is also more likely to have substance abuse problems. Children raised in homes where physical punishment is common also have lower self-esteem, higher rates of depression, and poorer academic success.

Some critics of spanking believe that any form of spanking is child abuse. There is certainly a fine line that separates physical abuse from acceptable discipline. However, it is never acceptable to strike a child with an object, or to use force that is strong enough to leave marks on the child's body. It is also inappropriate to pull a child's hair or ears, jerk the child by the arm, or shake the child. Any of these actions can cause significant injuries, even if those injuries are unintended. Since spanking becomes less effective over time, it often escalates and parents resort to more harmful forms of correction. Given the choice between effective forms of discipline that cause *no* pain (such as time-out and positive reinforcement) and a less effective technique that *inflicts* pain and potential injury, it makes little sense to resort to the more physical form of punishment. A good policy would be to avoid spanking or other forms of corporal punishment altogether.

Reinforcement

In the long term reinforcements are far more pragmatic choices than are punishments. The main role for punishments is to eliminate behaviours children should not have, but notice that punishments do not leave anything in their place. More simply, punishments train children what *not to* do, but not what *to* do. Imagine the parent who has nothing in her arsenal of parenting tactics but punishments. What is this parent's implied goal? Presumably, it would be to produce a child with no behaviours, since the only thing punishments serve to do is remove behaviours. Obviously, if a child is to become socialized, she must do a lot more than do nothing. She must do good things – she must engage in behaviours that are relevant and appropriate for her culture. Consequently, any parent who hopes to produce a socialized child must have strategies for increasing desirable behaviours, in addition to those designed to take away the undesirable ones.

For these and many other reasons, the most effective, most desirable, and most preferred method of affecting behaviour is the administration of reinforcements. Proper discipline cannot occur without extensive use of reinforcement, and children and adults of all ages respond to it. The youngest infant quickly learns that when she cries, an attentive parent will either change her soggy nappy or feed her. The parent's prompt response to the cry reinforces the infant's behaviour as an effective, useful communication skill, which has the effect of ridding her of an uncomfortable nappy or filling an empty tummy. Until more sophisticated forms of communication emerge, the cry is surely one of the most effective means infants have for getting parents to take action; and it is important for parents to reinforce their children's use of it.

As noted throughout this chapter, parental attention is one of the most powerful forms of reinforcement. Children thrive on attention from their parents, and they may go to great extremes to obtain it. It is unfortunate, then, that parents spend so much of their attention on children's misbehaviours. When parents spend most of their attention on children's misbehaviours, they are inadvertently teaching their children that a highly reliable way of getting attention from mum and dad is to misbehave. For many children, obtaining this unpleasant attention may far outweigh the fact that the attention is unpleasant.

The simple solution, of course, perhaps more easily said than done, is for parents to pay proportionally more attention to their children's appropriate behaviours. When parents spend their pleasant attention on appropriate behaviours, their children will come to associate those appropriate behaviours with the pleasant outcomes. Consider what we are saying: *you should pay more attention to your child when he or she is behaving normally*. All too often, we take for granted the normal behaviour of our children and focus attention on their transgressions. We are recommending just the opposite: focus attention on the normal behaviour, and ignore the transgressions as much as reasonable.

The rewards for good behaviour can range from smiles, words of praise and other signs of affection, to more tangible rewards such as special activities, extra privileges, and even – at times – material items. We are not referring necessarily to expensive items that can lead one into financial ruin, such as the latest in designer clothing or electronic game technology, but to more trivial items that are equally effective at demonstrating appreciation for desirable behaviour.

A common form of reinforcement employed by some parents is the use of a 'star chart' or 'sticker chart'. With this technique, the parent identifies a few age-appropriate behaviours and lists them down the left side of a sheet of paper, along with columns for the days of the week. The parent then places a star or sticker in the appropriate row and column each time the child demonstrates the appropriate behaviour. This technique works best if the parent is consistent in rewarding the child with a sticker immediately after the desired behaviour. For some children, the act of receiving the star or sticker is reward enough. For more pecuniary-oriented children, however, it is helpful to have some pre-assigned rewards that can be received after a certain number of stars or stickers have been awarded. For younger children, the list of expected tasks should be limited to no more than a few simple, developmentally appropriate activities such as using a spoon, putting away a few toys, and voiding in the toilet. For older children, the tasks can be more complex and the lists can be longer, and can include cleaning a room, helping with household chores, and feeding the dog or cat.

A more complex form of reinforcement is the 'token economy' system, because it uses both a form of positive reinforcement and a form of negative punishment. Positive reinforcement occurs whenever children receive tokens for engaging in behaviours that have been predetermined to earn them. So for every day that Nigel practises piano for fifteen to thirty minutes, he can earn a token. On days that he practises for an hour, he can earn two tokens. In contrast, negative punishment occurs whenever children lose tokens for engaging in behaviours that have been predetermined to have a token cost associated with them. Nigel may lose a token, for example, if he fails to pick his clothes off the floor after bathing. He may lose two tokens if he engages in name-calling or disrespectful behaviour. Parents can adjust the values of the various behaviours that are being reinforced or punished, depending on the family values they are trying to instil, by assigning different numbers of tokens to the various behaviours incorporated into the system. Token economies work best for school-age and early adolescent children. However, as is true in most disciplinary practices, in order for the token economy to be effective, the child must make the connection between the behaviours and the reinforcements/punishments resulting from them. And of course, the parent must be consistent in rewarding and penalizing practices.

Positive reinforcement is an extremely effective and powerful disciplinary tactic. But, as mentioned above, it can have the unintended effect of reinforcing misbehaviour when used inappropriately. The suffering father who was pushing the trolley in the supermarket at the beginning of this chapter, and who, in desperation, plied his screaming child with sweets in order to end the misery, has effectively reinforced the use of tantrums as a means of getting what the child wants. A short-term relief from painful social embarrassment has just resulted in a long-term setback. Care must always be taken to avoid reinforcing the wrong behaviours.

Beyond behaviours

All professional behaviour analysts, like *Supernanny*, and indeed all professional trainers of any sort, incorporate these foundational concepts into their efforts. These techniques are not magic, and they are not proprietary. They are simply basic behavioural principles at anyone's disposal. Besides behavioural professionals being more experienced than regular parents, there is probably only one major difference between the two groups: professionals *know* that behaviour analytic techniques work, indeed they make their living off them; while parents may feel uncertain or even sceptical about the efficacy of these techniques. For parents who don't feel confident in being able to use these techniques, there are many additional resources available from the internet, and popular press publications such as Glenn Latham's book *The power of positive parenting: A wonderful way to raise children*, and former president of the American Psychological Association, Alan Kazdin's book, *The Kazdin method for parenting the defiant child: With no pills, no therapy, no contest of wills*.

We acknowledge that our coverage in this chapter has been one-sided, with an exclusive focus on the techniques used in applied behaviour analysis. Our one-sidedness has been intentional, and only reflects our desire to familiarize parents with a set of basic disciplinary principles that are easy to use in the comfort of their own homes, with little formal training, and that are well known to work and to work well. Applied behaviour analysis is not only used in the successful socialization of typically developing children worldwide, but it is also one of the most successful techniques for managing children with severe mental or behavioural disabilities, including children with Down's syndrome and autism.

But there is obviously a lot more to children than just their behaviours, and many other systems of behaviour management have arisen which take into account children's thoughts, beliefs, and feelings. Some of these systems have been specially developed for working with children with severe behavioural problems, including those with 'oppositional defiant disorder' or 'conduct disorder'. In a fairly comprehensive review article, Sheila Eyberg and her colleagues itemize several of these systems, describing them collectively as 'evidence-based psychosocial treatments for children and adolescents with disruptive behaviour'. Targeted primarily at children whose behaviours are so severely out of line with expectations that they run the risk of not achieving normal socialization, these systems blend many aspects of applied behaviour analysis with approaches that focus on how children think and how children form relationships with others.

It is beyond the scope of this chapter to consider all sixteen treatments for disruptive behaviour disorders, but looking briefly at a couple of them may help interested parents understand how applied behaviour analysis techniques can be blended with other approaches. In *anger control training*, for example, children with disruptive behaviour problems meet once per week during the school day in groups of about six children. In the group, children read short stories about social encounters, and discuss the kinds of social cues given off by characters in the story, and also possible motives of the characters. Children learn how to solve the problems encountered by characters in the stories, read about and practise solving the problems of other story characters, and eventually learn how to apply the problem-solving strategies they have developed to their own social situations.

In *parent–child interaction therapy*, the focus is not so much on the child as it is on the relationship between the parent and the child. In this approach, families meet for weekly one-hour training sessions for about fourteen sessions. Parents learn two types of interaction patterns.

In learning a *child-directed* interaction pattern, parents develop skills for giving their children positive attention and for actively ignoring their children, depending on whether their children exhibit desirable or undesirable behaviours. In learning this pattern of interaction, the focus is on promoting 'positive parenting and warmth in the parent–child interaction'. Once parents have developed this skill set, they then learn how to give, and practise giving, clear and unambiguous instructions to their children, but also how to administer and follow-through with giving praise (positive reinforcement) and time-outs (negative punishment). Parents learn all these skill sets during the treatment sessions, and are coached by the therapist until they are judged to have achieved competency.

Certainly, there are many aspects of parenting that are challenging. Making appropriate choices for raising your child can be overwhelming at times. No aspect of parenting, however, is more troubling than the area of discipline. We all want our children to become respectable members of society, without the notoriety that follows the social deviants who make the headlines on the evening news. We also want our children to enjoy their childhood without living in constant fear of severe retaliation. How do parents teach children what is acceptable behaviour in society, without being tyrannical and overbearing? How do we balance enforcing responsibility and allowing our children the freedom to explore their horizons and establish their own identities? If you share these concerns, then you are already ahead of the game. And if you can train yourself to utilize forms of discipline that have been shown to have positive long-term outcomes, such as time-out or loss of privileges coupled with the use of praise and rewards, the outcomes of your years of parenting will be rewarding beyond all expectations.

The Bottom Line

- **What are the key dilemmas parents have to struggle with on this topic?**
  - Is punishment or reinforcement more effective in changing behaviour?

- What is the most effective punishment for tantrums?
- Does spanking have long-term harmful consequences?
- **What does the science say about this topic?**
  - Reinforcement of desired behaviours is superior to punishment for undesired behaviours, although punishment is sometimes necessary. In those cases, *negative punishment* (for example, removing privileges) is more effective than *positive punishment* (such as scolding or corporal punishment).
  - Negative punishment is the most effective treatment for tantrums. More specifically, completely ignoring the child during the tantrum works best for extinguishing the behaviour in the future. Responding to the child during the tantrum unintentionally reinforces future tantrums.
  - The research on spanking is contradictory, and it is difficult to show cause and effect. However, there are correlations between spanking and the child later resorting to domestic violence, aggressive behaviour, and substance abuse, as well as other undesirable behaviours. The research is clear that other forms of discipline (negative punishment and all forms of reinforcement) are more effective in eliminating undesired behaviours and reinforcing desired behaviours.
- **What do the authors advise?**
  - Reinforcement should be the discipline technique of first choice. While punishment may sometimes be necessary (for example, when the child is deliberately disobedient), it should be coupled with reinforcement for appropriate behaviours. The parent should always attempt to use a loving, compassionate approach when disciplining the child.
  - Ignoring tantrums is quite challenging, and it is frustrating to recognize that ignoring the behaviour does not have immediate results. However, it is important to remember that the goal is not just to stop the tantrum once, but to reduce their likelihood in the future. If the parent is patient and consistent in ignoring tantrums, the tantrums will disappear faster than if the parent responds to them each time.

- Because spanking can be potentially harmful, because it can sometimes escalate to the point of causing injury, and because other forms of discipline have been shown to be more effective, the authors recommend abandoning the use of spanking as a discipline technique. If the parent is compelled to strike out, we recommend going into the bedroom and striking a pillow. The parent will feel better, and the pillow will be unlikely to suffer any psychological harm.

Recommended reading for parents

Kazdin, Alan E. (2008). *The Kazdin method for parenting the defiant child: With no pills, no therapy, no contest of wills.* New York: Houghton Mifflin.

Latham, Glenn I. (1994). *The power of positive parenting: A wonderful way to raise children.* Brigham City, UT: Brigham Distributing.

Violence in the media

Dixon

As the parent of both a teen and a preteen, I find myself worrying daily about the opportunities my daughters have for getting themselves into trouble as a result of the media resources they use. My worries over media violence are just the beginning. The sheer volume of information that must be managed exceeds by leagues what was only imaginable ten years ago. Clearly, humans come insufficiently equipped to process the bandwidth of information in which they have begun to immerse themselves – a fact which was prophetically chronicled by science fiction writer Greg Bear in *Darwin's Radio*, who characterized the next stage of human evolution as the capacity for modulating two information streams simultaneously.

As the number of avenues of information our children must navigate increases, so will their chances of making a wrong turn. Consider YouTube, a veritable storehouse where you can upload just about any personal video-recording you make, so long as it is not vulgar or offensive (no porn, no graphic violence, no offensive videos, no copyrighted media, etc.). YouTube is a fascinating sociotechnological device. But my fear is that it serves not only as a vehicle for impressionable youth to distribute their most banal and embarrassing experiences to global audiences, but also as an incentive for performing banal and embarrassing experiences in the first place.

Consider text messaging. As pragmatic as text messaging is for us to communicate with our children while they are away from home, at least for those who have mobiles, the very same technology provides a number of inconveniences. For one thing, children can receive text messages they don't want, directly from individuals they don't know. Recipients of abusive texts may become victims of cyber-bullying. Texting with graphics makes it easy to send photos of oneself to friends and acquaintances, but sometimes these photos can be forwarded with indiscretion and end up in the hands of non-friends and non-acquaintances. The daughter of a colleague of mine recently shared a picture of herself in a bathing suit with a couple of her friends, and discovered just how quickly her skin-clad image could end up in the hands of some very insalubrious individuals. Modern mobiles with integrated high-resolution cameras even allow a child's image to be captured by an incidental stranger, without the knowledge or consent of the child or the parent.

Parents of adolescents may find it disconcerting that texting while driving has become a popular pastime of the foolhardy. Talking on the mobile while driving used to be sufficiently worrisome for parents. Now texting while driving requires that drivers divert not only their attention from the road, but their gaze as well. A 2005 Australian study showed that teen texters who drove spent twelve out of every thirty seconds with their eyes diverted from the road. This amounts to spending 400 per cent more time with eyes off the road than when not texting. Clearly, the combination of texting, driving, and being young represents a lethal combination. Texting while driving is illegal in many parts of the world, but some adolescents have never met a law they didn't like to break.

Consider MySpace and Facebook. These wonderful social networking sites allow children and adults to maintain relationships with old friends, with new friends, with online friends, and with on-ground friends. But as socially facilitating as they are, these sites also vastly overexpose children to informational contact with strange people. Unwitting children may be enticed to share personal information such as their names, addresses, and phone numbers. Online role-playing experiences such as Second Life and World of Warcraft also allow children to assume avatar-guised alternative personalities and to interact with complete strangers who are similarly guised.

Obviously, the benefits derived from media technology are phenomenal, but so are the problems that follow in their wake. Rapid information technology development can be intimidating and daunting. Overwhelmed parents may try to isolate their children from media sources altogether. Although this may be an effective strategy for infants and toddlers, it may eventually backfire for older children who are increasingly likely to find themselves behind in information technology developments.

So what comfort and guidance can science provide in the midst of so much change? As it turns out, not much. Science is ill-prepared to study most media technologies because they are too newly arrived on the scene. By its nature, science is methodical and deliberate. Media technologies emerge swiftly and abruptly. It is very much a case of the tortoise trying to keep up with the hare. By the time science has resolved one media-related concern, media technology has leapt forward three versions hence. On most accounts, science has been able to manage little more than description at this point, having only just begun to define the issues and delineate the scope of the problems. But given the importance of media technology in the socialization of our children, I expect science will have much more to say over the next several years. Until then, we are on our own in protecting our children from the fallout of the technology explosion. As a stopgap, I list a number of safety recommendations culled from various child advocacy websites at the end of the chapter.

Media content

But science has a great deal to say about at least one aspect of children's interface with media, namely, the impact of violent content. Based on the corpus of science to date, we can conclude with virtual certainty that *exposure to violent media increases tendencies toward violent thinking and behaviour in our children, regardless of age*. No other phenomenon in psychology can be concluded with g consensus. Accordingly, violent media content is something we must find a way to resolve. It bombards us with disconcerting portrayals and objectionable images we would be better off never having entertained. We should surely praise the efforts of regulatory bodies for developing rules and ratings for the distribution of violent media. But I dare say this may amount to too little, too late. At this point, we may be better off developing strategies which strike at the heart of violent media demand, at least for the most egregious and offensive varieties. But as we will see, even this task is not easily accomplished.

With such a focused and targeted conclusion as our founding premise, why not stop now, for what else is there to discuss? But in science one does not get away with simple statements of fact. When assertions are well founded and further debate is unlikely to be productive, the issue simply moves up to a higher level of abstraction. In the present case, points of contention ensue at the fuzzy boundaries where media, politics, policy, and the essence of being human overlap. Here is arguably where the most important science has yet to be done.

Of course, concern about the impact of media on impressionable young minds is not new. As long as there have been media portrayals of offensive imagery, perhaps traceable to the earliest vestiges of human literacy, or even to storytelling and artwork in human prehistory, doting parents have probably mobilized their efforts toward protecting their young from being exposed to it. But then, if you didn't want your kids to see something, you simply covered their eyes. Now, as dependent as we are on information technology for our own well-being, eye-covering is a much less pragmatic strategy. At perhaps no other point in the timeline of humanity has there been such a capacity for information technology to tap into the human passion for recreation and communication. But the information technology boom has also generated an epic battle between profit-motivated corporate free-market economies and otherwise culturally sanctioned prohibitions against violence, aggression, and social marginalization. What is more, today's child is expected by her peers to be fluent across all forms of media technology. Accordingly, each of your attempts to block your child's access to media runs the risk of getting her marked by her peers as 'weird'. Who ever heard of a kid who's never watched *Bugs Bunny*? So there are competing cultural pressures at work in the role of media in the socialization of your children.

A brief history of the science of objectionable media

The first wave of scientific investigations of objectionable media can be traced back to the endeavours of American social psychologist Albert Bandura. Bandura's work in the early 1960s, which ranks among the top twenty most revolutionary studies in the last fifty years of child psychology, was the first to demonstrate experimentally that simply viewing videotaped violence could produce aggressive activity among young viewers. In what are now quaintly described as the 'Bobo doll studies', Bandura demonstrated that children who viewed a videotape of an adult model behaving aggressively toward an inflatable Bobo doll, such as by punching, kicking, or verbally berating it, were more likely to behave aggressively under similar conditions than were children who did not observe the aggressive model. Bandura further built upon this effect by showing that children who observed the aggressive model get rewarded for his or her actions were more likely to behave aggressively than were children who observed the aggressive model get reprimanded. The take-home message from Bandura's work was that televised media influences children, and that the content of children's actions is likely to mirror the content of the media to which they are exposed.

Research throughout the 1960s and 1970s built on Bandura's work, and extended his findings to include both commercial television and prosocial media. In one 1975 experiment, for example, first-grade children who watched an episode of *Lassie* in which a boy was observed helping a dog were more likely to exhibit helping behaviour than were children who watched television not portraying helping behaviours. The work was extended even further in the 1990s and 2000s to include video games.

All of this is fine. The findings are interesting, and they make sense. Surely the prudent observer would think it wise to incorporate these findings into mainstream media practices so as to promote the common good – either by promoting prosocial behaviour or by discouraging antisocial behaviour – wouldn't he? But things are never as simple as they seem, especially when free-market politics enters into the picture. This first became clear when the US Surgeon General created a working committee to investigate the prevalence of television violence in the 1970s, and to devise strategies for handling it. On this occasion, the foremost scientific expert on the topic, Albert Bandura, was blackballed by industry executives from participating in committee discussions. Thus it was obvious even four decades ago that the fledgeling science of objectionable media would face a long-term, formidable foe, in the name of capitalism.

Meta-analysis and television violence

Ever since the destructive potential of television violence was first revealed, scientists have continued to study the issue. There have been so many scientific studies published that researchers have moved to a new level of analysis to keep abreast of all the findings. This new level of analysis is called a meta-analysis, where 'meta' means *after, transcending*, or *beyond*. When a scientist undertakes a meta-analysis, what she is really doing is lumping all previous analyses of a particular topic into one big super-analysis. Just as government leaders give an annual state of the state address, meta-analytic researchers give a sort of state of the science address.

The most famous meta-analysis of television violence is the 1994 study of Haejung Paik and George Comstock. Even though it is a fairly old study, it is still cited in the modern literature. It has stood the test of time. Paik and Comstock reviewed the results of 217 prior scientific studies, all published between 1957 and 1990. The range of human participants studied included boys and girls, and men and women, and they ranged in age from 3 to 70 years. The studies included real experiments: where, for example, an experimental group watched an aggressive video and a control group watched a neutral video, and then both groups were observed to see which one aggressed more frequently. The studies also included survey-based investigations in which people were asked how much violent television they watched and how frequently they behaved aggressively. In sum, the number of studies represented in the Paik and Comstock meta-analysis was quite large.

Paik and Comstock's results are complex, and far beyond what we can cover here. But to summarize briefly in their words, 'There is a highly significant positive association for the magnitude of the effect between exposure to portrayals of violence and antisocial behavior.' They measured the effect with a statistic called 'r', which is a common, technical metric used to measure how strongly two things are correlated with one another. Their overall r, collapsing across all 217 studies, was .31. An r of .31 means that there is about a 10 per cent overlap between the two factors being studied (which, for the reader who likes details, is determined by taking the square of r, or r^2). Another way of thinking about it is that 10 children out of every 100 are more aggressive as a result of viewing television violence.

Putting it into perspective

The fact that only 10 per cent of children are affected by television violence raises interesting questions about how to frame the results. Should we be bothered that 10 out of 100 children are adversely affected by exposure to television violence? Or should we be happy that 90 out of 100 are immune? After all, 10 per cent is not a very big number.

In a 2001 article published in the flagship journal *American Psychologist*, Brad Bushman and Craig Anderson framed the question nicely: is the correlation between television violence and aggressive behaviour of lesser, equal, or greater magnitude than other correlations judged to be major public health concerns? Here is a little test for the

Below are six pairs of factors that extensive research has found to be correlated. They are ranked from most highly correlated (top) to least highly correlated (bottom). Where would you insert the television violence–aggressive behaviour correlation?

1 Smoking and lung cancer
2 Condom use and sexually transmitted HIV
3 Exposure to lead and children's IQ scores
4 Calcium intake and bone density
5 Doing homework and succeeding academically
6 Self-examination and breast cancer prevention

The answer (see Figure 1) is that the correlation between watching televised violence and aggressive behaviour is second in magnitude only to the correlation between smoking and lung cancer (which is about $r = .40$). It even exceeds the correlation between condom use and prevention of sexually transmitted HIV (which is about $r = .20$). If you would not question the science that shows that wearing condoms helps prevent the spread of HIV, or that taking calcium supplements increases bone density, how could you question the science that shows that television violence increases the risk of aggressive behaviour? Yet, the impact of television violence on the aggressive actions of our children has not received the same kind of public health attention as have other important health epidemics. Why not?

Bushman and Anderson suggest that one answer is that corporate-sponsored mass media outlets simply haven't portrayed television violence as an important public health concern. In fact, news stories about media violence have actually *declined* over the last twenty years. And among stories that *have* been distributed, the negative impacts of television violence have increasingly been *de-emphasized* since about 1985. Could it be that corporate-owned media outlets have profits to lose if they acknowledge television violence as a public health concern? Many news agencies are subsidiaries of larger corporations that also generate profit by distributing and syndicating violent television programming. In free-market, capitalist economies, might it amount

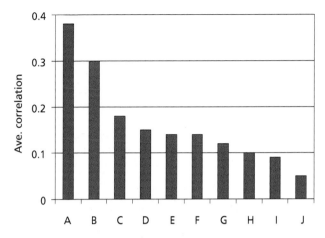

A. Smoking and lung cancer
B. Media violence and aggression
C. Condom use and sexually transmitted HIV
D. Passive smoking and lung cancer at work
E. Exposure to lead and IQ scores in children
F. Nicotine patch and smoking cessation
G. Calcium intake and bone mass
H. Homework and academic achievement
I. Exposure to asbestos and laryngeal cancer
J. Self-examination and extent of breast cancer

Figure 1 **The relative strength of known public health threats**

to 'biting the hand' when a corporate-owned news agency reports negatively on a sister-company's media products? This seems a reasonable possibility to me; but I am not an insider, and so I simply don't know. I will leave it to the reader to draw his or her own conclusions.

These public health concerns notwithstanding, Paik and Comstock reported other findings that may be of interest to parents of television-watching children. For example, the effect is slightly higher for boys (r = .36) than for girls (r = .26). This means that whereas 13 out of every 100 boys will be affected by television violence, only 7 out of every s will. But keep in mind that although girls are not as affected as boys, the correlation for girls is still, overall, just about as high as the correlation between condom use and HIV prevention.

The results also show that the effects do not go away as children get older. If you look at Table 1, adapted from the Paik and Comstock article, you will see that preschoolers are affected by television violence more than any other group. This may not be particularly surprising. But you may be very surprised to learn that college students are more affected than any other age group except for pre-schoolers. It appears that violent television portrayals are not just a problem for the youngest children, they are a problem for children across their youth.

Table 1

Age group	r	% of viewers affected
Preschool	.46	21
6–11 years	.31	10
12–17 years	.22	5
18–21 years	.37	14
Adults	.18	3

Finally, readers with preschool- and early school-aged children may be interested to know that exposure to violence in cartoons and fantasy programmes produces stronger effects than exposure to violence in any other type of programme. The correlation between aggressive behaviour and cartoon/fantasy violence was $r = .52$, meaning that 28 out of 100 cartoon watchers could be expected to demonstrate aggression increases. This is an important finding because it has been argued by some that violent television needs to be realistic to affect behaviour. Cartoons and fantasy programming are among the least realistic of any television programming, and yet they still have an impact. To be fair, we should recognize that cartoons and fantasy programmes are most likely to be viewed by preschoolers and young children, the two most susceptible age groups; but we should realize nevertheless that some of our least dramatic and most 'fun' programming can still enhance aggressive behaviour among our children.

Meta-analysis and prosocial television

Paraphrasing *Hamlet*, it is probably fair to conclude that 'The telly is neither good nor bad, but content makes it so.' Just as antisocial television increases antisocial behaviour, so it goes that prosocial television increases prosocial behaviour; although there is less research on the latter. In the only meta-analysis I could find, Marie-Louise Mares and Emory Woodard discovered that the effects of viewing prosocial television were not quite as strong as those of viewing violent television, but there were desirable effects nonetheless. Their analysis reports on the outcomes of thirty-four studies, including both experiments and surveys, and within those thirty-four studies they tested 108 different effects involving 5,473 children. The prosocial measures they studied included *positive interactions* (including things like 'friendly play' and 'peaceful conflict resolution'), *aggression* (which should be reduced by exposure to prosocial television), *altruism* (including sharing, offering help, and comforting), and *stereotype reduction* (because stereotypes involve elements of prejudice and discrimination). Mares and Woodard hypothesized that watching prosocial television should increase positive interactions and altruism, and decrease aggression and stereotyping. This is exactly what they found.

Across all four of these outcome measures, collapsing across both experimental and survey-based studies, across both genders, across all ages, and across all other aspects of the studies reviewed, prosocial television enhanced prosocial behaviour ($r = .23$). This means that in general, 5 out of every 100 children exposed to prosocial television behave prosocially as a result of that exposure. Prosocial television seems to have the strongest effect on altruistic behaviour ($r = .37$), and the weakest effect on aggression ($r = .16$). In addition, girls ($r = .20$) are slightly more affected overall than boys ($r = .13$). Finally, there appears to be a general decline in the effects of prosocial television as children get

ven-year-olds are most strongly influenced by pro-
\[evision, but the amount of influence decreases
ɔꞑarply until about age 12, and then more gradually after
that. Note that this is a different age trend than we saw
with violent television exposure, which revealed a resurg-
ence of influence as children reached college age. Unfortun-
ately, Mares and Woodard do not list the actual magnitude
of the effects at each age, so we cannot discern the specific
effects at each age.

The fact that television is so influential shouldn't really
surprise any of us. After all, television advertising is the
bread and butter of the marketing industry. If television
advertisements didn't produce a change in consumer beha-
viour (for example, encouraging people to buy a certain
toothpaste, or getting people to change their minds about a
political candidate), marketers wouldn't spend millions
of pounds on such a futile endeavour. Yet, there has been
denial by media corporations in response to these non-
flattering scientific findings. They would have us believe,
for example, that their violent programming produces no
negative consequences for the populace. If you think about
it, this is supremely ironic. Many of the companies who
argue that violent media have no negative impacts on our
children are the same ones who use advertising to get us to
spend money on their violent media! If media don't influ-
ence people, why would companies use media in an effort
to do so? Clearly, it is hare-brained to hold both beliefs
simultaneously.

Violent gaming

The case for television violence effects has been made fairly
strongly. But what about the effects of video-game violence?
Can we generalize from television to gaming? There are
plenty of ways in which the two platforms differ. For one
thing, viewing television is a fairly passive experience, while
gaming is highly interactive. Games depend on inputs from
gamers, and the gaming experience is different for gamers of
different skill levels. For games that involve 'killing', higher-
skilled gamers do more killing than do lower-skilled ones;

whereas lower-skilled gamers are more likely to be killed. In contrast, the outputs of television are the same regardless of the skill level of the viewer, and the only inputs television requires come from the power switch and the channel changer.

Unlike watching television, many types of games can produce time-warping, immersion experiences for gamers, who may come to feel as if their personal identities are linked in some ethereal way to their characters' identities. As a gamer myself, I can relate to this time-warping phenomenon. I recall vividly, when in graduate school, my experience of playing a primitive (by today's standards) role-playing game called *Bard's Tale*. It was the middle of summer, and I had no classes to attend. I woke up and had breakfast with my wife. I began to play *Bard's Tale* as she was getting ready for work. She left for work at about 7:30 a.m., and I remember making eye contact as she left the apartment and sending my salutations from afar. She returned a few minutes later, and I greeted her upon her return. I asked if she had forgotten something. But it wasn't minutes later. It was hours later. In fact, nine hours later, and my wife was returning home at the end of the day. I had spent my entire day playing *Bard's Tale* in complete temporal oblivion. Although I had been a television viewer my whole life, no television experience had ever produced such complete engrossment to the point of costing a day. A simple, unassuming collection of programming code had fully entrapped me.

Video games also differ from television in how much attention and emotion they demand. Modern video games require immense allocations of attention in order for players to complete levels, clear screens, and obtain objectives. Television programmes can usually be tracked with minimal levels of attention. Gamers are also connected to their media emotionally, sometimes to the point of inducing pathological anxiety and anger. Also, unlike with television viewers, whose emotionality attenuates at a programme's end, gamers may maintain a game-induced emotional state indefinitely. When they are not gaming, gamers may obsess about the game until they can jump back in, they may plot out their tactics for when they next log on, or they may read background literature from outside sources to become better prepared. Especially seductive is a relatively new genre of gaming experiences called *massively multiplayer online role-playing games* (MMORPGs). In MMORPGs, thousands of players from around the world log onto a single virtual reality, where they meet and partner with hundreds of acquaintances they have met during game play. They may form hunting parties and fighting guilds, and work cooperatively to complete quests, obtain objectives, and battle monsters. MMORPGs have risen to a level where they truly compete with real reality for a gamer's emotional commitment and enthusiasm. Among the most popular MMORPGs today are *World of Warcraft*, *Ever-Quest II*, *Lord of the Rings Online*, *Dark Age of Camelot*, and *Final Fantasy XI*.

In sum, if a medium as passive and uninvolving as television can induce aggressive behaviour in children, then a medium as interactive and engrossing as video-gaming is sure to induce aggressive behaviour in children. The scientific literature confirms expectations. There have been several studies on gaming violence and children's aggression, although generally there have been fewer than with television owing to the shorter life span of the gaming medium. Still, sufficient numbers of studies permitted three meta-analyses.

The two most frequently cited meta-analyses include one by John Sherry, and one by Craig Anderson and Brad Bushman. Both were published in 2001. Sherry's meta-analysis was based on thirty-two studies, whereas Anderson and Bushman's was based on thirty-five studies. However, there was probably considerable overlap among the two sets of studies covered because the meta-analyses were both conducted at about the same time. Both meta-analyses included experimental and survey-based studies.

The video-game-based meta-analyses had a slightly different emphasis from the television-based ones described earlier, primarily because the former focused on more than just aggressive behaviour, and included additional outcome measures such as *aggressive thoughts*, *aggressive feelings*, and *physical arousal*. The television meta-analyses focused only on behaviour. In addition, the Anderson and Bushman video-game meta-analysis included studies that looked at prosocial behaviour.

The results of the two meta-analyses were comparable to one another, and generally permit the conclusion that video-game violence contributes to aggression. But interestingly, the effects of video-game violence are smaller than the effects of television violence. In the Sherry meta-analysis, for example, the strength of the effect was about $r = .16$, suggesting that about 3 out of every 100 video-game-playing children become more aggressive as a result of playing video games. This isn't a very large effect, but it is close to the size of the effect of doing homework on children's academic achievement. The outcomes measured in the Sherry meta-analysis were lumped together, so it isn't possible to distinguish the effects of gaming on aggressive behaviours from the effects on aggressive thoughts and feelings.

But results were separated out in Anderson and Bushman's meta-analysis. For the outcome of aggressive *behaviour*, the effect of video-game violence was $r = .19$; for aggressive *thoughts* it was $r = .27$; for aggressive *feelings* it was $r = .18$; and for *physical arousal* it was $r = .22$. Finally, for the outcome of *prosocial behaviour*, the outcome was $r = -.17$. Notice for this last effect that there is a minus sign in front of the number, which means that playing violent video games was *negatively* related to prosocial behaviour. Or put another way, the *more* violent video games children played, the *less* likely they were to demonstrate any prosocial behaviour. These results pretty much align with Sherry's, and show that, overall, somewhere between 3 and 7 children out of every 100, depending on the specific measure, experience some kind of aggressive impact as a result of playing violent video games.

The case against media violence effects

As alluded to above, when scientific findings have major public policy implications, people come out of the woodwork to fend off attacks on what they perceive to be their liveli-hood. So although some people have come out in strong support of the media violence findings, others have strongly opposed them. On the 'pro' side, a number of key public policy agencies in the US have entered the fray. In 2000, for example, six major US medical and public health profes-sional organizations issued a 'Joint Statement on the Impact of Entertainment Violence on Children', which concluded, definitively, that there is a 'causal connection between media violence and aggressive behavior in children'. These organizations are extremely powerful in the US, and include the American Academy of Pediatrics (an organization not without its own faults, see Chapter 5), the American Academy of Child and Adolescent Psychiatry, the American Medical Association, the American Psychological Associa-tion, the American Academy of Family Physicians, and the American Psychiatric Association. But the US is not alone in its concern about the impact of media violence. In June 2007, for example, the UK banned the video game *Manhunt 2* for its 'unrelenting focus on stalking and brutal slaying' (a ban which was overturned six months later).

A lot of naysayers have also made public appearances. Among the antagonists, not surprisingly, have been the for-profit media and broadcasting industries. But, with these people there is such a conflict of interest infiltrating their perspective that they undermine their own credibility. However, a handful of scientists have also been fairly criti-cal of the media violence effects literature. Because there are no obvious conflicts of interest in their perspectives, it is worthwhile to review their counter-arguments, if for no other reason than to set the stage for presenting the counter-arguments to the counter-arguments (see below). As the reader may have guessed, I am not much enamoured with the case against the media violence effects research.

The first argument against the media violence findings is usually that the effects are small. We have already considered whether a problem can be considered significant if only 5 (or 3) out of every 100 kids exposed to media violence are affected by it. The argument has some validity. Admittedly, it does seem like a pretty small effect. But the argument loses ballast when taking into account the sheer numbers of affected children at the national level. If 5 out of every 100 kids are made more aggressive by media violence, then about 275,000 Canadian children, 97,000 Australian children, and 600,000 UK children should be monitored by parents, teachers, and law enforcement for enhanced levels of aggression. This amounts to nearly 1 million affected children in these three countries alone. The effects may be small, but the public health concerns are not.

A second common argument is that experiments involving violent media are contrived, and therefore invalid. Because they take place in the artificial world of the laboratory, they cannot possibly apply to real-world settings. This also seems like a reasonable argument. But if this were true, then it would apply to all laboratory research, including that which has produced scientific advances for the treatment and prevention of polio, smallpox and rubella. Surely we would not argue that because a study is conducted in a laboratory it is necessarily bogus. And in any case, what evidence can the critics proffer that laboratory measures of aggression are *not* accurate reflections of real-world settings?

A third criticism goes something like, 'if media violence is so bad for children, then why haven't we seen worldwide epidemics in crime rates with the massive, wholesale introduction of first-person shooter games and MMORPGs?' This is a fair question. But it is precisely this question that one hopes would serve as the basis for additional research. In my way of thinking, this question doesn't underscore a criticism as much as it underscores an opportunity. It merely highlights that we are only beginning to understand the nature of aggression in children. Aggression in children is almost certainly a product of very complicated sets of factors which include, among other things, children's genetic predispositions, their intelligence, the styles of parenting they are exposed to, their diet and nutrition, their educational opportunities, their history of illicit drug use, and their peer pressure. Most children exposed to media violence do not become societal criminals. But this fact does not imply that media violence has no effect on aggressive behaviour. It only means that we have much to learn about the conditions under which it does. If only 5 out of every 100 children exposed to media violence behave more aggressively as a result of that exposure, then we are 5 per cent closer to understanding the nature of youth violence.

How does media violence gain access to our children?

In the past few pages, I have documented scientific research which shows that exposure to media violence produces a small but reliable impact on children's aggressiveness. But we have not really considered *how* it does so. Scientists have proposed four specific mechanisms which they believe help explain the effects of media violence. Each has its own theoretical origins and research history. But each almost certainly works in congress with the others and contributes to the very complex phenomenon of childhood aggression. Each theoretical mechanism also has a rather technical name that has effectively distanced itself from accessibility by the average person. In no particular order of importance, these mechanisms include *observational learning (imitation)*, *priming and automatization*, *arousal and excitation transfer*, and *emotional desensitization*.

Observational learning (imitation)

This is probably one of the most highly acclaimed and most easily understood ways that children are believed to pick up aggressive behaviours. It comes from the aforementioned work of Albert Bandura and his Bobo doll studies, where it was shown that simply seeing an adult hit, kick, or verbally berate a self-righting inflatable doll is enough to provoke children into copying those behaviours. It is not exactly clear why humans are so inclined to imitate others. But we know that even newborns will imitate simple facial expressions when adults make faces at them. Some scientists have theorized that imitation is a basic primate ability, hard-wired through evolution, which allows organisms to pick up relatively sophisticated behavioural routines with relative ease and relatively little expenditure of energy. Imitation can be found throughout all species of higher primates. Among humans, it is the preferred method of instruction for teaching complex behavioural routines such as found in dance, team sports, the arts, and skilled trades. It would be impossible to know how to do most complicated actions without the benefit of a model to emulate. Although it primarily serves an adaptive function, the down side of imitation is that we can also acquire behaviours that are maladaptive, including drinking, drug-using, smoking, and fighting.

Priming and automatization

The concept of 'priming' really just refers to the basic experience we have that whenever we think of one concept or idea, we sometimes automatically think of a related concept or idea. When we think of breakfast, we may think of poached eggs. When we think of the coast, we may think of seagulls. Sometimes a particular fragrance may bring to mind events from our past. For me, the fragrance of musk oil reminds me of the girl I had a crush on in seventh grade. I think of her freckled face and her long brown hair. I think of the frilly leather coat she used to wear when she walked down my street. Each of us has a set of inter-related concepts that we store in our memories. Thinking of any one concept triggers a recollection of the linked concepts, and we begin to think of these triggered concepts as well.

As it pertains to aggression and media, it is easy to imagine how viewing a violent television programme or playing a violent game can prime us to think aggressive thoughts or have aggressive feelings that we didn't have prior to exposure. If we go out into the world immediately following exposure to violent media, the principle of priming dictates that we are likely to find ourselves imposing our aggressive predispositions onto the various social situations we encounter.

Priming is necessarily a temporary phenomenon, however. Otherwise we would never stop thinking about the concepts that were primed. So when aggressive thoughts and feelings are primed by violent media, they are also relatively short-lived. But it is also a phenomenon of priming that ideas or concepts that are repeatedly primed become more easily accessible over time. The more you think about a concept or idea, the easier it is to think about that concept or idea in the future. This is why it is easier for you to generate the name of your boss or spouse than it is to generate the name of your first infant school teacher. You may be able to generate the name of your first infant teacher, but it will take longer because you haven't thought about it in such a long time. Repeated exposure to violent media (or violence in the home, or violence in school) is liable to make it easier to access aggressive thoughts and feelings in the future. This is the automatization part: when children find themselves in some kind of social conflict, those whose aggressive thoughts and feelings have been primed again and again will have more ready access to those aggressive thoughts and feelings, and they will be more at risk for acting on them should an opportunity arise for doing so.

Arousal and excitation transfer

Arousal refers to an aggregate of physiological and bodily changes that go along with entering a state of excitement. These changes include having an increased heart rate, breathing faster, getting 'butterflies', and having sweaty palms. We can get aroused by good things, such as when we are romantically involved or thinking about something that makes us happy; and we can get aroused by bad things, such as when something frightens us or makes us angry.

However, getting aroused doesn't mean that we will necessarily become aggressive. The problem, as captured by the *excitation transfer* part of the theory, is that arousal can exacerbate any previous tendencies we might have had toward behaving aggressively. That is, if the conditions are such that we run the risk of becoming aggressive, either because we have learned aggressive responses through imitation or because our aggressive thoughts and feelings have been primed, then getting aroused just makes it more likely that we transfer our excitation toward an aggressive response. Getting aroused strengthens the likelihood of doing whatever we are already doing. If we are having aggressive thoughts and feelings, then arousal and excitation transfer only make it worse. Fortunately, as with priming and automatization, arousal doesn't last very long. It usually dissipates after a few minutes. So its impact on aggression is generally limited to the short term.

Emotional desensitization

The idea behind emotional desensitization is that when a person gets exposed over and over again to an emotionally objectionable or revolting object or action, he tends to become less affected by that object or action over time. His negative reactions to it gradually decline. Emotional desensitization is a normal process, and it is adaptive for many of us who have careers dealing with objectionable or revolting things on a day-to-day basis. Accident and emergency doctors, police officers, and slaughterhouse workers are surely grateful for the role of emotional desensitization in allowing them to carry on with their daily lives (as are parents of newborns with lots of dirty nappies). Desensitization is also the primary and most successful technique for treating individuals with severe anxiety and phobic disorders. In the technique of 'flooding', for example, phobic individuals are immersed, under closely monitored conditions, in a bath of real or imagined stimuli that are the source of their fears. After flooding, most patients show a significant decline in their fearful responsiveness to fear-provoking stimuli, at both an emotional and physiological level.

But although emotional desensitization can play an adaptive role in our lives, it can also produce maladaptive outcomes as well. The evening news may deaden our sensitivity to the kinds of sickness, starvation, pain and suffering that are so typical of living conditions in the developing world (even when those living conditions are found in developed nations). After watching the evening news every day, we may begin accepting these horrible conditions as facts of life, and we may eventually lose our drive to do anything about them. Desensitization may reduce empathy, and may even reduce our tendencies to evaluate violent actions as morally objectionable. Accordingly, the idea here is that as children become more and more accustomed to media violence, they also become more and more desensitized to it. Over time, violent scenes may elicit fewer negative reactions from children, who may increasingly judge violent actions to be commonplace. Once they are deemed commonplace, prohibitions against committing them are correspondingly reduced, and aggressive behaviours may become acceptable responses.

Conclusions

The scientific literature on the impact of media violence generates a clear picture of the negative role played by media violence in our society. Media violence is, on average, a very bad thing. But as a scientist, who is also a parent, an avid television watcher, and an MMORPG-er, I cannot in good conscience issue an across-the-board dictum that children should avoid television and gaming altogether. My main rationale is that there is reason to believe that prosocial television and prosocial gaming could do good things for our children. Prosocial media could improve the human condition.

But I am not even sure I could make an absolute, across-the-board recommendation when it comes to media with antisocial content. *Most* children appear immune to aggressive thoughts, feelings and behaviours when exposed to this kind of media. But *some* children do not. The safest bet, of course, is to prevent children's exposure to violent media altogether. Parents have direct control over their children's exposure to media in their own homes, and if they feel strongly enough about the matter, then by all means they should construct daily routines that facilitate alternative forms of entertainment. Family reading, family game-night, family bike-rides, and family day-hikes are superb alternatives. In addition, parents who are ambitious and vigilant enough can do their own research to identify prosocial forms of media, and undertake the efforts necessary to ensure that these forms of media are the ones their children have the easiest and most frequent access to.

But redirective tactics like these fail to take into account the draw that various forms of violent media have for children, fuelled, among other things, by peer pressure. Younger kids may *want* to watch cartoons that have violent content. Older kids may *want* to play *Call of Duty* and *Halo*. Parental admonitions notwithstanding, children are shaped by their cultures, and it is against these cultural attractions that parents will necessarily struggle. I recall the story of a psychologist friend of mine who, with her psychologist husband, vowed never to let her young son have a toy gun, or any other sort of war-making toy. By the time the boy was in preschool, he was playing cops and robbers merely by forming his hand into the shape of a pistol, and making gunshot sounds at people around the house. There are also pragmatic limitations to a strict prohibitionist approach. For one thing, the long arm of parent supervision does not extend far beyond the boundaries of the home. There is a high probability that as children develop friendships with their peers, they will be exposed to some form or another of violent imagery that parents will find less than satisfactory. At first, typically around late preschool age, it may be in the form of pretend play. At school age, it may be in the form of watching television or violent-themed DVDs at a neighbour's house. In adolescence, it may come in the form of playing first-person shooter video games.

All of this is not to suggest that you should throw your hands in the air and give up. Rather it is to illustrate that there will probably be set-backs to your supervisory efforts as you attempt to shelter your children from media violence. Covering your children's eyes may work in the short term. But by preventing children from having access to what they want, you are surely increasing their interest in attaining it. In the long term, your direct control over their choices will diminish, anyway. This is simply part of growing up. Still, there are strategies and tactics you can employ to minimize media violence exposure. For example, if a child is obsessively longing for a particular video game known to contain strong violence, you may find it productive to negotiate to a more expensive non-violent game (or two cheaper ones) instead. Parents can also work with other parents toward maintaining consistent inter-parental patterns of supervision as children visit one another's homes. It is better to make your expectations of other parents known in advance than to resent the choices they make after the fact. It is also easier to develop a zero-tolerance, non-violent media culture if all parents in the neighbourhood are in agreement. In this way, for borderline programmes and films, such as those rated 'PG', parents will automatically know to request permission from one another before letting children watch. Hence, it is a good practice to keep handy the names and phone numbers of your children's friends' parents. Of course, not all neighbourhoods and not all inter-parental relationships are conducive to this kind of community involvement.

In addition, there are many different kinds of parent–child relationships, and parental success in limiting exposure to violent media may vary accordingly. Children are simply born different from one another (see Chapter 6 on temperament). For lucky parents, children may go along easily with proscriptions about media violence, and not think twice about it. For other parents, especially those with oppositional children, quite a battle may result from efforts to impose restrictions on attractive but violent media. These children may take a stand and declare their right to make their own choices about whether and when to consume certain kinds of media. Parents are ultimately responsible for letting children make such choices; but depending on the maturity of the child, parents may very well decide to loosen their restrictions as they deem appropriate on a case-by-case basis. In some cases media 'violence' may be quite mild in comparison with others, and it may not be worth the family disharmony to hold fast to zero-tolerance policies. Negotiation toward the least violent media options may be the preferred strategy here.

These small-scale case-by-case strategies for managing children's interfaces with violent media notwithstanding, perhaps the most productive, long-term strategy for minimizing the impact of violent media is to target the problem at its source. Media violence is a cultural problem, and so interventions should be aimed at a cultural level. Obviously, we cannot count on the media industry to regulate itself. Rather, any cultural shift will need to emanate from the grassroots efforts of consumers. The wholesale boycotting of retail distributors who sell objectionable media may be one route to success. Boycotts have been fruitful in the past. As a result of a 1987 boycott for its use of 'rainforest beef', coupled with millions of dollars in lost profits, the Burger King retail chain revised its list of wholesale beef vendors and stopped purchasing beef from cattle raised on rainforest land. In 2005, a small group of girls from western Pennsylvania launched a 'girlcott' against Ambercrombie and Fitch (A & F) for distributing a line of girls' clothing with offensive phrases such as 'Who Needs Brains When You Have These?' After five days of negative media coverage, A & F pulled two offending lines of shirts from their shelves. Although A & F may have actually benefitted from the extensive press coverage in overall sales, the girlcott succeeded in eliminating the objectionable media from the stores.

Central government education ministries can take a stand, and in some places have already done so, in limiting the impact of violent media. For example, Canada's *National Media Education Week* (http://www.mediaeducationweek.ca/involved_ideas.htm) allows opportunities for classroom discussions about the power of media in children's lives. Australia and the UK have incorporated media literacy as part of their national core curriculum for primary and secondary school children. But, parents should be vigilant in ensuring that the contents of these media-oriented curricula fit with what they view as the most important assaults on their children's well-being. If the curricula are not fully satisfactory in working to minimize media violence, parents should work within and with the local school system and national ministries to reorient the curriculum accordingly.

Motivation for change at the national level can often come from media attention or boycotts (or girlcotts) at the local level.

Recommendations

Because the explosion of media technology has been so all-encompassing, parent-support websites aimed at keeping children safe have been similarly numerous. What follows below are suggestions from these websites that you can keep in mind as you help your children negotiate the myriad of media technologies.

Media violence: television and films

- Consider establishing a daily routine with ample amounts of family time that is not linked to media consumption.
- When consuming television- and film-based media, watch programmes with your children and evaluate them together. Probe your children's level of understanding of the programmes. Children of different ages understand television programmes differently. Clarify misunderstandings.
- Designate an approved list of programming options, and let your children choose from this list. Obtain a large variety of recorded high-quality children's programming for use when high-quality television programming is not available.
- Familiarize yourself with media rating guides, especially as they pertain to age appropriateness, violent content, profanity, and sexual situations. These vary somewhat internationally, and may or may not be governmentally sanctioned or regulated.
- Make agreements with the parents of your children's friends about what is an appropriate level of supervision. Agree to call one another before allowing children to be exposed to borderline media when your children are visiting one another's homes.

Media violence: video games

- As with television and films, familiarize yourself with media rating guides especially as they pertain to age appropriateness, violent content, profanity, and sexual situations. These also vary somewhat internationally, and may or may not be governmentally sanctioned or regulated. The Entertainment Software Rating Board provides a system used widely throughout the US and Canada (http://www.esrb.org/ratings/ratings_guide.jsp), whereas the Australian Classification Board (http://www.classification.gov.au) and the British Board of Film Classification (http://www.parentsbbfc.co.uk/guides_Videogames.asp) provide video-game ratings in their own respective venues.
- Discuss rating guides with your children before allowing them to shop for video games. Be prepared to negotiate down to less violent but more expensive video games if deemed appropriate. Take into account your children's maturity levels before absolutely prohibiting all manner of violence. Some 'violence' can actually be quite mild in comparison with others, and it may not be worth the family disharmony to hold fast to zero-tolerance policies.
- Make agreements with the parents of your children's friends about what is an appropriate level of supervision. Agree to call one another before allowing children to be exposed to borderline media when your children are visiting one another's homes.

Social networking sites and chat rooms

- Place the computer in a family room so that online activities can be monitored.
- Ensure that children know the difference between information they can share and information they can't, and that they know to always avoid sex talk.
- Try not to be too hard on children if they have mistakenly given out confidential information. They may avoid talking to you about similar issues in the future.
- Use the site's privacy settings to restrict who can access your child's site or who can start a chat session.

- Familiarize yourself with your child's favourite social networking sites. Consider creating your own account and becoming your child's online 'friend'.
- Learn the language of chat.
- Periodically, review your child's friend list, and ask probing questions about 'friends' your child doesn't know personally. Show the same interest in your child's online friends as in his or her real-life friends.
- Steer younger children (8 and below) toward 'safe' sites that take extra precautions and put in place extra safeguards to prevent inappropriate dialogue. Take a look at *Whyville.net* and *Imbee.com*, for example.

Cyber-bullying

- Discuss cyber-bullying with your children in an atmosphere of support that doesn't include automatic and necessary removal of internet access.
- Have them show you any abusive or offensive messages they have received, and keep a record of them.
- Tell them never to respond to abusive messages or phone calls. This is what the abuser is hoping for.
- Familiarize yourself with cyber-bullying policies within your school system, your internet service provider, and your mobile phone company. Report instances of abuse to these agencies as appropriate.
- Manage what your children view, what they do, and who they communicate with, both through available blocking software and through household policies. A standing policy should be that the parents are *always* allowed to look at the dialogue taking place on the computers in the house.

The Bottom Line

- **What are the key dilemmas parents have to struggle with on this topic?**
  - The overarching issue is whether children should be allowed to watch violent television programmes, and/or play violent video games.

- A related issue concerns the risks posed by other forms of media technology, including text messaging, video text messaging, YouTube, and social networking websites.
- **What does the science say about this topic?**
  - The vast majority of scientific research has been conducted on the effects of violent television and violent video games on children's aggressive thoughts and behaviours.
  - Complex and comprehensive 'meta-analyses' have shown, conclusively, that exposure to media violence *causes* an increase in children's aggressive thoughts and behaviours.
  - The overall size of this effect is small, but it is very large by public health standards, and it affects millions of children worldwide.
  - Any negative effects of other forms of media technology on children are not known because they are not yet the subject of widespread study.
- **What do the authors advise?**
  - Parents should familiarize themselves as much as possible with all forms of media technology, especially those media formats used most frequently by their children.
    - Parents should learn how to text-message with their children, and then get in the habit of communicating using text-messaging media.
      - Parents should become 'friends' with their children on social networking sites such as MySpace and Facebook.
      - Parents should also review their children's sites frequently, both for content and for keeping an eye on who their children's online 'friends' are.
    - In terms of media violence, parents might want to get involved at a macroscopic level, and join or develop grassroots movements aimed at elevating the content of local media programming, in an effort to minimize chronic exposure to media violence.

- Parents should become familiar with media rating systems for television, films, and video-game programming content.
- Parents should use these rating systems to establish exposure standards for their children to follow, both while they are at home and while they are away.
  - Older children should be involved in discussing their own standards to the extent that is practical, depending on the kinds of media they prefer and their own level of maturity.
  - From a practical standpoint, parents with older, or strong-willed children may wish to have a back-up plan to fall back on if their front-line defences fail. Non-negotiable stances sometimes backfire on parents.
  - Parents may wish to adjust standards according to the various viewing or playing contexts their children are found in. And standards can be revisited as children grow and mature.
  - Parents may consider making alliances with other parents in an effort to establish neighbourhood-wide standards to be implemented when children view or play media with violent content at various locations.
    - Allied parents may wish to establish a regular pattern of communication with one another, and to discuss the appropriateness of particular programmes or video games.

Parents' psychological health: effects on children

Strahan

Case studies: Samir, Elizabeth and Audrey

- Samir is a 52-year-old father of three, still married to his first wife. He is a successful businessman. For the last few years he has been battling a serious depression, and recently his wife persuaded him to seek therapy. One of the first comments he makes in his session is that he works hard every day to make sure that his irritability and sadness don't affect his youngest child (the two elder ones being away at university). 'It's not my daughter's fault that I'm depressed and I try to act as normal as I can', he says. Still, he feels guilty about his lack of energy and enthusiasm as a parent. He has attended therapy sessions for the last few weeks and is feeling better.
- Elizabeth is a 40-year-old mother of three, married once and divorced once. She has been unemployed for several years and she receives disability payments because of a chronic pain condition. She confesses that she is highly addicted to pain medications, of which she takes far more than the prescribed amount. She admits to spending much of the day sleeping, and her live-in boyfriend takes care of cooking and cleaning, works two jobs, handles family finances, and has taken on the responsibility for controlling her medications. This is because, when she is taking medications, she gets confused and has twice taken an overdose of narcotics, ending up receiving emergency treatment. She attended one therapy session and has not returned for a follow-up appointment.

- Audrey is a 58-year-old mother of five who has been married three times and is now divorced. She is receiving disability payments due to a diagnosis of bipolar disorder. When she is in an acute manic state, she travels across the country, demanding that truck drivers at roadside rest areas have sex with her; this has resulted in numerous arrests. She reluctantly agrees to see a therapist occasionally for follow-up support and has finally agreed to take her medication on a regular basis after many failed attempts to cope without it.

I present these three case studies as illustrations of the wide diversity of parenting behaviours that fall under the topic for this chapter. Clearly, the experiences of Samir's, Elizabeth's and Audrey's children will vary enormously, despite the fact that they all have parents with a psychological disorder. I chose these three individuals (after changing their names) because they have children who are now young adults and because I know something of how their children are doing. Not surprisingly, Samir's children are faring rather well, and Elizabeth's and Audrey's children are struggling more with the tasks of schooling, jobs, and building stable relationships. Perhaps more surprisingly, Audrey's children are doing far better than she is.

It may be unusual to include this kind of chapter in a parenting book. After all, most people read parenting books in search of techniques that can help them solve particular problems. But more and more parenting research demonstrates that the key parenting variables have to do with who the parents *are* and how they handle their own problems, rather than simply what approaches they take to specific child-rearing situations. I offer this chapter in response to that line of research.

All of us know people who are trying to be good parents despite dealing with psychological distress. It might be depression, or a phobia, or grief following a death. They may be overcome by depression or an obsessive-compulsive disorder or even a serious social anxiety disorder that prevents their functioning effectively in the world outside the home. So often these parents (or their spouses) worry about what their problems will do to their children.

This chapter will address that question. The emphasis is on individual parents' psychological problems – we will be discussing the issue of how marital conflict and divorce affect children in a separate chapter.

Key concepts in examining parent illnesses and how they affect children

For decades scientists have studied children who grew up in highly stressful and negative environments, including war zones, refugee camps, and crime-ridden neighbour-hoods, and we have learned a lot about what happens in their development. Naturally, these children are more at risk for developing psychological problems in their own right. This is also true for children whose parents have psychological disorders. These children have a higher rate of psychological disorders themselves. For example, the average child growing up in any family has about a 20 per cent risk of developing some kind of psychological disorder (ranging from phobias to conduct disorder). If the child has a parent with a psychological disorder, the risk jumps to somewhere between 30 and 50 per cent. It makes sense that these children are more vulnerable, given the emotional, financial and logistical strains that psychological disorders create in the home.

The more interesting component of these studies has been on the topic of resilience, or how children can bounce back from adversity. It is clear that, even in very difficult circumstances, many children do well both socially and academically.

The factor that parents can do least about is the genetic component. Nearly all psychological disorders studied have some genetic component. So, for example, Samir's and Elizabeth's and Audrey's children will all carry higher risk due to their genetics. But even for parents with bipolar disorder, much can be done to lessen the likelihood that their children will develop the condition. Here are some examples of these kinds of protective factors:

- Caregiving arrangements – if there is a single parent with depression, for example, but the child is mostly cared for by a non-depressed grandparent, that will help to protect the child against developing problems. The scientific evidence on what helps children cope is clear: even if the parents are extremely impaired, if the child has a loving and stable adult in their life, their chances of being successful in life are much better.
- Extent of mental illness – as you can see from the case studies above, people differ enormously in the severity and time span of their mental illnesses. Samir had a severe depression, but it was time-limited and he was having it treated. Audrey had a severe disorder and it had gone on for decades, largely untreated much of the time. As you might expect, children whose parents have more severe and more persistent mental illnesses have more trouble adjusting effectively.
- Resilience factors: internal strengths. Children are born with different temperaments, as we learned in Chapter 6. Those with easy temperaments will have an easier time dealing with adversity. Other internal strengths such as high intelligence, a good sense of humour, or excellent social skills will help the child to handle their difficult situation more effectively. Some of these internal strengths can be taught. For example, a child can learn to stop worrying, can develop a broader perspective on problems, can develop social skills, and so on.
- Resilience factors: external supports. This means the loving and stable adult(s) already mentioned. It also includes a wide variety of other supports. For example, families who are connected to a religious group can receive considerable internal and external support from their religious lives. Teachers, best friends, and perhaps even online support systems (this is less well documented) can help the child to cope better. External support works best if it is predictable. I often work with patients in hospital whose families want to know how to schedule their visits. I encourage them to pick particular days, because it is far more powerful support for their family member to know that Jose will visit on Tuesday

and Thursday evenings than to know that he will be visiting roughly twice a week. This is also true of finding supports for children growing up in difficult circumstances.

- Types of therapy: we know that talk therapy ('psychotherapy') helps people with most psychological disorders do better than if they simply took medication. Many types can be useful, but as far as parenting skills (and most of the specific disorders, with the exception of depression) go, the best research support is for cognitive behavioural therapy (or CBT). Thus, I will be highlighting that approach in this chapter.

Depression

Depression in parents of babies

Depression among parents is quite well studied, partly because of high-profile cases of postpartum depression, and also because of some long-term studies monitoring how depressed mothers interact with their children. But the effects of a mother's depression can start even before the child is born. It has been found that depression during pregnancy already leads babies to be more at risk. The mother's prenatal stress hormone levels are high, and these high levels of stress hormones are then found in their newborn babies. These 'depressed' babies have been shown to be more at risk for birth complications and to have increased difficulty calming themselves down. Just imagine the negative spiral that can follow: a depressed mother already feels sad and guilty, her baby is more difficult to soothe and sleeps less well, the mother becomes more and more sleep-deprived, and so on.

Most important in understanding depression is that it is self-perpetuating. It has a nasty habit of cutting people off from the very behaviours that would help alleviate the depression. For example, the new mother who knows that she is depressed will probably feel worthless and ashamed of being depressed. She receives congratulations about the 'happy event' while feeling numb inside, and she also feels guilty about her irritability and moodiness. Thus, she will often remain silent about her sadness and depression, which cuts her off from talking to those around her. The silence feeds the depression and makes it stronger.

Depression also makes people feel less competent, and since new parenthood is guaranteed to make one feel incompetent anyway, the depressed new parent gets a double dose. A new mother, sunk in depression and feeling defensive, may be reluctant to allow her extended family members or paediatrician to offer her suggestions or to 'give her a break'. In many cases, depression will cause her to misinterpret offers of assistance as evidence that others don't trust her to do a good job.

There are many effective treatments for depression, too, but in order to access them the new mother must admit she is depressed and must seek help. If she is already overwhelmed with the sleep deprivation and the challenges of caring for a newborn baby, seeking help can seem like an impossible task. Finally, depression makes one withdraw socially, and so the social demands of asking for help are more overwhelming than they would be normally.

New fathers, too, are vulnerable to depression. New parenthood is a time when people who are immigrants or otherwise cut off from extended family networks feel particularly lonely and isolated, which is another risk factor for depression. Postpartum depression shows up in about 10 to 15 per cent of all deliveries, although a milder form called the 'baby blues' occurs in 40 to 85 per cent of all deliveries (the baby blues usually go away in a few days).

I admit, I am getting worried that I will upset my readers with this. It *is* depressing to think that even before a baby is born, the mother's depression can be transmitted to the child, and that parents can suffer from depression merely as a result of having a baby. The bright side of this comes from the research on resilience, and from the recommendations below. These are based on good scientific evidence and will help your child to thrive despite any depression that might run in your family.

I want to emphasize one major intervention for postpartum blues: start getting physical exercise as soon as possible after the birth of the baby. Even walking briskly as little as ten minutes a day will boost your mood and will help conquer the depression. Walking is good for both you and the baby, and even in cold weather the baby can be bundled up and put in a baby carrier or jogging buggy so the two of you will be mobile. Research has shown that 'aerobic' physical activity is a potent antidepressant. Some new parents who are too exhausted to even bathe wonder how they can gather the energy to walk. Start with very short walks if you are this exhausted, and if you can call a friend to look after the baby while you take a twenty-minute walk and then a shower, so much the better. Anti-depressant medication and talk therapy are also helpful, as is practical support from friends and family.

Depression in parents of toddlers and older children

Depression can come and go, or it can be chronic. Researchers have studied how parents who are depressed interact with their children, and have compared those patterns to how non-depressed parents interact with their children. Some of the major findings are as follows:

- Depressed parents are less likely to interact with their children.
- Depressed parents express more hostility.
- Depressed parents show more irritability and sadness with their children.
- Depressed parents are less likely to respond to children's behaviour, focusing instead on their own internal world.
- Depressed parents tend to withdraw from confrontation with their children.
- Depressed parents show pessimistic views of the world and rate themselves poorly, and their children may copy those world views and that self-image problem.

This adds up to a pattern of relationships that are not as close as the parent would have if she or he were not depressed. Fortunately, depression responds well to a variety of treatments, both through talk therapy and through medication.

Recommendations

1 Recognize that you are dealing with major depression. This can be very tricky, because we all live stressful lives. Knowing when we have slid over the line from 'very stressed' to 'very depressed' can be extremely difficult. If you are not sure, discuss your symptoms with your family doctor, and do it as soon as possible.

2 Be willing to talk with others about how stressed you are. Talking over the things that seem embarrassing or shameful, such as your worries about being incompetent, is a powerful antidepressant. Talking with other new parents can be enormously helpful when you realize that so many of them have the same kinds of feelings you are having. Internet parenting support groups can be very useful for this kind of support.

3 As mentioned above, extensive research has shown that 'aerobic' or 'cardio' physical activity is a potent antidepressant. It is difficult to increase your level of physical activity when you are depressed, but this should always be part of the treatment of depression, if you are physically capable of exercise.

4 Medication can be very useful but does take some weeks to take effect, and sometimes it can require multiple attempts before you find a medication that works for you. Work closely with your family doctor or psychiatrist if you decide to take an antidepressant medication. If the physician keeps adding on more and more medications, get a second opinion.

5 Long term, you will get better results and fewer recurrences of depression if you don't just take medication, but instead engage in talk therapy ('psychotherapy'). This can be in addition to or instead of the medication. In most forms of therapy you will work on the thoughts, behaviours and social patterns that feed depression. It is

essential that the therapist is someone you can trust. The best predictor of successful treatment for many disorders, including depression, is a therapist who is warm and caring, and who communicates well with the depressed client.

6 For all the psychological disorders, what matters to your children is not the *diagnosis* but rather your *behaviour*. So if you are clinically depressed and still managing to get out of bed, get the children off to school, go to work, and so on, your depression will have a less damaging impact on them than if you are depressed and spending the day in bed. Granted, these are not easy things to do when you are severely depressed. Similarly, even if you are incapacitated for a month or so but you are fortunate enough to have a partner or parent who can move in and keep the household running, that will result in fewer negative effects on your children.

7 If you are not the one with depression and are concerned about a family member or friend, raise the issue with them. Don't be surprised if they respond irritably – that is part of the depression. Let them know that you are having a hard time raising the question, and that you care about them and want to be supportive.

8 Be supportive of their efforts to find treatment. Often they are so depressed that they will be grateful to you if you help them take the next few steps. For example, you could offer to attend the first session with them when they go to meet a new counsellor. You could offer to baby-sit for their children every week when they go for treatment, or help them find someone who can do that for them. Remember how paralysing depression can be, and do your utmost to smooth out obstacles to treatment.

9 Finally, if you are a friend or family member, be there for the children as much as possible. Schedule regular times to be with them. Take them to the zoo once a month. Give them a chance to talk about how hard it can be to live in their house (but do not try to make them talk if they don't want to). Being around adults who are able to get joy out of life and who just have fun will be a great gift to those children.

Anxiety disorders

Along with depression, anxiety disorders are the most common psychological disorders. Many of us have anxiety problems that we choose not to treat. Public speaking phobias, spider phobias, phobias about visiting the dentist, or music performance anxiety are examples of very common anxieties. I once had a student, Jess, who had a severe spider phobia. If she was up during the night and spotted a spider when she went to the bathroom, she would respond by standing still and screaming until one of her roommates arrived to kill the offending creature for her. She reasoned that letting the beast out of her sight would give it an opportunity to crawl away and attack her another time, but she was too paralysed by fear to react in any other way. She never weighed the potential danger from the spider against the potential for homicide perpetrated by one of her sleep-deprived roommates!

People with these kinds of anxieties will generally not seek treatment for their phobias until they find themselves incapacitated or highly distressed by their symptoms. So, for example, Greg did not see his public speaking anxiety as a problem that was treatable. It was not until he passed up a very desirable opportunity for a promotion at work, because of the presentations he would have to make if he were promoted, that he realized he had a problem, and it was his wife who pushed him to seek treatment.

Anxiety disorders can take many forms ranging from mild to severe. Panic attacks, obsessive-compulsive disorder, and extreme social anxiety can all make a person unable to function as a parent. Additionally, we know that parents who are very anxious can transmit their anxieties to their children by their own example (along with having passed along a genetic tendency to become anxious). So, for example, Greg's children will learn from him that getting up in front of a crowd and talking is a terrible thing, and that it is only natural to want to avoid it. Consider how different it would be for Muthoni's children, who know that their mother gives lectures daily to hundreds of university students. If she comes home in the evening and describes funny things that happened in her lectures, her children get a very different message from Greg's children about the nature of public speaking.

Researchers have been studying how anxiety disorders in parents affect children. One recent study in Australia, led by Erin McClure, found that mothers with anxiety disorders had children who were twice as likely to develop anxiety disorders compared to children in the general population. When they looked at mothers suffering from both anxiety disorders and depression, that risk was trebled. This kind of study does not tell us whether the risk to children is primarily genetic or primarily due to what the child learns by watching their parent.

Recommendations

1 Seek treatment. If you are a parent with a tendency to be highly anxious, you should know that anxiety disorders are highly treatable. For example, panic disorder responds very well to a fairly short course of psychotherapy using cognitive behavioural therapy (CBT). In this way, you are teaching your child that problems can be tackled head-on, and you are freeing yourself and your family from the burden of what will otherwise be a lifelong struggle with an anxiety disorder. Again, the therapist needs to be warm and caring, and also needs to push you to confront your fears over time.

2 Seek good, non-anxious role models for your children. Using the examples from earlier in this section, if Greg's children were to be around Muthoni on a regular basis, it would encourage them to get over their inflated fears of public speaking.

3 Desensitize yourself to fears. Suppose you have a fear of water that stems from the time when you were 9 years old and your brother Daniel splashed so much water in your face that you thought you were drowning. Even if you do not choose treatment to get over your fear of water, you could gradually get over it by making yourself spend more time near and in the water until you were once again able to enjoy splashing about.

4 Recognize that your risk assessments are inflated. People with anxiety disorders have a well documented tendency to see risk everywhere, and this can make them overly restrictive and controlling with their children. That can lead to resentment from the children and it could backfire by causing the children to rebel excessively. Instead, talk to friends and family members whose judgement you trust and ask them to let you know if they think your anxiety is causing you to be overly restrictive with your children.

5 Be honest with your children about your own problem and encourage them to face things they fear, knowing that the more they allow themselves to be controlled by fear, the stronger the fear becomes.

6 If you are a friend or family member, the same recommendations already made for depression, above, apply.

7 Finally, if none of the above appeals to you but you like writing, a technique called 'Expressive Writing' has proven to be extremely helpful in reducing distress and improving levels of emotional and physical health. Pioneered by James Pennebaker and colleagues, this simply involves writing openly about your deepest fears, traumatic events, and hopes.

Alcohol and other substance abuse

Children whose parents abuse substances have higher risks for developing all sorts of health problems and behaviour problems (including substance abuse, conduct disorders, criminal behaviour, school problems, and so on). A recent large study led by Cynthia Osborne of the University of Texas found that children's futures were at risk regardless of which parent was the substance abuser, and that a child with two substance-abusing parents was particularly at risk. Additionally, she found that having a substance-abusing father in the home led to a far greater risk to the child's healthy development than if the father abuses substances but does not live with the child.

Additionally, substance abuse is dangerous to the children. This is because the parents have so much less control over their impulses, and are much more likely to use violence toward their children. Parents who are under the influence of alcohol and drugs are also much more likely to be neglectful of their children – for example, failing to notice that the child is playing with matches.

Often, substance abuse occurs in parents who have other disorders as well. For example, parents may deal with an untreated depression or anxiety disorder by drinking heavily. This takes a stressful situation and makes it even more difficult for the child. It also increases the odds that the child will become a 'young carer' who takes responsibility far beyond his years – for example, ensuring that his substance-abusing mother pays the rent.

With substance abuse, we again see the amazing resilience children can have. Despite neglect and abuse from parents, despite the poor role models their parents make, and despite having had to miss out on the better parts of childhood, there are many of these children who turn out to do quite well in life. Again, the presence of a caring adult who is consistently in the child's life seems to be a critical factor.

I was recently approached by Jenny, a university student who was distressed about her younger half-sister, Ashley. Ashley was living with the student's mother, who consumes large amounts of alcohol and is nearly comatose most of the evening. Jenny has made the decision to stay in the home until Ashley finishes school, and Jenny makes sure that the younger girl gets good meals and does her homework. She also makes sure that she and Ashley have time to talk about how their mother is doing and how they want their lives to be different from hers. Jenny was reassured by learning about the research on resilience. Despite the poor role model set by their mother, Jenny's responsible approach speaks even more strongly to Ashley, and her chances of a successful outcome are much enhanced by Jenny's surrogate parenting.

Recommendations

1 Treatment of substance abuse is considerably less effective than treatment for anxiety and depression,

but still it improves the odds of a good outcome. That treatment could either be through a standard drug treatment programme or through a self-help programme such as Alcoholics Anonymous or Narcotics Anonymous. What matters most is not the specific treatment, but which approach is more acceptable to the person with the addiction.

2 If you have a partner with a substance-abuse problem and he or she refuses to seek treatment, it would probably be better for your children if your partner moves out (or if you and the children move out). This is never an easy decision, but separating may improve the odds that your children will do well in life.

3 If you have a family member who is a substance-abusing parent, even if they resist treatment, you can improve their child's chances by making a conscious decision to be that child's safety net. Offer to baby-sit on a regular basis. Spend every Sunday afternoon with the child, or help them with their homework twice a week. The child will benefit far more if she knows she can count on you to be there on specific days than if you pop in at random times throughout the week. This is a very difficult decision to make, as it limits your freedom to do as you please, but it could make all the difference in the world to that child.

4 Be willing to accept a 'harm reduction' approach to the substance abuse. For instance, if the parent refuses to give up the substance abuse, but is willing to agree to use the drug just on weekends, that would be far better for the child (and the parent) than abuse that goes on all week. Sometimes relatives insist that only complete abstinence from the drug will do, but being a purist on this matter may not be best for the children involved.

5 Don't give up on the parent even if you get extremely frustrated and downhearted. Some will make changes only after many years of failed attempts to change. Conversely, it is important that you are willing to set limits so that your own mental health and safety are not compromised (for example, you can insist that they do not use drugs at your home, or that they can't borrow money from you).

Schizophrenia and bipolar disorder

Schizophrenia and bipolar disorder are two of the most serious psychological disorders. Here again we can find parents who have these diagnoses but function fairly well as parents. If they are taking medication and keeping their disorder in check, the negative effects on their children may not be that significant.

On the other hand, these disorders make normal functioning much more difficult, and can lead to many problems with parenting. As with depression, schizophrenia in pregnant women leads to increased risks of problems for their newborn babies. Mothers with schizophrenia show the same tendency as depressed mothers to be less responsive to their children. In addition to causing a parent to become less responsive, delusions can cause parents with schizophrenia to harm their children inadvertently. For example, a parent may become convinced that all food except brown rice is poisoned, and might deprive her child of important nutrients because of this delusional thought, or she might take her child out of school with the idea of keeping the child pure, which could result in loneliness or social isolation for that child.

It is important to keep in mind that the problems created by these disorders can become much less damaging to the child if a good support system is in place. If a mother has schizophrenia, but she has supportive and stable relatives living nearby, her children will have a safety net and should do better than if she and the child live far away from any helpful relatives or friends. Sometimes other family members are very negative influences, in which case the child will do better if the support system is made up of trusted friends from school and the neighbourhood.

Bipolar disorder has symptoms including deep depression and periods of euphoria and irritability. When we look at the research on how a parent's illness affects the children, this seems to be one of the most detrimental disorders. Children of bipolar parents have about *three times* the risk of developing a psychological disorder compared to children in the general population. It makes sense if you consider that a bipolar parent is extremely unpredictable. Untreated bipolar disorder leads to behaviour that could be wildly out of control, sexually promiscuous, and irresponsible, followed by periods of apathy, unresponsiveness, and gloom. Then there are times when the bipolar parent is 'normal' and functions well. Thus, the child never knows what to expect, and cannot even take comfort in the role of being a 'young carer', since sometimes the parent is doing well and resents the child taking charge.

Both schizophrenia and bipolar disorder have the additional problem that their treatment involves drugs that create unpleasant and sometimes dangerous side-effects. Because of this, people with bipolar disorder or schizophrenia often resist taking the medications, and they may end up in hospital. This means the family may deal with multiple hospitalizations per year. One factor that really helps is when these parents receive psychotherapy. Parents who do are more successful overall; the therapy helps them to stay the course with the medications, and helps them handle the emotional storms created by the illness, and the therapist can also be a sort of guide through the mental health care system. The research is clear that this works better than simply prescribing medications.

As I mentioned before, in order for therapy to work, the therapist must be someone who is interpersonally warm and who treats the client with respect and kindness (while remaining professional). If your therapist is not meeting those criteria, speak out and get a new therapist assigned.

Recommendations

1 If you have bipolar disorder or schizophrenia, it is imperative that you set up a good support system that will be able to help your children. This might involve relatives, friends, or teachers. What matters is that the people are trustworthy and willing to take an active role in the life of your child (on a scheduled basis). Anyone's children benefit from this kind of mentoring. Since your children are particularly vulnerable, being careful to set up this kind of arrangement will benefit them especially.

2 If you have bipolar disorder or schizophrenia, make sure you have a good therapist who is someone you can talk with. This could be a psychiatrist, psychologist, counsellor, social worker, or nurse, but it should be someone who is trained and who knows something about your situation.

3 If you have a friend or relative who has one of these disorders, the recommendations are similar to those for many of the disorders listed above. Encouraging treatment, being there for the child, and being supportive to the parent are all going to help that family to succeed.

4 Do not take lightly the many problems that can be created by medications. It is tempting for a family member to say 'just buck up and take your medications and everything will be fine', but the reality is not that simple. The more you learn about the medications, the more helpful you will be able to be to your friend or family member.

5 Take advantage of any local support groups for family members of individuals with these disorders. There you will learn concrete steps you can take to help manage situations, you may learn about new medications or treatments for the disorders, and you will feel better knowing about how others have coped with their situations.

Other disorders

The textbooks are full of psychological disorders that we don't have time to address in this kind of parenting manual. The general principles listed above should apply to all of them: being supportive, encouraging treatment, helping buffer the child's response to their parent's illness, and so on. Additionally, it is important to keep a perspective on the child. Rather than being terrified at the impact of the disorder on the child, remember that she or he has many strengths, and that at least 50 per cent of children even in the most dysfunctional families adjust well despite their upbringing. With your help and support, and the child's natural resilience, you can increase the odds of a successful outcome even further.

The Bottom Line

- **What are the key dilemmas parents have to struggle with on this topic?**
  - How will psychological disorders in the family affect my child's well-being?
  - What can I do about it?
- **What does the science say about this topic?**
  - Resilience and good mental health can be taught.
  - Even if the child is exposed to some very difficult circumstances, there are ways to lessen the impact on the child. The right attitude can 'arm' that child to deal more effectively with the adversities encountered.
- **What do the authors advise?**
  - Avoid communicating to the child that a difficult family situation is a catastrophe that will scar him or her permanently.
  - Convey an attitude of hardiness (see Chapter 12) and work to improve supportive relationships for the child.

Recommended reading for parents

Addis, M. and Martell, C. (2004). *Overcoming depression one step at a time*. Oakland, CA: New Harbinger Publications.

Burns, D. (1999). *Feeling good handbook*. London: Penguin Books.

Butler, G. and Hope, T. (1995). *Managing your mind: The mental fitness guide*. Oxford: Oxford University Press.

Davis, M., Eshelman, E. and McKay, M. (2000). *The relaxation and stress reduction workbook* (5th edn). Oakland, CA: New Harbinger Publications.

Hilliard, E. (2005). *Living fully with shyness and social anxiety: A comprehensive guide to gaining social confidence*. New York: Da Capo Books

Knaus, W. (2006). *The cognitive behavioral workbook for depression*. Oakland, CA: New Harbinger Publications.

Your child's psychological health: nurturing strengths and handling problems

Strahan

Case studies: Keenan, Jenny, Elliot and Yasmin

- A friend asked me some time ago about whether she needed to be concerned about her son. Keenan was about 5 years old at the time, and a 7-year-old boy neighbour had come over to play. Some weeks after the visit, Keenan told his mother that the other boy had touched Keenan's penis, and my friend was wondering whether this experience was going to have harmful long-term effects on Keenan. She thought perhaps she should make an appointment for Keenan to see a counsellor.

- Jenny is 8 years old. Her parents are concerned because she tends to be a fearful girl, and they don't want her fears to prevent her from enjoying life. She worries about what children think of her at school, and she worries about forgetting to do her schoolwork. She worries about doing work incorrectly, but she also worries about whether her teacher will be irritated with her if she asks questions. She worries about what will happen if lightning strikes her home, whether there will be a flood or an earthquake, and whether terrible things will happen to her parents and the family cat. She watches the evening news on the television and her parents wonder whether they should prevent her from watching it.

- Fourteen-year-old Elliot has been refusing to shower on days that correspond to odd numbers. Even when he arrives home, sweaty and muddy after playing with his friends, he will only take a shower when the date falls on an even number. He is also having more and more diffi- culty with his homework, since he takes hours writing and re-writing assignments. He reveals that he has developed a fear that forming the letters imperfectly will cause harm to anyone whose name or nickname starts with that letter. Thus, if he mis-forms either the letter M or K, it could cause something terrible to happen to his mother Kelly. His parents are both meticulous and somewhat anxious people, and they are not sure whether his behaviour is 'just a fad' or whether it needs psycho- logical treatment.

- Yasmin is 16 years old. She was always a difficult child but lately she has begun to play truant from school more frequently, and she openly defies her parents' instruc- tions. Her parents are quite certain she has been drinking large amounts of alcohol and possibly also using illegal drugs. They found some odd-looking pills in her room, but decided to destroy them, fearing what they might have in their house. They also decided not to confront Yasmin about the pills, knowing that she would yell at them about their invasion of her privacy. She sometimes gets in such a rage that she talks about killing herself or killing them in their sleep. They are at their wits' end, fearing that anything they do will lead to a bad outcome. They talk to their family doctor, who puts her on medication, which does not seem to make much improvement.

Parenting is a tremendous challenge, and perhaps no parenting dilemma is as difficult to handle as the question of how to respond to concerns about your child's mental well-being. Asking for advice from friends and family members may confuse the picture further, since any parent who asks for advice will receive it in abundance, and often it will contradict what the unfortunate parent was just told by another trusted friend. Furthermore, no parenting manual will be able to cover the variety of questions that you will have about your child's emotional well-being.

This sounds rather daunting, but a basic knowledge about what makes children survive and thrive will make the task slightly less difficult. When a parenting dilemma arises, if you are well versed in the basics, you probably will be able to create a response that will make sense and will be as helpful to your child as possible.

Key concepts about children's mental health

Building some baseline knowledge about children's mental health is a good way to start. To do this, we need to think about what makes children as stress-resistant and resilient as possible. We also need to think about the major categories of psychological disturbances, and which sorts of treatments are helpful to children having those problems.

- *Developmental assets*. This concept has grown up along with the literature on what makes children resilient (see Chapter 11 on parents with psychological problems). The number of assets listed will vary depending on the researcher. One nice example of such a listing, tailored to the child's age, can be found at www.search-institute. org. Examples of developmental assets are 'family support', 'other adult relationships', 'school boundaries (school provides clear rules and consequences)' and 'neighbourhood boundaries'. The problem with this type of inventory is that it lists a number of assets that it would be ideal for any child to have, but it does not always readily suggest actions that parents can take in order to improve their children's stress-resistance. It also does not prioritize the assets, and many parents do not have the energy or time to implement all of them. Finally, some of the assets are only partially under your control (for example, you cannot make your daughter feel proud of herself, but you can provide her with opportunities to decide what she is good at and find ways to pursue those interests).

  Fortunately, the research leads to some very strong conclusions that will help you sort out which of your decisions and actions will have the greatest positive impact on your child. I will describe these below under the topic 'Raising kids who are stress-resistant'.

- *Internalizing disorders*. This is one of two major categories of psychological disorders in children. These are disorders where the child tends to withdraw inward or express his or her distress in quiet ways. Depression and the anxiety disorders are classic examples of these kinds of problems.
- *Externalizing disorders*. This is the other major category. It includes disorders where the child is rebellious, destructive, or simply highly active and out of control. Attention deficit hyperactivity disorder (ADHD) and conduct disorder are examples from this category.
- *Behavioural problems – chronic or acute*. These include a number of common behaviours such as thumb-sucking, bed-wetting, nail-biting, and so on. In many cases, these do not rise to the level of a psychological disorder, although psychological treatments are generally the best approaches to take if the child does not naturally give up the behaviour as she grows. Always keep in mind the child's age and developmental level when you consider these problems. Let us take the example of bed-wetting. It is an inconvenience, but would not be a cause for alarm if the child is 4 years old. By the age of 10, the parent should be much more concerned, and treatment would be necessary. One way to start the process would be to look up Schaefer and Millman's classic handbook, *How to help children with common problems*. I think every child should be sent home from hospital with a copy of this book; it is a wonderful resource for parents. If using their recommended approach does not work, or if you have trouble implementing a plan, seeing a psychologist or counsellor for assistance would be a good next step.
- *Scepticism about medication as a cure-all*. A lot of behavioural and psychological problems are mismanaged when people give the child medication but do not follow up on recommendations for counselling or psychotherapy. Remember that many drugs originally tested on adults have never been tested for safe use with children, and in the case of some of them (for example, the SSRI antidepressants), use with teenagers can be harmful.

- *Types of psychological treatment*. Historically, there has been a variety of schools of thought within psychology. Those that have the best support for use with children are cognitive behavioural therapy (CBT) (for a variety of disorders) and interpersonal therapy (for depression). It matters greatly whether the therapist has good social skills and is able to relate reasonably well to the child (within reason – some angry adolescents sink sullenly into their jackets and refuse to like even the most personable psychologist).
- *Get several opinions if there is any doubt about the diagnosis*. Don't just assume that the child's paediatrician will be knowledgeable about psychological disorders. I have seen instances where the family doctor diagnosed a child as having 'bipolar disorder', when in reality she just had a difficult temperament.

Raising kids who are stress-resistant

Let us start this section by talking about rat pups. Scientists have been using them to understand how we humans develop our stress responses. Dr Liu and colleagues at McGill University in Montreal published a major article in 1997 showing how the mother rat's licking and grooming of her young pups led to the pups having far more effective stress responses. Later studies confirmed that rat pups whose mothers did not lick them, or who were deprived of contact with their mothers, developed chronic stress hormone elevations. Additionally, scientists have learned that the rat pups who develop the healthiest body responses to stressors are those who are exposed to significant stressors while still pups (for example, the researchers put a strange adult male rat in the cage with them), but whose mothers soothe and lick them after the stressful event.

You may be sceptical about research on rat pups being applicable to children, but in this case the findings are quite relevant. For one thing, this work dovetails nicely with the findings of the developmental assets/resilience research. Children will always have stressful experiences, and our task as parents is not to attempt to shield them from all stress. That would be counterproductive. Rather, our task is to shield them if possible from stressors that would be beyond their coping resources, to talk with them about the stressful events that do occur, and to help them develop 'buffers' against stress (which are the developmental assets).

I do not want you to take away from this chapter the idea that you should just throw your child into highly stressful situations on purpose, as long as you soothe them later. We simply don't have evidence that there would be anything to be gained from this, and there is potential for harm to the parent/child relationship. But if you take a normal life stressor, geared to your child's developmental level, and make sure that you are responsive and affectionate, and talk with your child about how they handle the situation, that will provide the best chance that your child will develop stress hardiness.

For example, if your child is 10 or 11 and wants to go on a camping trip but is fearful about it, this would be an excellent opportunity to encourage her to attend. Listen to her concerns; you don't need to agree with them, but be careful not to belittle the child for having them, or she will not talk with you in future when she has concerns about more dangerous topics. 'I'm scared about going camping', should be met with a response like 'I remember feeling scared about that, too. What is worrying you most about it?' Many parents who want their children to be fearless respond instead with something like 'Nonsense, there's nothing to be afraid of', which cuts off communication with the child and gives her the message that she cannot talk with you about these sorts of things. Then, help your daughter find ways to reduce her anxiety. For example, you could see whether one of your daughter's friends could also go on the same trip. This way the experience can be shared with someone else, and the next time she will probably be eager to go whether or not her friend is able to accompany her.

So what can a parent do to promote the best possible chance for a child to thrive? The research in this area has come up with some strong recommendations. There are several key elements that greatly improve children's odds of success in life. These are as follows:

1 The physical presence of a parent in the home at key times, such as after school and at bedtime, is enormously helpful to the child's development.
2 The closeness and warmth of the relationship between the parent and child. This includes physical affection but even more the ease with which the child is able to talk with the parent. It does *not* include the ease with which the parent can talk with the child (see 4 below).
3 Parent expectations for the child that include avoiding substance abuse, doing well in school, etc.
4 A home environment that is relatively free of stress, conflict and aggression. Interestingly, there is clear evidence that parents should avoid talking with their children about anxiety-provoking topics (for example, financial worries and conflicts with ex-spouses). The parent may have a strong need to talk, but the child should not be the one to whom the parent unburdens herself/himself.

A marvellous resource for parents interested in teaching their children to be as resilient and stress-resistant as possible is *The optimistic child*, by Dr Martin Seligman. Dr Seligman outlines a simple but effective programme for improving your child's ability to bounce back from disappointments and difficulties.

Raising kids who are socially adept

Some children are naturally gifted when it comes to social interaction and will thrive socially no matter what kind of home environment they grow up in. Others are naturally socially awkward and will have to work harder to get along in life. These differences are 'hard-wired', but if your child is not skilled in the social graces, you should realize that there are things you can do to promote better social skills in your children.

1 Don't automatically take your child's side. If the child comes home upset with the teacher, help her to think through why the teacher may have done what she did. For example, assume your 7-year-old boy comes home from school, upset because the teacher thought he was talking during a test, when actually it was the boy next to him who was attempting to start a conversation. You as a parent have some choices about how to respond. You could:

   a Spring to your child's defence and call or write to the teacher to express your unhappiness. This is likely to encourage the child to develop a sense that 'they' (authority figures) do not have good reasons for their actions, and will also lead your children to believe that you will fight their battles.

   b Tell your child that life is unfair and he should get used to it. This leaves your child feeling vulnerable and isolated, knowing that he cannot look to you for help in solving social problems.

   c Start a conversation with your child about why it might have seemed to the teacher that he was cheating, and what he can do in the future to handle such misunderstandings. Helping him to get some perspective on others' motives is a great way of building empathy and understanding. It also begins to show your child that tricky social situations are problems that can be solved.

2 Find ways to immerse your child in a variety of different social situations, with differing expectations at each one. Sports teams, family gatherings, dinner with colleagues, and church or community functions all have different expectations, and your child will benefit from learning to be comfortable in a wide range of different settings. Then make sure you find time to talk with your child about what happens, particularly if your child feels threatened or uncomfortable in a new situation. He will feel better if he knows that everyone feels awkward when they are the new one in the group, and will benefit from your advice on how he can get to know others (for example, by inviting another child in the group to your home to play).

3 Play team sports and board games with your child. These are ways to learn about following rules, taking turns, and getting along with others. If, for example, you are upset about a call by one of the game officials, you can be a role model for socially responsible behaviour. Remember that children do not do the things you tell them to do. Rather, they copy your actions.

4 Coach your child, by example, in two very basic components of resilience: take events as challenges that can be overcome rather than terrible catastrophes, and use humour to cope with unpleasant events. If your child sees you reacting to frustrations at the office by blaming others and calling them names, or by drinking too much, your approach to stress will speak more loudly than anything you tell your child to do.

5 As superficial as this may seem, make sure your child is dressed reasonably well and is well groomed. The research is clear that other children are more likely to reject a child who looks odd or dirty or is dressed in an unusual way. This is not a surprising finding, as even adults are more favourably inclined toward another adult who is well dressed and well groomed. Be careful, though – this does not mean that your child needs to wear the latest expensive designer clothes. Choose outfits that are attractive, but inexpensive, and that allow your child the freedom to play outdoors.

6 Also on the issue of clothing, remember that how a child is dressed sends powerful messages both to the child, and to the rest of society. Many current fashions eroticize little girls. The same parents who buy their 6-year-old daughters sexy outfits because they think they are 'cute' will need to deal with teenagers who expect to be appreciated mostly for their sexual attributes. Likewise, for little boys, fashions can help turn them into mini-warriors whose ideal of manliness reflects only the narrowest gender stereotypes. The fantasies you encourage in your children by what you buy them and what they watch when they are young will be reflected in their behaviour. The parents who buy their son a Star Wars costume for a fancy dress party should not be surprised

when their boy begins leaping about the room attacking others with his plastic light sabre.

Parent training programmes

These are outstanding resources. The more intensive ones (with longer time in class) tend to be most effective. Parents who take these programmes not only see benefits as their child's behaviours improve, but the research consistently shows that the parents' own mental health and sense of well-being improve once they learn new skills for managing their child's behaviours more effectively. There are a number of these programmes available throughout the UK. Perhaps the best researched are the 'Incredible Years' training programmes, but there are a number of other approaches (such as the Positive Parenting Programme or 'Triple P', and Strengthening Families, Strengthening Communities). These programmes share many of the same basic elements, and all of them have good research support. It would be more useful for most families to pick one that is convenient in terms of time and place, rather than to try to choose between them. Check with your primary healthcare provider for details on how to access these programmes in your area.

Common behaviour problems

This category includes all kinds of difficult situations or habits, such as bed-wetting, thumb-sucking, having problems sleeping through the night, etc. When behaviour problems emerge, no matter what they are, one useful way to think about them is by asking the following questions (derived from an approach called 'Functional Analysis of Behaviour', which owes much to B.F. Skinner but has been used by observers of human nature both before and since Skinner):

- What benefits is the child getting from this behaviour? Usually these involve one of four types of benefit. The major categories of benefit include obtaining tangible rewards (as with stealing), obtaining social attention (as with clowning in class), escaping from an aversive situation (as with a child who escalates misbehaviours because he knows if he does it enough he will be kicked out of school), and obtaining sensory stimulation (as with nail-biting or thumb-sucking).

- What positive means could accomplish the same ends? For example, can the class clown be enrolled in acting classes, or given a job at school that involves communicating with others?
- What system of rewards or punishments can be set up to promote good behaviour? If the class clown is enjoying taking acting classes, classes could be made contingent on good behaviour in school. Usually, rewards are more effective than punishments.
- Once a system is worked out, the parents and teachers (if school is where the problem takes place) need to communicate on a regular basis, and follow through on the plan or modify it if it is not immediately successful. Most behaviour plans do require some tweaking in order to make them more effective.
- Schaefer and Millman's classic book *How to help children with common problems* is an invaluable resource with detailed instructions on how to set up behavioural programmes for these sorts of problems.

A word about spanking and other forms of corporal punishment

Don't. The scientific evidence is abundantly clear that spanking is not effective in improving desirable behaviours in your child. It also tends to boomerang and can hurt the relationship with the parent, as well as increasing the likelihood that the child will be aggressive towards others. There are many more effective strategies that are far more useful and carry less risk of negative outcomes. Chapter 9 in this book will give you considerably more information and suggestions on the topic of how to encourage good behaviour in your children. Interested parents and clinicians are also encouraged to read Elizabeth Gershoff's review on this topic (see list of references).

Bullying

Both boys and girls can be guilty of bullying, though with boys it is more often accomplished through use of force or threat of force, and with girls it usually involves interpersonal nastiness such as name-calling or spreading rumours. Many schools are instituting programmes designed to help children withstand bullying and to eliminate the problems. These programmes are showing good initial results. If your child has a problem with being bullied or with bullying, keep in mind that this is a problem for which collaborating with the school is essential. Try to keep an open mind, meet with the teachers or school psychologist, and work jointly with them to develop a plan that you can support whole-heartedly.

Depression and bipolar disorder

The mood disorders, depression and bipolar disorder, are among the most frightening to parents. They involve the transformation of your child from an open, playful, happy child to a gloomy, morose, withdrawn, sullen, and even sometimes suicidal child.

One of the biggest problems with getting treatment for children and adolescents lies in the fact that parents do not see the mood disorder in their children. Others (teachers, neighbours) may see the changes, but parents are too emotionally invested to see what is happening. Most often, parents underestimate the problems that their children are having. This means that depression often goes untreated until the adolescent is at a very serious stage of the depression.

When I began working as a therapist I was amazed at how difficult it was to ask some of the most important questions of a depressed client. 'Are you thinking of killing yourself?' 'Does it all seem hopeless to you?' We are socialized not to ask those questions, believing that somehow we will 'put ideas into their heads' and drive people toward suicide. That is a completely unfounded concern and runs opposite to what you should be doing.

In fact, if your child might be suicidal, one of the best things you can do is pick up on the hints he might be dropping about how 'nothing is worthwhile', 'it all seems useless', etc. You must have the courage to ask your child whether he is down and depressed, feels despairing, and whether he is considering harming himself. Most depressed children in that situation report that it is a relief to have someone ask them about this – finally. Then your task is to find them a therapist whom they will like and respect. Work hard to find another psychologist, counsellor, or social worker if the first one does not 'click' with your child fairly soon. It is crucial that the child has a liking for the therapist, as therapy will only be effective if the child feels respected by the therapist, and likes and trusts the therapist.

Currently available major studies show that teenagers who are depressed do better if they receive cognitive behavioural therapy (CBT) for depression than if they are given antidepressant medications (which can actually increase the risk of suicide in teenagers). They show quicker improvement with the cognitive therapy, and they also report liking their treatment more if it involves talking, solving problems, and learning new social skills – activities that are important components of CBT.

Bipolar disorder is an even more difficult situation. There is currently a trend toward diagnosing bipolar disorder in younger and younger children. A recent review of trends in the US found that there was a forty-fold increase in the number of bipolar disorder diagnoses in the ten years from 1997 to 2007. It is not clear exactly what this means – it could mean that the actual prevalence of the disorder is increasing, it could mean that American psychiatrists are over-diagnosing it, or it could mean that American psychiatrists were under-diagnosing the disorder in the past (or any combination of the above). Whatever the case, parents need to be very careful and need to ask hard questions when a doctor suggests a diagnosis that is currently 'trendy'. As we know from past experience, all this attention to one diagnosis makes doctors overly willing to use the diagnosis, along with the potent and sometimes dangerous drugs used to treat it. There are in fact cases of children with bipolar disorder, but parents should keep in mind that there are dangers associated with over-diagnosing a disease just as there are problems associated with under-diagnosing a disease.

These are some recommendations if your doctor or someone else suggests that your child has bipolar disorder:

1 Get a second (and even a third) opinion. You would do well to consult both a reputable child psychologist and a reputable child psychiatrist who are organizationally independent of each other, and pay close attention to how their opinions overlap or differ. *Never* allow your child to receive medication for bipolar disorder just on the basis of one medical evaluation, even if you are desperate to find a treatment for your child's behaviour.
2 Recognize that the symptoms of bipolar disorder overlap considerably with many other childhood disorders, particularly attention deficit hyperactivity disorder or ADHD. Thus, it is easy for practitioners to misdiagnose.
3 Be aware that many of the medications being used to treat paediatric bipolar disorder have not been tested on children, and some have very difficult and even dangerous side-effects.
4 Also, be aware that antidepressant medications being used for children may make it more likely that the child will have a diagnosis of bipolar disorder in the future.

In sum, mood disorders such as depression and bipolar disorder are serious and both their treatment and their neglect can have serious consequences. CBT therapy from a therapist who is reputable is vital and is more likely to be helpful in the long term than is antidepressant medication. Also, it is very tricky to diagnose bipolar disorder correctly in children, and even if you have confidence in your physician, it is crucial to get a second opinion on a diagnosis that has such profound consequences for your child.

Anxiety disorders

In contrast to mood disorders, anxiety disorders are easier to diagnose and the treatments are more straightforward. Some of the most common anxiety disorders in children include separation anxiety, specific phobias such as fear of dogs, social phobias, and obsessive-compulsive disorder.

Just as with adult anxiety disorders, children's anxieties grow out of 'catastrophic' thoughts about terrible things that may happen. For example, if your child is fearful of dogs, it may be because she heard on the evening news about a child who was killed by a dog. This causes her to overestimate the danger of dogs, and if she then starts to avoid all dogs, she could become more and more fearful of all dogs, so the phobia would grow.

Fortunately, the best treatment for most fears is very simple. Psychologists call it 'exposure', meaning simply that the child comes into contact with the thing they fear. It is fine for parents to use this principle at home if the phobia is not too intense. For example, a child who is afraid of dogs could watch another child petting a (friendly, safe!) dog and could eventually be brought closer to the dog, until she ultimately agrees to pet the dog. If your child is so fearful that he is trembling or crying or otherwise refuses to be exposed to the feared object, it would be better to work with a trained psychologist or counsellor. The therapist can determine what is maintaining the fear and the parent does not need to play the role of the ogre – leave that to the professional!

The same basic principle applies to other anxiety disorders as well, but obsessive-compulsive disorder and similar serious disorders need treatment by a trained therapist. Parents could inadvertently damage relationships with their children by forcing them into actions that the children are not yet willing to accept.

Medication is sometimes useful for anxiety disorders, but in general it adds little benefit and brings risks along with it. Once again, as with depression, cognitive behavioural therapy (CBT) has been shown to be both safe and effective in treating anxiety disorders, and it should be the treatment of choice. If your primary care physician suggests using medication without referring your child to psychological treatment, you should be willing to *ask why*.

Substance abuse

The news on substance abuse with children and adolescents is much less positive than it is for depression and anxiety. While anxiety and depression usually respond well to treatment, with substance abuse, the picture is less hopeful. Once a substance abuse pattern has developed, it alters the child's brain in some important ways, and it makes it much harder to get rid of a pattern of drug-abusing behaviour.

For substance abuse, prevention is much more productive than treatment. Things that you as a parent can do in order to decrease the likelihood of your children abusing alcohol or drugs include:

1 Don't abuse substances yourself.
2 Watch the subtle and not-so-subtle messages you send your children. If you typically come home from work grumbling about how awful your work was and eager for that first beer as soon as you walk in the door, you are sending an unmistakable message about the importance of beer as a relaxation strategy, and how the rest of your day was misery. Your child will pick up on and copy these attitudes.
3 Model alternative ways of having fun and coping with problems. Invite friends over to play games, meet a friend for a cup of coffee, and play sports or go for a walk when you are stressed. These approaches teach your child about how to have fun and manage stress without turning to alcohol or drugs.
4 Know your child's friends, and support the most positive friendships from an early age. This is one primary strategy for keeping your children out of trouble. As long as your child's friends are staying away from drugs, that will make it less likely that your child will get involved. It is not foolproof, but will help enormously.

5 Talk with your child about what other kids their age are doing and saying. If you get in the habit of having conversations with your child, and let them know you would disapprove of any drug use, your child will be less likely to abuse drugs.
6 Have a warm and positive relationship with your child. This is more important than many other elements – if your child feels he can talk with you, and knows you will always care, he is much less likely to get into trouble with alcohol or drugs.

The Bottom Line

- **What are the key dilemmas parents have to struggle with on this topic?**
  - What should I do if someone suggests my child has an emotional problem? How is that assessed?
  - What can be done if there is a family genetic tendency toward disorders such as anxiety or depression?
  - What are the best treatment approaches?
- **What does the science say about this topic?**
  - Resilience and strong mental health can be taught in children. Parents can greatly reduce the likelihood that their children will develop problems by taking an active role, particularly if there is a family genetic history of anxiety or depression.
  - Parent training programmes are excellent resources for any parent who wants to develop new skills.
  - Treatment of psychological disorders often does not require medications in children, though there are some disorders for which medication is very useful.
  - Work closely with a psychologist or counsellor; if your child likes that person, treatment will be more effective.
- **What do the authors advise?**
  - Take a parenting class such as the Incredible Years programme. It will benefit the whole family.
  - Read the Seligman book listed below.
  - Understand that you can teach valuable skills even if you have a tendency to be depressed or anxious yourself.

- If there are ongoing difficult issues such as a parent with bipolar disorder or schizophrenia, or behaviour problems in the child, take the time to get additional support from family and friends.

Recommended reading for parents and paediatricians

Barrett, P. and Ollendick, T. (2004). *Handbook of interventions that work with children and adolescents: Prevention and treatment*. Chichester: Wiley. (Note – this is a scholarly book geared to clinicians.)

Chen, J. and George, R. (2005). Cultivating resilience in children from divorced families. *The Family Journal: Counseling and Therapy for Couples and Families*, 4, 452–455.

Christopherson, E. and Mortweet, S. (2003). *Parenting that works: Building skills that last a lifetime*. Washington, DC: American Psychological Association.

Groopman, J. (2007). What's normal? The difficulty of diagnosing bipolar disorder in children. Retrieved November 2007 from www.jeromegroopman.com/articles/whats-normal.html

Schaefer, C. and Millman, H. (1994). *How to help children with common problems*. London: Jason Aronson, Inc.

Schor, J. (2004). *Born to buy: The commercialized child and the new consumer culture*. New York: Scribner.

Seligman, M. (2007). *The optimistic child: A proven program to safeguard children against depression and build lifelong resilience*. Boston, MA: Houghton Mifflin Co.

Neuropsychology for parents: ADHD and head injuries

Ziccardi and Strahan

Human neuropsychology is the study of brain structure and function. It is a vast science, and just the weight of its textbooks make that painfully obvious to the neuropsychologist in training. For the purposes of this book, we thought it was particularly important to focus on two issues that often face parents. These are encapsulated in the following questions from parents:

- My daughter Jenna, a bright 9-year-old, seems to be having trouble focusing in class. The teachers think she should be evaluated for some kind of attention deficit disorder. What should I do?
- My son Geoff is 11 years old and loves playing sports. I've read some recent reports about children's brains and whether heading the ball is dangerous. Should I be concerned?

In this chapter, we will address the question of how parents should react if they have concerns about their child's capacity to focus attention. We will also look at what the science of neuropsychology says about how sports injuries can affect the developing brain. Both of these issues are excellent examples of how scientific consensus has mostly been reached (in the case of attention deficit disorder) and is still evolving (in the case of head injuries in football).

Attention deficit hyperactivity disorder

While on vacation with my wife and two sons, I was preparing to take the boys out of the hotel one afternoon so that my wife could take a nap. I instructed my 6-year-old to put on his shoes while I finished with some other task. Five minutes later, I checked on him, only to find him still in socks. There was no television playing, no toys scattered about, and no book in his hand. He was simply distracted each time he started to get his shoes. I again told him to put on his shoes, and even set them before him. I went to the bedroom to check something and returned to find him still in stocking feet. At this point I raised my voice and implored him to finish the job. He informed me that I did not need to keep telling him to put on his shoes. I ultimately guided him 'hand over hand', or else he would still be in his socks in a Toronto hotel.

This type of dressing dance will be all too familiar to parents who attempt every morning to make sure their inattentive offspring do not leave the house naked.

Attention deficit hyperactivity disorder (ADHD) is a neuro-developmental condition in which a person has difficulties with attention/concentration, excessive motor activity, and/or impulsivity. Estimates suggest somewhere between 3 and 5 per cent of school-age children have this disorder. The symptoms of ADHD divide into two clusters: inattention symptoms and hyperactivity/impulsivity symptoms. Three types of ADHD are recognized: ADHD, combined type, ADHD, predominantly inattentive type, and ADHD, predominantly hyperactive-impulsive type.

Diagnostic criteria for ADHD

First, a word of warning: many, many children have the symptoms listed below. Please do not become too alarmed as you read these criteria. The issue with ADHD is a matter of degree. So yes, most of our children will go to their rooms and forget that they were supposed to be getting their shoes. But they won't usually go to their rooms three times in a row, each time forgetting about the shoes.

The diagnosis of ADHD is made not just on inattentive behaviours, but on how frequently they occur and how significantly they disrupt the child's ability to make friends, do well in school, and pursue goals that are important to the child. As another example, I tell parents that most children at some point in time will decide to give themselves a haircut, with unflattering results. The child with ADHD may impulsively repeat this experience several more times, forgetting how dismal the outcome was.

Attention deficit hyperactivity disorder, for clinical purposes, is defined by:

I. Either (1) or (2):
    (1) Six (or more) of the following symptoms of inattention have persisted for at least six months to a degree that is maladaptive and inconsistent with developmental level:
    Inattention
    1 Often fails to give close attention to details or makes careless mistakes in schoolwork, work, or other activities.
    2 Often has difficulty sustaining attention in tasks or play activities.
    3 Often does not seem to listen when spoken to directly.
    4 Often does not follow through on instructions and fails to finish schoolwork, chores, or duties in the workplace (not due to oppositional behaviour or failure to understand instructions).
    5 Often has trouble organizing tasks and activities.
    6 Often avoids, dislikes, or is reluctant to engage in tasks that require sustained mental effort (such as schoolwork or homework).
    7 Often loses things necessary for tasks and activities (e.g. toys, school assignments, pencils, books, or tools).
    8 Is often easily distracted by extraneous stimuli.
    9 Often forgetful in daily activities.

(2) Six (or more) of the following symptoms of hyperactivity-impulsivity have persisted for at least six months to a degree that is maladaptive and inconsistent with developmental level:

Hyperactivity

1 Often fidgets with hands or feet or squirms in seat.
2 Often leaves seat in classroom or in other situations in which remaining seated is expected.
3 Often runs about or climbs excessively in situations in which it is inappropriate (in adolescents or adults, may be limited to subjective feelings of restlessness).
4 Often has difficulty playing or engaging in leisure activities quietly.
5 Is often 'on the go' or often acts as if 'driven by a motor'.
6 Often talks excessively.

Impulsiveness

1 Often blurts out answers before questions have been completed.
2 Often has difficulty awaiting turn.
3 Often interrupts or intrudes on others (e.g. butts into conversations or games).

II. Some symptoms that cause impairment were present before age 7 years.

III. Some impairment from the symptoms is present in two or more settings (e.g. at school/work and at home).

IV. There must be clear evidence of significant impairment in social interactions, school, or work.

The best neuropsychological model for understanding ADHD symptoms is based on the notion of the brain's executive system. Executive skills refer to one's ability to plan, organize, direct, and execute actions. Think of a CEO of a large company. He rarely 'produces' tangible work. At the end of the day, he has not typed any letters, packed any boxes, or loaded any trucks. However, his job has been to tell all the other parts of the company what to do, how to do it, and when to stop doing it. The 'executive' in our brain resides in the frontal lobes. This part of our brain makes decisions, assesses various courses of action, and puts these plans into motion. It relies on other brain skills, such as memory, language, and motor coordination, to get results. A person with ADHD will struggle with making a plan, persisting with a plan, or knowing when to stop acting out a plan. Parents often nod in agreement when others describe how frustrating homework becomes with their ADHD child if the parent is not literally 'at the child's elbow'. Try to cook dinner while also giving homework help, and the child's difficulty with planning and 'stick-to-it-iveness' becomes readily apparent. 'Clean your room', 'set the table', and 'get dressed' are other common tasks that these youngsters struggle to complete without nearly constant supervision by the harried parents.

A common refrain from parents is that their child seems to know school material when studying the night before a test but 'goes blank' come test time. This is again an outcropping of the inability to guide oneself through purposeful behaviour. Even if the child has learned the material thoroughly, recalling it during a specific test time can be difficult.

The ADHD child in a testing situation will struggle to direct and organize his attention internally to retrieve the relevant test knowledge. Even in a non-distracting environment, managing internal distractions can make it difficult to produce an accurate appraisal of the child's knowledge from group testing. This fact often leads to children with ADHD being suspected of learning disabilities based on group standardized testing. It should be noted, however, that these children are more likely than other children to have learning disabilities and other problems, in addition to ADHD, a fact that makes comprehensive assessment so important.

Assessment

The process by which we diagnose attention disorder symptoms has progressed quite a bit over recent years. Most often, families seek out their physician, frequently on the advice of school personnel. The physician will often gather input from parents, educators, and a psychologist before making a diagnosis of ADHD. Much ado has been made about teachers 'diagnosing' ADHD, as this is considered a biological diagnosis and thus beyond the scope of a teacher's expertise. In some instances there have actually been legal actions brought by parents who felt their child's teacher was diagnosing medical problems and proposing medical treatment. Many school administrators now hammer home to their staff that they cannot tell a parent 'your son needs Ritalin' or make similar comments. I have found that the current catchphrase is for school personnel to tell a parent that the child needs 'a physical' or 'to see his doctor'. More than one baffled parent has replied by asking if their child is 'sick' and has left the conversation somewhat confused by the recommendation. The teacher's input remains vital to making an accurate diagnosis, however.

Parents obviously have the primary role in the diagnostic process; if they choose not to seek consultation, no diagnosis or intervention can be carried out. Children with ADHD often are seen as having hearing problems in their preschool years. Parents call and call the child, only to wonder, 'Can she hear me?' To date, I have yet to see a collaborative programme between audiologists and psychologists or physicians aimed at identifying possible ADHD children who seem not to hear, yet who always pass the early hearing tests.

By early school years, parents begin to see attention difficulties for what they really are. I always ask about children's ability to follow the family's 'morning routine' during the first few years of school. After several months, most children in early years learn the parents' expectations about the 'morning routine' before school. Whether it is to eat breakfast before dressing or making sure one's book bag is ready before watching the television, most children easily learn these steps. Children with ADHD routinely require prompting to stay on task and complete these familiar routines. As with my son in the opening paragraph, they know the expected steps but need much guidance to complete them. After-school routines and chores also reveal these weaknesses in ADHD children. Moreover, asking whether these problems exist with mundane, non-academic tasks underscores that the problem is not only with academic tasks. This can be an important clue in differentiating between ADHD and a learning disability.

During the evaluation process, physicians often send the family for a psychological evaluation once medical causes are ruled out. Allergies, medication side-effects, thyroid dysfunction, and neurological illnesses (e.g. seizures) should all be considered by the physician as potential causes for inattention. In many cases, teacher and parent rating scales (such as the Conners' or SNAP-IV-R questionnaires) will be administered through the physician's office. Based on medical examination and parent and teacher reports, a physician can then diagnose and treat a child's inattention symptoms. However, many other psychological disorders often need to be formally ruled out as well, thus prompting the need for more formal investigation by a psychologist. Complicated family and emotional situations (e.g. a recent divorce, or other changes in the family structure such as the birth of a new baby), suspected pervasive developmental disorder, or the presence of other behavioural problems are common reasons for more detailed psychological investigation.

The psychological evaluation is usually completed over several sessions. It consists of clinical interviews with the parents and child, psychometric testing with the child, and perhaps classroom teacher consultation. Interviews are used to exclude other possible causes for inattention, such as anxiety about some home stress, performance anxiety regarding school, or social difficulties. Early developmental delays and medical issues are also closely reviewed as these can point to more global problems – for example, pervasive developmental disorders such as autism. Interviewing younger children (below age 10) is intended more to build rapport and evaluate mood, behaviour and language, as these children are mostly not self-aware enough to describe their attention problems. Older children can be of great assistance, however, as they may have received feedback from friends, coaches, and other adults which indicates inattention.

Psychometric testing involves using different instruments to measure a child's intellectual strengths and weaknesses. Intelligence testing is designed to shed light on the child's learning potential. There are many parts to the various IQ tests available to the psychologist. All of the more comprehensive tests include measures of the child's immediate attention skills, verbal information learned over time (e.g. vocabulary knowledge), and non-verbal problem-solving skills. Achievement testing involves measuring a child's acquired academic knowledge – that is, how well do they read, spell, write, and do arithmetic compared to their peers nationwide. School personnel are often trained to use norms or averages based on school year or grade level. In the US, a student entering third grade, for instance, may be described as reading on a 'mid-year second grade' level. Psychologists may use age-norms, however, going on the premise that a young third grader has had less opportunity overall to acquire some of the information contained in the test. Either approach is suitable for assessment with younger children.

Treatment

The mainstream approach to treating ADHD symptoms is medication. This approach has been well studied in multi-group experiments (more on this in a moment). There are a variety of medications currently in common use for treatment of ADHD symptoms. Several variations exist for many of these medications (such as controlled release versus more rapid release), making for difficult choices for the physician and parents. Although many studies are touted as showing the efficacy of one medication versus another, there is no clear winner among these medications. Parents must recognize and accept that there is a trial and error element to selecting a medication once a child has been diagnosed.

Multiple studies over the years have shown good treatment outcomes with medication for more than 70 per cent of all correctly diagnosed children. Improvement can often be seen in self-control behaviours, academic performance, social skills, and self-esteem. These effects are noteworthy to caregivers, peers, and the child receiving treatment. However, it is not uncommon to have to try several different medications before unpleasant side-effects are minimized and the child's treatment response is acceptable. Parents must accept an active role in working with their physician if their child is to be effectively treated.

Regarding medication effectiveness, a 1999 study (by the MTA Cooperative Group) demonstrated the efficacy of using medication to treat children with ADHD. In the study, 579 children were given medication, or intensive behavioural counselling, or a combination of medication and behavioural interventions, or else 'standard treatment' by community professionals. The study found that medication alone was better than the counselling interventions. Moreover, the combination treatment did not produce any better outcome for the child's ADHD symptoms than did medication alone. However, those who received the counselling plus medication option did improve in their other symptoms, such as in their mood.

I am often questioned by parents when I propose medication as the first order of intervention after making an ADHD diagnosis. Psychologists are not trained to think of medication as the first order of treatment for behavioural problems. However, the research and clinical evidence is overwhelming that ADHD has distinct biological underpinnings and medication must be recognized as a prominent aspect of treatment.

It is important for parents to understand that psychological intervention can be useful to parents and children in certain cases. Any child with another psychological condition in addition to ADHD (such as oppositional defiant disorder or an adjustment disorder) will almost certainly need some combination of behavioural intervention and medical management. In the MTA study, it was noted that those groups that received parent training along with medication placed high value on the training. In addition, those families reported improvement in other indirect positive behaviours. For example, they felt that they were calmer and had reduced anxiety levels, and they reported that their children showed less oppositional behaviour and they had better parent–child relationships. Recent studies such as Karen Jones's work in Wales demonstrate real benefits of parent training programmes in improving both ADHD and conduct disorder symptoms in preschoolers.

Outcomes

Children treated for ADHD have far better long-term outcomes than children with the disorder who are not treated. Multiple studies have shown this positive finding on a variety of variables. One specific question often pondered by parents is whether medical treatment will increase the risk of future substance abuse. All current studies clearly dispute this notion. In fact, children with ADHD who are not treated have a higher overall rate of substance abuse compared to their treated peers. One group of researchers succinctly concluded as much: 'Our results also indicate that medication status is an essential modifier of the ADHD–SUD (substance use disorders) association.'

They found that adolescents with *untreated* ADHD were significantly more likely to have problems with alcohol, marijuana, hallucinogens, stimulants and cocaine than were adolescents who received treatment, although not more likely to use tobacco. Both groups were more likely to develop substance abuse problems, including tobacco, than were children who were not diagnosed with ADHD. They suggest that the success of drug treatment in reducing the behavioural and emotional difficulties associated with ADHD may thus reduce a principal cause of substance abuse. They reach the conclusion that drug therapy for ADHD does not put a child at risk for later abuse of either prescribed medications or recreational or illegal drugs, but rather may play a role in reducing the likelihood of such problems.

Summary and conclusions

Attention deficit hyperactivity disorder is a neuro-developmental disorder affecting between 3 and 5 per cent of children. Common characteristics include distractibility, forgetfulness, disorganization and impulsivity. Left un-treated, these children are at risk for social, academic and personal psychological difficulties. Parenting is also drama-tically more frustrating without treatment. Outcome studies suggest that untreated adolescents are more likely to abuse drugs. More broadly, these children certainly struggle more to reach their potential as students without treatment. Medical intervention is currently the most effec-tive mainstream approach to treating the disorder, although families benefit from psychological treatment and training as well.

Preventing and treating head injuries in children

With all the health decisions facing parents, why include a specific section on head injuries? We are including this topic for the following reasons:

- Increased awareness and improved safety behaviours by parents can make a huge difference to your child's long-term health and well-being.
- It is also an area where many myths prevail.

First, let us look at the consequences of head injuries. These vary tremendously. Some children and adolescents who have mild head injuries (also called 'concussions') have nothing more than a temporary increase in irritability and trouble concentrating (this is called 'post-concussion syn-drome'). They recover fully and do not seem to show any ill effects in their schooling or in their personality. Sometimes parents or coaches who see this pattern decide that con-cussions are not much of a problem.

However, with moderate or severe head injuries, or with a child who has repeated concussions, the picture can be quite different. Both of us (Ziccardi and Strahan) have worked in rehabilitation hospital settings for many years. There we routinely see young people who were involved in car accidents and who were ejected from the car. This usually leads to devastating head injuries. Many of these young patients never fully recover, and the head injuries may mean that the child who previously earned excellent marks in school may now have to struggle for average marks, or worse. Additionally, head injuries can lead to personality changes that are even more damaging than the intellectual effects. Some of these young people become intensely irritable, impulsive, and more likely to act out in angry or irresponsible ways. They can suffer lifelong consequences in their ability to lead satisfying professional and social lives. Learning to cope with that kind of head injury, and its consequences, requires working cooperatively with the family, the entire healthcare team, and the school.

Fortunately, these kinds of severe head injuries are rare, particularly when children wear seatbelts and use car seats, wear helmets when biking, and take other similar precautions. A parent reading this kind of book is already quite aware of the usual safety guidelines for children in cars. For example, in 1989 it became compulsory that children wear seatbelts in the UK. Wearing seatbelts and using child safety seats have resulted in a huge improvement in the death rate and the rate of head injuries.

What are the common situations in which otherwise conscientious seatbelt wearers fail to put seatbelts on their children? One of these is when they are driving a very short distance. Unfortunately, 60 per cent of car accidents are reported to occur within ten minutes of the child's home. We strongly recommend that parents, grandparents, and anyone riding with the child on a regular basis agree in advance to be very conscientious in seatbelt use. This will make it easy on children and parents alike, as the automatic process of buckling up takes over. Generally the child does not even consider engaging in a power struggle on this issue, which is clearly non-negotiable.

The problem of repeated mild concussions is probably the single area within paediatric neuropsychology that is prone to the most misinformation. Some coaches who work with children, and some parents, are so focused on athletic success that they forget to consider the child's long-term well-being. More and more evidence is accumulating that repeated concussions can have a devastating effect on the brain. This is true whether the athletes are children, young adults, or professional players.

What can be done to reduce risk?

This is not a settled issue in sport science, yet. Let us look at the example of football (or 'soccer', in North America). In 2004 the Canadian Academy of Sport Medicine issued a position statement on children playing football (soccer). Some of their major recommendations were as follows:

1 'Soccer should be regarded as a contact sport in which players are at risk for head injuries and concussions . . .'
2 'Players, parents, and coaches should be aware of the signs and symptoms of a concussion . . .'
3 'All concussed athletes should be examined and treated by a doctor familiar with diagnosis and treatment of sport related concussions . . .'
4 'Children should minimize heading the ball until there is a better understanding of the effects of heading . . .'

(www.casm-acms.org)

Note that they are not making recommendations about headgear. Much recent research has been done on the topic of protective headgear. A 2008 study by Dr Scott Delaney in the *British Journal of Sports Medicine* found that adolescent football players who wore protective headgear cut their risk of concussions in half. Other important findings from that study were that most athletes who had concussions did not realize that they were concussed, and that girls were more prone to concussions than boys.

A recent overview (Gray *et al.*, 2009) available online describes the controversies surrounding whether heading the ball is truly harmful, and whether headgear should be required. Scientists have not yet come to agreement on these matters, although it appears that there is good evidence for the use of headgear.

Our emphasis on one sport is intended to highlight the evolving nature of scientific controversies in football/soccer.

It is *not* intended to suggest that this sport is more dangerous than others, which would be quite untrue. In fact, a recent summary of traumatic brain injuries in US children between 2001 and 2005 shows that the most dangerous activities for children's brains were horseback riding, riding 'all-terrain vehicles', playing ice hockey, and ice skating.

The other most controversial topic in this area has to do with 'return to play' after a head injury. This refers both to returning to a particular game after having a blow to the head, and also to permitting the young athlete to return to competition after having a concussion. Guidelines on these questions are still evolving, but there is clear consensus that any athlete suspected of having a concussion should not return to play that day. There should be formalized sideline assessment (which can take just a few minutes). Athletes who have had any loss of consciousness should be assessed medically as soon as possible, and should not return to play for at least one week.

What do we recommend?

1 The weight of the evidence seems to be converging that wearing protective headgear (and often, mouthpieces) for *any* contact sport is appropriate and necessary, and it will help to reduce risks. This is of course also true for a host of non-contact sports such as bicycle and horse riding, and skate-boarding.
2 Even with headgear, athletes in contact sports will still suffer concussions. As they progress in their athletic careers, very careful attention needs to be paid to both the dangers and benefits of continuing play. This should be a conversation that involves the young athlete as well as the parents and the sport physician or neurologist who has treated the young athlete for concussions.
3 Naturally, using seatbelts and car seats routinely is a crucial parenting behaviour; it is one of the few that leads to tremendous potential benefit at very little cost or effort.

The Bottom Line

- **What are the key dilemmas parents have to struggle with on this topic?**
  - One of these is whether to use medication for a child with ADHD.
  - Another controversy is how best to prevent head injuries (particularly whether headgear helps).
  - How soon, and whether, a child should return to a sport after suffering a concussion.
- **What does the science say about this topic?**
  - ADHD responds best to medication, though behavioural treatments do help other psychological symptoms such as depression, and parents find parent training classes *extremely* helpful in managing these children.
  - Seatbelts and car seats are essential when anyone is riding in a car.
  - Though the jury is out on football/soccer headgear, there is increasingly more evidence that protective headgear should be the norm in any contact sport and also in other sports with a high potential for head injuries (such as horse riding).
  - The decision to continue in a sport after sustaining head injuries is a very complex one which must be handled case by case, as there is not yet sufficient scientific consensus.
  - Coaches and athletic trainers need training in sideline assessment of head injuries, and should follow one of the established sets of guidelines, for example those published by the American Academy of Neurology.
  - The young athlete should not return to play for at least a week after sustaining a concussion.
- **What do the authors advise?**
  - *Always* use seatbelts and car seats, even for very short trips.
  - Your child should wear protective headgear for all contact sports. This will be easier if you work with your coach to provide evidence and make it mandatory in your child's sports leagues.

- If your child has had serious concussions in a sport, have a series of thoughtful conversations with them, and a neurologist. You should discuss whether the long-term damage outweighs the benefits of participating in that sport.
- Have open discussions with your child about safety and driving, and be a good role model for your child (no mobile phone conversations while driving, for example).

Parenting adolescents: handling the transitions from childhood to adulthood

Banks

As a family physician, I have the privilege of providing care for not only children but their parents as well, and one of the things I notice in particular is that as children reach adolescence, I see the children less and the parents more often. I now understand why. After the parents have struggled for years to do everything right and raise their children to be functional and acceptable members of society, Adolescence rears its ugly head and appears to undermine all of the parents' good work. What once was a cherubic, well-mannered child with rosy cheeks and a winning smile is metamorphosed seemingly overnight into a hairy creature with an attitude, raging hormones, and complete absence of personal hygiene skills. This sudden loss of control on the part of the parent, coupled with the realization that all of those years of loving effort have just fizzled like a wet firecracker, is enough to drive the parents to emotional and physical distraction and prompts frequent visits to the physician.

I am sometimes able to patch these festering wounds of hopelessness by reassuring the parents that adolescence is a temporary condition through which all must travel and from which most escape relatively unscathed, but the parents are not always convinced. The fact of the matter is that adolescent children *are* a challenge, and parents are often ill equipped to deal with the challenges.

In the next few pages, we will attempt to highlight some of the important issues in raising your adolescent child, although to do the topic justice would require an entire book dedicated to the adolescent.

The changes

To understand the challenges that parents of adolescents face, it is helpful to understand a little about the changes that our children are experiencing during this period. Whether we like to admit it or not, it is also difficult to be an adolescent child.

Adolescence begins with the onset of puberty and lasts until approximately age 21, at which point the young person has completed most of the physiological changes and has managed to establish a sense of identity. For boys, the process begins usually by the age of 11½, although early developers may start as early as 9 or 10 years old. Girls usually start the process about a year earlier.

Outwardly, we see the gradual development of the secondary sex characteristics. In girls, skeletal and muscle growth start immediately and peak by the time that menstruation begins, while in boys this growth spurt begins a little later and continues throughout puberty. Body composition also undergoes changes during puberty, with the percentage of body fat increasing in girls and decreasing in boys. While this sometimes seems an injustice to girls, it is nevertheless a change that is necessary to help them develop the curves and contours that distinguish them from their male counterparts.

Although these physical changes are often awkward for the child, even more challenging are the psychosocial changes that occur. Adolescence is hallmarked by the over-powering drive for independence. While this phenomenon is sometimes interpreted as ingratitude by the parent, it merely reflects the natural struggle of the child to achieve a psychological, social and physical identity separate from the family. Oddly enough, this is a good thing, since the child needs to develop a sense of individuality and function independently in the real world. Nevertheless, it sometimes seems counterproductive that the adolescent breaks free to become an individual, only to join ranks with his or her peer group and conform to their standards.

In addition to the physical and social changes that mark adolescence, the child must pass through a series of other developmental stages that enable him or her to achieve a successful transition into adulthood. With the physical changes come a keen preoccupation with the changing body and a sense of self-consciousness that at times can be overwhelming, but at the same time the child craves attention to reaffirm self-worth. The child becomes concerned with attractiveness, although this may be surprising to many parents who find the clothing trends, piercings and hair styles appalling. By late adolescence a relatively stable body image has emerged.

To the dismay of some parents, the changes in physical characteristics parallel a growing interest in sexuality. Fortunately, in early adolescence, sexual interest usually exceeds sexual activity. This is an opportune time for parents to intervene with sage advice and wise instruction, but the discussion should be two-sided and should include input from the child. This guides the parent and suggests how much information may be needed or desired by the child. By including the child as a participant in the discussion, it also reaffirms that the parent values the child and recognizes that she is indeed maturing; listening to her establishes trust and lays the foundation for continued communication as the blossoming child passes through later stages of adolescence, when communication becomes even more critical.

By mid-adolescence (ages 14 to 16) the sexual drive surges. Peer groups become less important as individual relationships form and dating begins. At this stage sexual experimentation may occur. As adolescence concludes, the young adult has typically managed to establish a sense of sexual identity and is capable of intimacy and, in some instances, even commitment. Parents need to be mindful of these trends, since parental attention and communication are effective in delaying sexual activity among many teens. See Chapter 15 for more on how your values as a parent influence your teen's behaviours and choices, especially in relation to sexual activity and drug use.

Obviously, the adolescent child must endure a great many changes that prepare him or her for adulthood. A number of internal conflicts arise as the hormonal and physical maturity clashes with the childish intellectual and emotional maturity. While the body is ready for courtship and propagation, the heart and mind are not quite prepared for the expanding responsibilities of adulthood. During the adolescent's struggle to achieve individuality, the teen's hormonal and emotional ups and downs can bewilder the concerned parent. Fortunately, most teens handle these internal changes quite well and adapt to the challenges that face them. For those who struggle, however, the changes can be softened by loving parents who take the time to communicate without domination.

Altering the parenting approach

Prior to adolescence, the parenting role was focused on teaching right from wrong, instilling values, modelling responsibility, and deflecting imminent disasters by anticipating foolhardy behaviours. With adolescents, however, the parent picks up the additional task of encouraging independence while maintaining subtle but consistent control. This allows the teen to make some non-critical mistakes and establish an identity. The parent must also help the adolescent develop critical thinking skills and independent judgement, preparing the child for the time when constant parental supervision is absent. This is a juggling act, admittedly, since appearing too controlling will have negative effects on how the child accepts the parent's input. However, multiple studies show that when parents appear to be involved and aware of the adolescent's whereabouts, the child tends to modify his or her behaviour somewhat and is more likely to avoid certain risky behaviours. Thus the parent has managed to exert subtle control without being tyrannical, and the child has managed to exercise some independent decision-making.

The ultimate goal for parents should be to ease the child's transition from adolescence to adulthood. This requires attention to a number of important factors. In their work as specialists in adolescent medicine, Drs Victor Strasburger and Robert Brown outline four important elements that help create independent, mature young adults.

The first key element is good family communication. This is a crucial issue that makes us or breaks us as social beings and as parents. Maintaining open lines of communication with your child establishes that you are approachable and available when needed and gives the message that you are interested in what they have to say. While the adolescent is unlikely to share all of her thoughts and dreams (which is good, since the parent probably would be unable to handle all of that information and still maintain sanity), at least she will be more likely to come to her parents with truly important issues. The parent, on the other hand, must fight the natural urge to be judgemental and dogmatic. Rather than suggesting that the child is not thinking clearly – or at all – the parent might respond diplomatically by acknowledging the teen's ideas and then suggesting alternatives. 'I certainly understand why you think that. But it's not what I've found. Maybe you could ask a couple of other adults you respect and find out what they have to say about revising before exams?' Now the child has other options and can choose to follow the parent's advice without feeling defeated or bullied by the parent. Obviously, the adolescent will sometimes choose to ignore the parent's advice and follow her initial plan; and unless this is a life-or-death matter, this is probably OK. Children should learn from their mistakes, just as adults do. But because there has been communication about the matter, the parent can now anticipate potential problems and be ready to provide rescue services if needed. Communication sometimes requires that parents display a little humility.

This does not mean that parents should not try. It is still permissible, and in fact obligatory, for parents to communicate expectations to their teenagers. When trying to persuade the child to complete certain tasks, parents should be specific with directions; otherwise the child will interpret vague instructions liberally and to his convenience. The instructions should also be complete. One cannot assume that the teen will display initiative and follow through with everything, unless the parent gives complete instructions. It is not enough to tell the child to take out the rubbish. The parent needs to say, 'Before lunch, gather up all of the rubbish from under your bed and add it to this bag; then tie the bag up and put it in the bin outside, or you will be unable to go to William's house this afternoon.' This leaves little to the imagination, and there is not much room for misinterpretation. Spelling out consequences for failure provides a little leverage to the request, as well.

The second key element to creating independent young adults, according to Strasburger and Brown, is to enhance the teen's self-image. Adolescence is a time when self-esteem soars like Icarus to the sun, then plunges abruptly to all-time lows when the waxen wings melt. How effectively the teen recuperates from these ups and downs will affect, to some degree, the stability of the adult personality. Self-esteem and self-image do not develop overnight but begin forming in early childhood; waiting until the child reaches adolescence before providing any parental influence would be a disservice to the child. While the parent may not be able to change the child's personality at this late stage, it is still important for the parent to help the teen mould the personality to fit more comfortably into societal expectations. Parents should help find a positive niche for the developing child, pointing out his strengths and encouraging him to pursue interests that enhance those strengths. Praise is as important for adolescents as it is in younger children and should be used liberally, while criticism should be used sparingly and should be tempered by diplomacy. Correcting the teen without insult allows him to maintain his dignity, and that, in turn, leads to a better adjusted child who is ready to handle the transitions into adulthood.

Some children have a natural inclination for greater self-esteem, supported by their levels of popularity among peers. This popularity is often a result of athletic ability, physical attractiveness, clothing and outgoing personality, and this affirmation boosts self-confidence and solidifies the sense of identity. However, while popularity breeds envy, it does not necessarily make the child likeable. In fact, the 'popular kids' are often the first to try smoking, drinking alcohol, or using other unsavoury substances, and suspicious parents should keep a close eye on the situation.

Of course, sometimes a child's self-esteem gets a nudge, or an all-out shove, from Mother Nature. As early as the 1920s, studies were suggesting that boys who matured physically at an earlier age were more likely to be considered attractive, outgoing, relaxed and in control. These were the boys who developed into leaders and athletes and who managed to attract the opposite sex without effort. On the other hand, those whose physical maturity lagged behind were considered less attractive, more attention-seeking, demanding, talkative and often annoying. These were the boys who, later in life, continued to have feelings of inadequacy.

The opposite seemed to be true for girls, in these studies. In keeping with the unfortunate tradition of double standards and sexual inequality, girls who got a jump-start on their physical development were less popular and were understandably less cheerful, expressive and poised than the girls who were developing in synchrony with their ages. These findings were based on only a small number of subjects, and subsequent studies suggested that these differences may be influenced more by social class or cultural attitudes. Other studies suggested that these differences actually begin prior to the onset of puberty and that there may be a genetic reason why kids differ in their attitudes to as well as their rates of physical development. Whatever the reason, it is clear that some of the things that we do as parents help our teens develop a strong sense of self-esteem; other factors, which occur naturally, may help or impair the teen's self-esteem and self-image. However, if the parent knows to look for such signs as delayed physical development, it is possible to intervene early and help that teen get past the obstacles.

The third key element to creating independent young adults is teaching logical thought and effective decision-making. This is a challenging task for adults. To many parents, it seems like their teens do not think at all, so trying to teach them how to think maturely is a fruitless effort. This couldn't be further from the truth – adolescents think all the time, which is what makes them so challenging. The problem arises when parents think that they can force the adolescent to see things from their more experienced perspective. That is nothing less than delusional, and the battle of the wills begins. The secret to success is that the parent needs to give the teen some autonomy in decision-making, while still maintaining control and setting reasonable limits. I call this 'regulated independence'.

Certainly, some things should not be negotiable. Issues of safety, for example, should never become areas for debate, and the parent should state this clearly. The child needs to know that she is loved too much to permit her to make choices that would endanger her or others. It is appropriate to discuss this with the teen, because she needs to know that the parent has legitimate reasons for these rules and that this is not just another one of those power struggles between parent and child. However, this then gives the parent the perfect opportunity to ask for the teen's input regarding other options. 'I'm sorry, Belinda, but I can't let you participate in the Tazmanian Machete Dance Festival. Do you have any idea why that would be a bad idea?' After the teen starts listing the possible hazards, including loss of appendages, facial features and significant quantities of blood, it is helpful to continue the discussion in this manner: 'You are absolutely right. Now can you think of anything else you would like to do tonight that would not require a trip to hospital?' The parent has effectively squelched an inappropriate activity, while giving the teen an opportunity to think through the consequences and make an independent choice that would be more appropriate for her well-being.

On some occasions the parent might need to be a little more creative, particularly when it is clear that the adolescent is set on having her own way. Rather than giving her too much leeway, it might be necessary to provide a more structured set of choices that would give her a modicum of freedom while staying within reasonable boundaries. For example, the parent might say, 'I'm sorry, but I'd rather you didn't go to the beach with your friends this weekend. Perhaps you would be interested in seeing a film, or going to the shops, or maybe a trip to the library to check out the new arrivals!' What teen could refuse this plea? By giving the child a series of choices, the parent has effectively set limits but is still allowing her to exercise some free choice.

The crystal ball and the watchful eye

Raising adolescents involves not only courage and skills in diplomacy and communication, but it also entails a little premonition, as well. Much of parenting involves anticipating potential disasters and intervening in a timely fashion, and this is just as critical when dealing with adolescents. When children are small, the parent can focus on simple issues like moving priceless antiques out of the reach of tiny, inquisitive hands, padding the corners of coffee tables to prevent head injuries, and covering electrical outlets to prevent electrocution. As children graduate to adolescence, however, this task becomes more complicated, because more of the teen's time is spent outside of the home and away from direct parental supervision.

Early in adolescence, peer influence becomes an important force in the teen's life. During this period, it is common to see the teen engage in activities that would not normally be endorsed by the parents. This is even truer in situations where parents are neglectful, or where family bonds are weak; in these situations, peer groups become more influential, and teens may increase their misbehaviour in order to find out what limitations actually exist. These ties to peer groups can be enduring, and behaviours can be significantly influenced. However, not all peer influences are bad. Some behaviours, such as smoking, for example, may be either encouraged or discouraged by the child's peers, and this can have a profound effect on a teen's future health behaviours. It is therefore critical that parents remain aware of their children's friendships and encourage them to associate with those who would most likely be positive influences.

Because of their perceived invulnerability, adolescents are natural risk-takers. Parents must recognize that their child, regardless of his demeanour at home, has the potential to transform into Mr Hyde when away from home. Some risky behaviour results from the inability to foresee or recognize the dangers in the behaviour, while other risky behaviour may result from inadvertent carelessness; however, in some teens, these risky behaviours arise from sheer recklessness. Many parents throw up their hands in despair and exclaim that they have no control over their child, but in reality much of this potentially destructive behaviour can be curtailed by close monitoring or counselling by the parents, if only they recognize when to intervene.

Since most injuries and deaths in teenagers result from car and motorcycle accidents, it is critical that parents discuss these issues with their teens and stress the importance of wearing seatbelts. In many of these cases, alcohol or other drugs are involved, and conversations about using good judgement and not riding with friends who have been drinking (and, of course, not getting behind the steering wheel if they themselves have been drinking) can have a beneficial effect.

A considerable problem for teenagers is that of violence. We all cringe when we hear news reports about classroom stabbings or gang-style attacks, but these are extremes. In the US, unfortunately, the reality is that adolescents are more likely to be victims of violence than any other age group, and homicides are the second leading cause of death among adolescents in the United States. Parents must be on their guard to prevent their children from becoming participants or victims in these horrendous situations. Certain factors place our teens at greater risk of violent behaviour, and parents should be aware of these risk factors. Not surprisingly, male adolescents are more likely to engage in violent behaviour than girls, although no one is immune. Children who go through puberty at an earlier age than their peers are more likely to participate in violent behaviours. This may be as simple as bullying their classmates, but in some cases it can extend to more severe forms of violence. Likewise, we see more aggressive behaviour among teens who lack a sense of future or who see their future as hopeless. Only by openly communicating with the teen can a parent get a true appreciation for this attitude and help alter the child's outlook on life. If the parent is overwhelmed by this challenge, then seeking professional help is certainly an appropriate choice.

Multiple studies have confirmed that in families where corporal punishment (spanking, hitting, or inflicting other discomforts) is used frequently, the child is more likely to engage in violent behaviours (see Chapter 9 for a more detailed discussion of discipline). The same is true for families in which children are exposed to domestic violence or child abuse. Other studies have consistently shown that repeated exposure to violence in the media – especially television and films – leads to aggressive and violent behaviour in adolescents (Chapter 10 looks at this issue in more detail). By monitoring and limiting the exposure to the media that so permeates our children's daily lives, parents can have a positive influence on violent behaviour. Other studies have demonstrated that adolescents are more likely to participate in violent behaviours if guns, alcohol or drugs are available in the home. Two-thirds of all violent adolescent deaths in the US are due to firearms, and a significant impact can be made if parents remove these weapons from the home.

Important medical issues for teens

Substance abuse

Perhaps most worrisome for parents is the risk for a teen's experimentation with alcohol, tobacco and other drugs. Experimentation is certainly a common problem in this age group, although it is not inevitable and can be greatly affected by positive parenting skills.

Among adolescents, the most commonly abused drugs are tobacco, alcohol and marijuana. The natural course of tobacco addiction unfortunately begins during adolescence, with two-thirds of British smokers beginning prior to age 18: 10 per cent of children between 11 and 15 years of age smoke regularly. Similar trends are noted among young smokers in the US. By age 14, over 58 per cent of American school children have tried smoking on at least one occasion, and this number increases to over 70 per cent of high school seniors (age 17–18). Many of these individuals will develop a number of chronic medical problems related to their smoking. Despite these high numbers, however, the parents are blissfully ignorant; some studies suggest that less than half of parents were aware that their children smoked. Among adolescent girls who smoke, a large number of them say they do so in order to lose weight or maintain their weight. Many others develop the habit because of peer influences. While parents often picture some seedy-looking, tattooed teenager lurking in the shadows and proffering cigarettes to innocent young children, this is generally not the case; many teens do not experience a direct external pressure to start smoking, but rather feel an internal pressure to try cigarettes when they see others do it. Others receive discouragement from their friends in an effort to prevent smoking initiation. However, the greatest influence on teen smoking may very well be smoking parents and siblings. Teens are more likely to smoke if their parents smoke or have a permissive attitude toward adult smoking, or if the parents are unlikely to punish the child for smoking. Proper role modelling is obviously critical in discouraging the adolescent from smoking – if parents do not model the desired behaviour, any amount of discussion is less likely to be helpful.

Even more of a problem is that of under-age alcohol consumption. According to the 2007 Youth Risk Behavior Survey, 65 per cent of American ninth graders have consumed alcohol on at least one occasion, and this number rises to 83 per cent among high school seniors. A quarter of English teens between 11 and 15 years of age had used alcohol in the week preceding a survey conducted by the Office for National Statistics. Since alcohol is involved in half of the adolescent deaths caused by car accidents, suicides and homicides (the major causes of death among teens), the gravity of this problem becomes obvious. While most of these teens will not become alcoholics, many of them will experience significant problems caused by alcohol.

However, when one of the parents has a history of alcoholism, the child has a three- to fourfold higher risk of becoming an alcoholic himself. In these situations, increased vigilance by the parent is important.

Of the illicit substances that are available, marijuana is the most commonly used among young people. In a 2000 summary of studies of drug use, 12 per cent of English children between the ages of 11 and 15 years had used marijuana, while 25 per cent of teens between the ages of 16 and 19 years in England and Wales had indulged. More recently, a survey of teens from Northern Ireland showed that a third of 14- and 15-year-olds had tried marijuana, and 10 per cent used it on a daily basis. Data from the US shows a similar problem. In 2007, 38 per cent of American high school students had tried marijuana, and nearly 20 per cent had used it within thirty days of the survey. This is particularly troubling since regular use of marijuana is associated with delinquency, low levels of parent–child communication, low levels of commitment to school, and a tendency for those teens to use 'harder drugs' such as cocaine and heroin. Marijuana has long been considered a 'gateway drug'; however, it is not clear whether the use of marijuana leads to the use of other substances, or whether children who use marijuana are just more likely to use other substances. Regardless of the association, it is clear that parental involvement is important in helping to prevent this problem.

The likelihood that an adolescent is going to experiment with substances such as drugs and alcohol depends on a number of factors, including how readily available that substance is and whether there are appropriate restraints. These restraints, in great part, depend on how much effort the parent has made at instilling values when the child was younger – these important lessons tend to stick with adolescents as they struggle with social issues, like nagging voices deep within their consciences. Emotionally supportive parents who communicate openly with their children have the greatest impact on preventing or limiting substance use, and the earlier the parent intervenes, the less likely it is that substance abuse will become a problem.

Sexual activity among teens

As adolescents begin dating and hormones begin surging, parents cannot ignore the fact that the teens develop a keen interest in sex. We see this even in the early stages of adolescence (around the age of 10 or 11), although the interest does not become an obsession until somewhere around the age of 14 to 16 years, when the teen starts developing a sense of sexual identity. This is also the period when concerns about sexual orientation may arise, although these inward struggles are often concealed from – or unrecognized by – the parents.

According to data from the 2007 Youth Risk Behavior Survey, about a third of US ninth graders and 65 per cent of high school seniors had engaged in sexual intercourse at least once, and 35 per cent of high school students were currently sexually active. Among adolescents in the United Kingdom, a 2000 study found that 30 per cent of males and 26 per cent of females had intercourse before the age of 16. Fortunately, condom use has increased, but there is still a large incidence of unprotected sex among adolescents. Naturally, this places the teen at significant risk of pregnancy. Teens in the US and the UK are far more likely to experience pregnancy than in any other industrial society, including Canada, the rest of Europe and Asia, according to a study conducted by UNICEF. This age group is also especially prone to sexually transmitted diseases, which, if untreated, can result in a number of long-term health problems as adults, and, in some cases, can be deadly. There is also a significant risk of sexual abuse in this age group, particularly if the child is already sexually active. While many of the abusive acts occur on 'dates', a surprising number are perpetrated by family members or family friends. This only stresses the importance of close parental monitoring and awareness of the child's friends.

How significant the interest in sex becomes at these early ages can be affected by a number of outside influences, including (once again) the media. Sexual topics are prevalent in most prime-time television shows and are the driving force behind many of the daytime soap operas and talk-shows, and these influences spill over into music, music videos, and teen magazines. Unfortunately, it is typically the pleasurable aspects of sex that are emphasized in the media, leaving the negative consequences such as sexual abuse, teen pregnancy and sexually transmitted diseases to be discovered first-hand. It is therefore up to the parents to regulate exposure and ensure that their teens receive a balance of accurate information, and it is imperative that these issues are discussed openly and honestly without being overly judgemental.

Enhancing body image

While it seems that some teens are intent on slowly destroying their bodies by the lifestyles that they practise, there is nevertheless a powerful drive to be physically attractive. These teens are often willing to go to extremes in order to accomplish this goal. Among adolescent males, some of the more frequent questions posed to me centre around nutritional supplements touted to enhance the physique. For years, athletes have taken amino acid supplements in order to improve muscle development. Some amino acids have been found to stimulate growth hormone, prompting body builders to take these supplements before a workout in order to enhance muscle growth. However, there is no evidence that taking oral amino acid supplements before exercise improves growth hormone release, and no studies convincingly show that amino acid supplements increase muscle mass and strength compared to strength training alone. There have also been no well designed studies that show improved muscle mass or strength after taking human growth hormone supplements. Since these are expensive supplements and probably have no benefit, their use should not be encouraged.

Other teens have been enticed to take oral creatine to enhance their physical performance. In fact, creatine may very well be the most commonly used performance-enhancing substance among adolescent athletes. Creatine, in combination with resistance training, may play a role in improving the maximum weight lifted by young men.

However, there does not appear to be an improvement in speed. Well designed studies have not shown a significant effect on women and older individuals, and there are also no long-term studies that look at possible harmful effects from the supplement. Thus, while there may be some benefit to certain types of athletes, the routine use of creatine is unlikely to be of much value.

A discussion of the adolescent body image would be incomplete without at least mentioning eating disorders, which are extremely prevalent in this age group. The reader is referred to Chapter 4, on 'Diet dilemmas and childhood obesity', for a discussion of these issues.

Acne

The bane of the adolescent existence is arguably the dreaded skin condition, acne. While not unique to adolescents, it is certainly more common in that age group and is the source of much misery. While acne occurs naturally at this age, it can be aggravated by a number of factors, including oil-based makeup, suntan lotion, hair gels, squeezing the pesky blemishes, scrubbing the skin too vigorously, and even menstruation. It always seems that the splotches appear at their worst just before a major social event, and there certainly are small studies suggesting that acne may be worsened by emotional stress. While there are no magic pills to make stress dissolve, there are a number of options for treating acne.

Acne is not caused by dirt, and the effect of diet is still very controversial. A few studies suggest a correlation with the Western diet (chock full of concentrated sugar), but most studies do not show a dietary effect, so avoiding all the tasty foods is unlikely to help acne.

Most teens will respond to over-the-counter agents such as topical benzoyl peroxide, although these products work better if applied to the entire face rather than just the blemishes. However, in the more severe cases, a physician may choose to prescribe topical agents containing sulphur, vitamin A derivatives, or antibiotics, or it may be necessary to resort to oral medications such as antibiotics. Some birth control pills are also effective in treating acne in adolescent women. In the more severe instances, a physician may need to prescribe a potent oral medication such as isotretinoin. However, because that class of medications has the potential for serious side-effects, it must be monitored closely by the physician. And because that medication can cause birth defects, it should never be taken by girls of child-bearing age unless they are also on birth control pills routinely.

Wrapping up

The challenges and temptations faced by adolescents can be overwhelming for them, as well as for the parents. If it is any consolation to parents, it is natural for the teen to distance himself from the family as a test of his newfound independence, and as a consequence of the maturing process he will sometimes experiment with lifestyle choices that would meet with strong disapproval from the parents. While this may be normal behaviour, it does not minimize the possible hazards. Unfortunately, the use of scare tactics will not work on the adolescent (in fact, they rarely work on older adults either, since many continue to smoke despite repeated warnings about the known hazards), but by maintaining open lines of communication and demonstrating a true concern without being dogmatic, it is still possible for the parent to have significant influence.

The good news is that science confirms the importance of parental influence, particularly with regard to the high-risk behaviours of teens. Merely asking the teen where he is going, with whom he will be spending time, and when he will be returning home gives the impression that his actions are being monitored. It has been shown in multiple studies that the perception of being monitored is effective in limiting adolescent substance use as well as limiting sexual activity, teenage pregnancy and violent behaviour. It is not necessary for the parent to lurk in the shadows, following and recording every move that the adolescent makes; just showing concern, communicating and asking questions is often enough.

Equally reassuring is the fact that, while peer groups are highly valued by younger adolescents, family once again becomes an important source of security for the child as he enters the latter stages of adolescence and peer groups become less influential. This reaffirms the importance of the family dynamic, regardless of how troubled that dynamic seems at times. Family is the one institution that supersedes all others. Its permanence, providing protection within the strong arms of unconditional love, support, and forgiveness, brings the adolescent – and the parents – through difficult times together, usually successfully, and always better for having tried.

The Bottom Line

- **What are the key dilemmas parents have to struggle with on this topic?**
  - Adolescent risk-taking behaviours can have devastating and long-lasting implications. How can this be prevented?
  - How can the parent channel the adolescent's drive for independence without suppressing the child's development?
- **What does the science say about this topic?**
  - Some experimentation and limit-testing is natural. However, parents who have frank, non-judgemental discussions about risks with their children, who maintain an interest in the child's whereabouts and the company they are keeping, who play an active role in monitoring and limiting exposure to media, and who maintain open lines of communication without being overpowering, are more likely to prevent significant risk-taking behaviours.
  - Adolescents should be given some autonomy of choice for decisions that are low-risk or unlikely to have negative outcomes. However, parents can maintain control over more important decisions by providing alternative choices and allowing the child to choose from those more acceptable options. Remaining aware of the adolescent's whereabouts has been shown to

influence children's choices positively and make them less likely to engage in risky behaviours.

- **What do the authors advise?**
  - Open and respectful communication seems to be the key to surviving adolescence – both for the child and for the parent. This requires effort and involves listening as well as expressing opinions. It is important for the parent to appear open-minded and non-judgemental, and compromise is often necessary, except when safety is at stake.

Recommended reading

The National Parenting Center (www.tnpc.com/parentalk/adoles.html) is an excellent, readable resource that addresses issues ranging from communicating with teens, to limit-setting, body image and dealing with stress.

Stepp, L. (2000) *Our last best shot: Guiding our children through early adolescence*. New York: Riverhead Books. (Laura Stepp is an award-winning journalist who explores the worlds of actual adolescents and places these stories in the context of current developmental theory.)

Children, family structure, and life choices

Strahan

This chapter is a series of answers to the question: 'How do our family structures and our values affect children's futures?' Some examples of ways in which this question might come up are:

- What is the impact of divorce and remarriage on children's well-being?
- In which cases is it better for parents to divorce, and in which would it be better for them to stay together for the sake of the children (assuming the parents are willing to do that)?
- How do adoptive parents improve the attachment or bonding process with their new adoptive children?
- What does the science of family psychology tell us about the children of gay and lesbian parents?
- How do parents increase the likelihood that they will be able to pass on to their children their most cherished values?
- How do we best talk with our children about topics such as sex, teenage pregnancy, smoking, and drug use?

Not long ago, an economist and a writer (Levitt and Dubner, 2005) came out with a book entitled *Freakonomics*. In it, they look at data that sometimes support and sometimes challenge widely held views about this fascinating, complex world of ours. One chapter of the book reports on studies looking at parenting and how parenting decisions affect child outcomes. For example, they examine whether taking children to museums results in children who are more interested in culture. The book presents the following basic conclusion: children are shaped most powerfully not by *what their parents do*, but by *who the parents are*. So, for example, if the parent is someone who loves reading, that trait will probably show up in the children. A parent who does not enjoy reading but who dutifully buys books for the child, in the hope that books will improve the child's mind, will probably not do much good (although that parent will be a boon to the publishing industry!).

Levitt and Dubner do describe some parenting actions that have significant effects, including keeping the child out of a bad school, increasing the child's chances of having positive peer friends, and of course avoiding abuse and neglect.

Looking through that lens of *who you are* rather than *what you do* is rather comforting. For example, if you are reading this book, you already have several huge factors in your favour: you are committed to being a good parent, you are reading a book, you are examining the scientific evidence on parenting, and you have the capacity to sustain attention through quite a few chapters. Thus, you have commitment, motivation, an analytic mind – all of these traits mean that your children will be likely to be more successful than those in the population at large.

In this chapter, the challenge becomes one of gaining a better understanding about how our life choices, and the values we hold dear, can come together to enrich our children's lives.

Marriage and divorce in children's lives

This is a very difficult subject in every way. It is hard for the parents who are asking the question of whether they should get divorced, it is a tough road to travel no matter how they answer that question, and it is hard for the children in most cases.

Let us begin with a few clinical anecdotes which illustrate the range of possible responses to the question of whether parents should get divorced.

- Jenny and Perry have been married for eight years. Their marriage has been a turbulent one, with episodes of intense jealousy, first from Jenny and more recently from Perry. Things have got much worse in the past few months since Jenny was seen kissing another man in a pub. Perry has been hurt and furious, has attempted suicide by driving off the road, and is now begging Jenny to stay with him and work on the marriage. The couple are having explosive arguments in front of the children, often including screaming, cursing at each other, and calling each other vile names. There has also been some pushing and shoving, though no outright physical abuse. The couple have three boys.

- Tariq and Jamila have been unhappy for years in their marriage. She has been having an email-based romantic involvement with another man; this romance has not progressed to physical intimacy, but it has caused her to become increasingly preoccupied with the idea of leaving Tariq. They are rather cold and distant towards each other, but do not argue in front of the children. They have two girls and one boy. Both of them are ambivalent about saving the marriage, and there is some mutual respect for each other, when I interview them separately. They feel stressed and tense about the need to maintain a 'good front'. They are both good parents who are deeply committed to doing what is best for their children

- Maria and Eduardo have never had a happy marriage. They married very young, had three children, and lately their marriage has been troubled by suspicion on Maria's part that Eduardo is having affairs. She has responded by becoming increasingly depressed and withdrawn. Eduardo tries to get her to talk about what is bothering her, but she responds very little either to him or to the children. The children, ranging in age between 8 and 16, have taken over many household duties and they help their mother get out of bed, remind her when it is nearly time for them to leave for school, etc. The parents never argue in front of the children, although Maria frequently says in front of the children that it would be better if she had never been born.

- Phillip has been divorced from his ex-wife for three years. They have four children, the eldest two of whom have 'taken sides'. One lives with Phillip and has no contact with the mother, one lives with the mother and has no contact with Phillip, and the parents share custody of the two youngest children, a boy and a girl aged 6 and 8. Phillip is a conscientious father, but he is so angry at the way his ex-wife's infidelity ripped apart his life that he believes he will be unable to trust another woman ever again. He finds it difficult to prevent himself from making sarcastic and hostile remarks whenever his two youngest children mention having had a good time with their mother and her boyfriend.

These scenarios are loosely based on real couples whom I saw in my practice some time ago. I offer them as examples because of the intense pain experienced by these couples, the question in each of them about what is best for the children, and the complexity of the life choices involved.

Stanley and Fincham (2002), Kelly and Emery (2003) and Constance Ahrons (2006) are among the many researchers who summarize the scientific literature on how divorce affects children. While most children of divorce are able to function effectively, divorce does increase children's risk of many negative life outcomes by a factor of two or three. The following basic points emerge from these reviews:

- Children of divorce are more likely to have behavioural problems.
- Particularly in the two years following their parents' divorce, children of divorce are more distressed than are children whose parents are still married.
- Level of parental conflict is the key dimension to measure. The parental behaviours that are most difficult for children to handle are jealous behaviour, quickness to anger, criticism of the other parent, and moodiness.
- Children whose parents are in low-conflict marriages (i.e. marriages where there is no yelling or acting out by

parents) do better if their parents stay together (even if the parents are unhappy), than if the parents divorce.

- Children whose parents are in high-conflict marriages, where the children can see the conflict, do better if their parents divorce.
- Divorce increases the risks of depression and acting-out behaviours for boys.
- Children of divorce are more likely to become divorced themselves.
- Children of divorce tend to show somewhat lower levels of educational, occupational and financial achievement later in life.
- There are significant financial stressors that accompany divorce and that have negative impacts on all members of the family.

It is clear that in cases where the couples are physically abusing each other, or where the children are being abused or neglected, separation is imperative. In some such cases, neither parent is competent to raise the children, and an aunt or grandparent or someone else would be a better choice to raise the child. But in most cases, if the parents are able to keep their disagreements under wraps, it is likely to be better for the children if the family remains intact.

Researchers have also looked extensively at the question of what sorts of custody arrangements are best for the child (see Kelly, 2006, for a good review article on this topic). These researchers have identified three major patterns that divorced parents can fall into. One of these is the 'conflicted co-parental relationship'. This involves ongoing anger and conflict fuelled by at least one of the parents. Often there is a pattern of one parent continuing to 'fan the flames' by ongoing attempts at litigation. This represents about a quarter of divorced couples, and their children are at greater risk for poor outcomes, because of the ongoing conflicts. Parents in the second category, who have a 'parallel co-parenting relationship', are emotionally disengaged from each other and have low conflict. Over 50 per cent of divorced couples fall into this category. The final category consists of the 'cooperative co-parents' (a quarter of all divorced parents), who are able to work together and maintain flexible communication, for the good of the children. Children from this last category often fare as well as those in intact marriages. The following basic findings should be taken seriously, at least in families where both parents are basically competent individuals who are able to control their emotions:

- Children prefer joint physical custody, with frequent contact with both parents.
- Children have better adjustment and academic achievement when they have frequent contact with both parents.
- Children do best if their parents are able to contact each other and work cooperatively to discuss parenting issues that arise.
- Witnessing overt conflict between their divorced parents leads to far worse emotional and academic outcomes. Even if the parents maintain a high-conflict pattern after divorce, as long as the children are not exposed to it, it will not harm them as much.

The science therefore provides some clinical guidance to therapists or friends working with couples considering divorce. For couples such as Tariq and Jamila, who are able to keep their unhappiness under wraps, their children will probably be best served if they stay together. It would be best for all if they were able to engage in marital therapy and learn better ways to communicate with each other, and perhaps even recover some pleasure in each other's company. Still, even if they are just coolly civil to each other, but warm and responsive to the children, that will generally serve the children's interests well in the long run. Couples such as Tariq and Jamila often consider divorce as a solution, but fail to consider the costs in time and money and heartache that accompany divorce. If they do decide to divorce, their children can be buffered from the ill effects of divorce if the parents engage in 'cooperative co-parenting'.

Perry and Jenny are quite another matter. Their arguments are explosive and create a sense of chaos in the home, and fear in their children. This couple came to see me after Jenny had already filed for divorce, and I focused primarily on finding ways to help them protect the children through the divorce process. Even the simplest discussions about how to protect the children resulted in much yelling and in one or the other storming out of the room. It was difficult for me to serve as a mediator because they were so caught up in the arguments. For couples who are so emotional and so out of control in their interactions, divorce is often the best solution for the children. One caveat is that sometimes parents with this kind of behaviour quickly become romantically involved with another partner who is eerily similar to the first. Thus, the children repeatedly witness parents fighting, only with new partners. This just compounds the children's emotional distress. Parents in this kind of marriage are exposing their children to increased risk for depression and acting-out behaviours, and higher future risks of suicide attempts.

With Maria and Eduardo, the issues are clouded by Maria's clinical depression. With proper treatment of her depression, the marriage may improve and the couple would then be able to learn some basic interaction skills. This would make them happier and more effective as parents. It is abundantly clear from the research that having a clinically depressed parent has a variety of negative effects on the child. One of these pathways is genetic, since a parent with a strong family history of depression will be more likely to have a child with a tendency toward depression. But many of the effects of parents' depression are probably caused by the way depressed people behave. Depressed parents tend to be grumpy, withdrawn, and irritable. They are less likely to explain things to their children and more likely to yell at them. They also tend to overestimate their children's behaviour problems and are less likely to be emotionally responsive to their children. Any or all of the recommended treatments for depression described in Chapters 11 and 12 (talk therapy, antidepressant medication, etc.) would help not only Maria, but her children and Eduardo as well.

In Phillip's case, the divorce has been final for years, but Phillip's emotional turmoil and his ex-wife's frequent attempts to initiate litigation to strip him of his joint custody status prolong the separation pains for his children. He is unaware of how tightly he clings to his anger, and he resists my efforts to work with him on forgiving and moving on. He believes that forgiving his ex-wife would mean that her sexual infidelity was acceptable. He fails to see what impact his ongoing hostility towards her has on his children and his own peace of mind. For Phillip, the divorce will not be completed until he decides to get over it and live his life looking toward the present and the future rather than the past.

Recommendations for couples considering a divorce

- If you have not already done so, talk to your family doctor and get a recommendation for a therapist who works with couples. Marriage therapy is generally not as successful as individual therapy, but it works far better than doing nothing.
- If you go to a couples therapist and she/he is encouraging you to air lots of old grievances, so that you are becoming angrier with each other rather than feeling better after a few sessions, *find another therapist*. Successful couples therapists work on active problem-solving, focusing on what you like and respect about each other, and learning positive patterns of communication. Airing grievances typically does little besides fanning the flames of dislike.
- Remember that there are lots of possible patterns of living. If your spouse refuses to go to therapy with you, you can always go on your own. Sometimes that leads to huge improvements in your overall satisfaction, because you learn to deal with your partner in ways that are more productive, you learn not to be bothered by things your partner says that used to be hurtful, and so on.
- There are many excellent self-help books that can be of real use to struggling couples. One of these is Heitler's *Power of two*, another is Christensen and Jacobson's *Reconcilable differences*, and a third is Gottman's *Seven principles for making marriage work*. These self-help

books share the virtue of being based on well established scientific principles rather than on one author's opinion.

Recommendations for couples divorcing or already divorced

In cases where divorce is inevitable or has already occurred, there are still a number of steps you can take to maximize the chances that your child will cope well with the situation. Some of these are as follows:

- Take advantage of excellent resources on this topic. For example, the Australian Psychological Society (www. psychology.org.au) provides an excellent booklet online entitled 'Parenting after separation', which summarizes the scientific literature on the effects of divorce on children.
- If you are able to have some 'divorce mediation' sessions, take advantage of them. They will be of benefit to you and your children in the long run, though they may be emotionally painful at the time.
- Be willing to talk openly about the situation with your children. But do it in a non-blaming way – for example, 'Daddy and I have decided that we're arguing so much that we need to separate.'
- Avoid criticizing the other parent and *especially* avoid giving your children details of the other parent's behaviour (e.g. infidelity). Save this for lunches with your co-workers. Older children may demand more of an explanation from you, but make every attempt to be as fair and neutral as possible when you answer their questions. They still love the other parent and you will put them in a very difficult emotional bind if you present your side in vivid detail.
- Examine whether your own anger or resentment or hurt are spilling out on your children. Sometimes a therapist or a trusted friend can help you work through this kind of problem.
- Treat the children as innocent bystanders and not as potential allies or enemies.

- Remember that it is natural for children to love both parents, no matter what the other parent has done. It is healthier for them to keep that love than for you to attempt to squelch it. It will only make your children resent you if they sense you are trying to control their feelings towards the other parent.
- Remember that the first two years following divorce are the most difficult time for your children. Try to provide them with additional support and time with people they love (extended family, good friends, neighbours) during that period.
- Maximize your child's resilience in the face of the divorce. Consider getting a copy of Martin Seligman's *The optimistic child: A proven program to safeguard children against depression and build lifelong resilience.*
- Make sure that you do not fall into the trap of 'catastrophizing' about how terrible the divorce will be for your children. Certainly, this event will be a difficult one for them, and it would be better if they had not gone through it. Still, most children of divorce cope well with the turmoil. Remember that children whose divorced parents are able to work together cooperatively can be as successful long-term as those whose parents stay together.
- Keep in mind the importance of your children staying connected to both extended families.
- Children whose parents are cooperative have stronger emotional ties to both extended families, which will provide them with a great source of strength and resilience in the future. This is yet another reason why you should work hard on cooperative relationships with your ex-spouse, as well as with his/her family.
- Be aware of how long divorce-related hostilities can persist. Children whose parents were in a high-conflict situation reported even twenty years later that they had withdrawn from relationships with both parents, in order to escape from the conflicting demands that were placed on their loyalties. The moral of the story is that you pay for your high-conflict divorce by worsening the relationship with your children.

Remarriage and relocation

Remarriage after divorce is common; half of parents are in a serious relationship a year after the divorce. Most children report wanting their parents to have a romantic partner, but the form that relationship takes is important.

For example, remarriage in the first year after a divorce is considerably more stressful to children than if their parents remarry three or more years after the divorce. Many children who have been through the remarriage of a parent say that the remarriage was *more* stressful than the actual divorce. Additionally, it becomes increasingly stressful to the children if their parents have a series of live-in partners who come and go, or a series of remarriages. Particularly if a parent remarries and has more children, the children from the earlier marriage often feel marginalized and less important.

Relocating to an area that is far from the non-custodial parent causes damage to the parent–child relationship, and it can increase hostility between the parents. Braver *et al.* (2003) looked at some of these ill effects on children. On a variety of measures, children whose parents had moved far away after divorce received less financial aid from the more geographically distant parent (compared to children who stayed geographically close to both parents), they worried more, they felt more hostility in their relationships, they suffered more distress, and they had worse self-esteem. The authors of this study also discussed possible negative health effects on these children.

Suggestions

- After divorce, keep your romantic life as low-key as possible for the first two years. Even if you are in a new serious relationship, your child does not need to know all about it, and should not be encouraged to form emotional ties with the new partner until long after you are certain that you want to move to a more committed relationship.
- If and when you do remarry, understand that your children may well not share your happiness. To expect

them to be happy for you is unrealistic. Understand that every new relationship (with your new partner, your ex-spouse's new partner, and both parents' new children or stepchildren) presents new emotional territory for your child to navigate.

- Do not move far from the other parent unless there is no alternative – your children need to have access to the other parent on a regular basis. No matter what you might think of your ex-husband or ex-wife, it is generally a very real loss to your child to lose contact with him/her. Moving more than a journey of about ninety minutes from the other parent is likely to create real problems for your child, as well as additional inconvenience to you.

Adoption and attachment

Some good friends of mine recently adopted Mia, a little girl from Colombia. They are kind and conscientious people, and they decided it would be good if they took her to an 'attachment specialist', as some of their friends were urging them to do. Once there, they were dismayed to learn that their beautiful little toddler was at high risk of developing an attachment disorder which could lead to lifelong problems with her social and emotional development. They began regular sessions, they liked the counsellor, and Mia is doing very well at school and at home.

How can we interpret this situation, in light of what we know of evidence-based reasoning? The casual observer might conclude that the attachment treatment was successful. That conclusion would be unfounded. There are a couple of points to keep in mind: first, *this is just an anecdote*. Second, we don't know how Mia would have turned out without the attachment counselling. Thus, we can reach *no* informed conclusions based on my friends' experiences.

In order to make factual statements about attachment counselling, we would first need to know how to define a successful adoption. Factors that scientists usually examine are the child's academic success, whether the child reports symptoms of poor adjustment (low self-esteem, suicidality, substance use, etc.), how close the child reports feeling to the adopted parents by the time that child is a teenager or young adult, etc.

By most of these measures, adopted children do quite well, even without any special counselling. It certainly matters how early they are adopted. For example, a child who was adopted at age 10 after being looked after in a variety of different settings and by different care providers is likely to do less well than a child adopted as an infant. It also matters what toxins or drugs the child was exposed to *in utero*. So a child whose mother smoked cigarettes, injected drugs, and drank heavily during her pregnancy is more likely to have the deck stacked against him no matter when he is adopted.

Still, with these caveats in mind, the long-term outlook for adopted children is quite positive. Generally, children under the age of 5 who were adopted as babies are similar to non-adopted children in temperament, mental functioning, and attachment to their parents. Starting at about age 5, later-adopted children do show more behavioural problems than non-adopted children in a number of studies. Still, when asked later in life about their feelings, late-adopted children tend to describe their adoption as a positive force in their lives.

One very interesting study was done in Sweden by Bohman and his fellow researchers (1996). They looked at three different groups of children and compared them to a 'control group' of children living with their biological parents. One of the research groups consisted of children who were adopted, one consisted of children living in long-term foster care, and a third group consisted of children living with their biological mothers – mothers who had originally planned to have the children adopted, but who later changed their minds and decided to keep the children. The scientists followed these children until young adulthood. When compared to the control group children, at the age of 15 the adopted children did not differ significantly in their grades or behaviours. However, both the long-term foster children *and* the children whose mothers had decided not to have them adopted were more maladjusted. More strikingly, when the children were about 23 years old, the researchers looked for evidence of alcohol- and criminal-related problems in all three groups. They found that adoptees and 'control group' children did not differ on this measure, but that those boys who had been in long-term foster care had considerably more evidence of criminal activity and alcohol problems.

Long-term studies in the US have found similar results, with adopted adolescents scoring normally not just in their behaviours but also on measures of identity development and self-image. It is important to note that both the Swedish and the US studies found more problematic behaviours in school-age adopted boys, compared to non-adopted boys, but those differences generally smoothed out by late adolescence. Another interesting finding from a number of studies is that teenagers who are adopted seem to be sent for therapy in higher numbers than are non-adopted children, even when they are showing relatively minor problems. This may have to do with adoptive parents' anxiety about the effects of adoption, or perhaps their increased receptiveness to the use of social services.

One issue parents often ask about is how much they should talk with their children about the adoption. Studies have shown that the best outcomes for adoptive children are in families where children are permitted to talk about adoption and ask questions about it, but where that theme is not particularly stressed by the parents. In other words, parents should be open to having those conversations but not become preoccupied with the theme of adoption and 'difference'. This may be difficult for parents who are highly anxious.

International and 'transracial' adoptions have been studied since at least the 1970s, when researchers looked at the adjustment of a group of Korean children adopted in the USA. There have also been many similar studies over the decades in a variety of European countries. For the most part, these adoptions show good success rates, with about 75 to 80 per cent of the adopted children showing good adjustment, good self-esteem, and a strong commitment to the adopted family. Those who did not fit in that 'good adjustment' category showed a variety of problems ranging from 'mild' to 'severe'. A recent study examining outcomes of internationally adopted children in Ireland is available on the internet with the title 'A study of inter-country adoption outcomes in Ireland'. This website can be found at the following address: http://www.adoptionboard. ie/booklets/A_study_of_Intercountry_Adoption_Outcomes _in_Ireland_(Main%20Report).pdf

I have previously alluded to the 'age at adoption' issue. It is clear that children who spend years in the foster care system do not do as well as those adopted at a younger age. Major policy reviews in the UK and other developed nations have encouraged policy development that makes it possible for children to be placed more rapidly in adoption situations rather than keeping them 'in care' for longer stretches of time. Still, there are cases where even teenagers benefit considerably from late adoption, with both the adoptive parents and the child being well adjusted, and well satisfied with the adoption process.

One last point about parents' educational status deserves to be made here. At least one major study found that adopted children showed slightly better adjustment in middle-class families with average education levels, as compared to children adopted by highly educated families. This may be due to the higher achievement pressures in the highly educated families. Thus, adoptive parents who are highly educated should be aware that they may be burdening their adoptive children with unrealistic expectations.

'Attachment therapy'

Getting back to my friends and their daughter Mia, we can assume that she has at least a 75 per cent chance of having a good adjustment, even without any special attachment counselling. Now, given that fact, what do we know about the role of attachment specialists and therapies that are intended to support the bonding process?

The picture here is less promising. Two major reviews in the USA and the UK (Chaffin *et al.*, 2006; Barth *et al.*, 2005) have examined this issue. Both reach similar con-clusions. Among these are the following:

- 'Attachment therapy' techniques are based on theories that have never been supported scientifically. For example, they assume that the children hold suppressed rage and this rage needs to be released or the child will fail to attach and may go on to develop very serious lifelong problems. There is no scientific support for this theory.
- 'Attachment therapists', particularly those who seek to treat children with serious behaviour problems, often promote a view of adopted children as carrying a huge burden of pathology, when this is counterproductive, increases parents' anxiety unreasonably, and there is no reasonable scientific evidence for this belief.
- 'Holding therapy' is still being promoted by some attachment therapists who believe it is necessary as a means of releasing rage in a controlled environment. With this technique, children are held, sometimes by several adults at a time, while being poked or tickled or squeezed in a way that is designed to cause an emotional outburst from the child. This type of therapy has been discredited, and it is likely to cause more harm than good.
- The mere fact that a child has been seriously neglected or maltreated earlier in life does not mean that they have a disorder. Many of these children are remarkably resilient and cope well.
- Well established cognitive and behavioural therapies (CBT) hold much greater chances of being successful than do 'attachment therapies'. These CBT techniques can be used successfully for the adopted children, if there is an emotional or behaviour problem, but they can also be used very effectively for the parents. For example, if adoptive parents are coached in how to be consistent in their expectations, and how to be emotionally warm and responsive even to difficult children, this bears the greatest promise of improved outcomes for these children.

I need to say here that there are certainly therapists interested in supporting adoption outcomes who do *not* use controversial techniques such as 'holding therapy'. They may be very useful to adoptive parents who are worried about how their children will adjust, or for parents who doubt their own parenting skills. What I would *strongly* caution against here is adoptive parents believing that their children need therapy and that they will not do well if they are deprived of that. Adoption is not an illness.

Gay and lesbian parents, heterosexual parents, and child outcomes

Historically, some of the same fears and concerns that have been held about adopted children have been attached to the biological or adoptive children of gay and lesbian parents. A number of studies have examined the long-term outcomes of children who grow up in these families. In addition to examining the outcomes measured in the general adoption studies (academic success, behavioural problems, self-esteem), these studies have often examined measures of sexual adjustment and gender identity. There is still a shortage of good, controlled studies, but the evidence is accumulating on this set of questions.

Thus far, the results have been quite clear. In terms of academic success, social adjustment, and gender identity, the children of gay and lesbian parents fare as well as do children of heterosexual parents. Some of them do report experiencing derogatory remarks about their families, but they also say that they have good relationships with their parents and they function normally compared to their counterparts who were raised by heterosexual parents.

One interesting finding about gay and lesbian adoptive parents is worth mentioning here. Leung and his colleagues, in 2005, examined outcomes for adoptees who were older or had 'special needs' such as developmental disabilities. They found that older children actually did better when they were placed with homosexual families as compared to hetero-sexual families. Adopted children in general did equally well with parents of either sexual orientation.

Parent values and religiosity

This topic is of concern for many parents. How does our value system affect our children? How can we transmit our values to our children? Whether we most value a particular ethical stance, such as tolerance and acceptance of others, or a specific religious orientation, or attitudes toward drug and alcohol abuse, there are a myriad of issues we care about that we would hope our children would also care about.

The question about how we can transmit values has several other questions embedded within it:

1 Is it possible to do this? In other words, we all know children who rebel against their parents' value systems. Perhaps the idea that we can transmit values is an illusion.
2 Is it desirable to do this? For example, if one of our chief values is that we raise children who are autonomous and think things through for themselves, we would want to be very cautious about consciously pushing our children in a particular direction.
3 Is the relationship bidirectional? In other words, if values can be transmitted between parent and child, can the children influence the parents' values, or do the parents simply influence their children's values?

As always, we want to appeal to the scientific literature to shed some light on these questions. The answer to the first question is a qualified 'yes'. There is ample evidence that parents consciously and unconsciously have effects on their children's values and choices later in life. For example, parents who are actively engaged in regular religious practice have children who tend to delay having sexual relations (for example, see Manlove and colleagues' work, 2006). These studies are just correlational, so we cannot assume that religiosity *causes* the children to wait longer before having sex. Other parenting actions that tend to promote children waiting longer before engaging in sex, and taking fewer risks, include:

• Being more aware of their children's activities and whereabouts

- Engaging in more family activities with their children
- Having trusting and close relationships with their children.

Wight and his colleagues conducted a major Scottish study (2006) in which they looked at a variety of parenting factors that were associated with children's sexual choices. They found that children who had the most spending money and whose parents monitored their activities least were most likely to have multiple sexual partners during the course of the study. Again, we need to be careful about what inferences we make – the spending money may or may not have caused the sexual behaviour. A closer examination of the data reveals that high levels of spending money are found among adolescents whose families are of lower socioeconomic status, whose parents are more likely to be divorced, and whose parents tend to be younger.

In the same study, the researchers looked at whether comfort and ease in talking with children about sex predicted sexual choices in the children. The situation here was rather complex, and it varied depending on the cultural group. For example, the Pakistani and Indian children were less likely to talk about sex with their parents. For boys in general, having either a great deal of comfort or very little comfort in talking with parents about sex was associated with increased sexual behaviour. For girls, comfort in talking with their fathers about sex was predictive of having a later sexual début and using condoms more consistently.

Another recent study by Chaoyang and colleagues (2002) examined how parents' substance use (cigarettes, alcohol and marijuana) influenced the likelihood of children using substances. As one might expect, they found that parents who used drugs were more likely to have children who used drugs. Additionally, they found that these children of drug-using parents said they felt less well equipped to refuse offers of drugs. Conversely, parents who did not use any drugs had children who felt better able to refuse offers of drugs, and who were less affected by whether their friends did or did not use these drugs.

There is also ample evidence that parents' religious or spiritual activities and values can have significant effects on the child's development. In a 2003 review, Mark Regnerus found that religiosity can buffer adolescents against depression, and it is associated with higher levels of positive health behaviours. Additionally, adolescent children of mothers who view religion as important report higher levels of closeness with their mothers than do adolescent children of mothers who don't find religion important. This literature is tricky, as studies differ in whether they examine 'private religiosity' or outward religious practices such as church attendance. Additionally, there are many forms of religiosity, some of which are associated with harsher parenting styles, while others support greater warmth and support of children. Thus, there are certainly many ways in which parents' choices and values influence their children's choices.

The second question I pose above is more the purview of philosophy than of psychology, but there are nuggets from psychological studies, such as those described above, that might be helpful in thinking it through. To the extent that we want our children to avoid risky behaviours such as unprotected sex with multiple partners, influencing their choices is ethically desirable.

It is probably some relief to those rare parents most interested in preserving the free will of their children that heavy-handed attempts to transmit values are most likely to backfire. A huge scientific literature going back many decades demonstrates that children of authoritative parents (as opposed to authoritarian or permissive or neglectful) have the best outcomes on nearly any dimension measured. Authoritative parents are those who show high degrees of both warmth and control. These are the parents who are affectionate, and also those who have firm rules and expectations. They are also those most likely to have children who are secure, well adjusted, and who can also influence their parents on important questions.

This gets to the third question above. Some research indicates that parents are significantly affected by their adolescents' ideals *if* the parents are authoritative and if there is active discussion going on in the house about issues that matter to both children and parents. This is really the ideal home, in my opinion; it is one in which the parents value the children's opinions enough to listen to them, one where the children feel free to discuss their opinions, and ultimately one where the children will grow up to be the most competent, secure adults possible.

These would be the homes where the authoritative parents would in effect be saying, 'I love you and expect you to do as I say, unless you convince me that there is a better course.' Contrast this with the authoritarian parent who says 'Do as I say!' or the permissive parent who says, 'Do whatever you like,' or the neglectful parent who says, 'Child? What child?!'

If there is one strong theme that I would hope you would take away from reading this book, it would be that authoritative parenting is associated with the most positive outcomes in nearly every psychological study, over many decades. To be an authoritative parent, you need to show much love and warmth, you need to respect your children as separate individuals whose viewpoints should be heard, and you also need to articulate and enforce clear rules consistently. When you have a particular parenting dilemma that you are wrestling with, you can either access the scientific literature yourself, or work closely with a friend or psychologist or health professional who can assist you in tackling these questions.

I wish you all the best in your quest to be an effective, evidence-informed parent who truly enjoys this marvellous journey that is parenting. I find it very comforting, in my own parenting, to know that the key points are that I show warmth and affection and keep expecting my children to follow the rules. That is the cake and the rest is all icing.

The Bottom Line

- **What are the key dilemmas parents have to struggle with on this topic?**
  - What impact will being adopted or having divorced parents have on my child?

302 PARENTING WITH REASON

- Do I need to seek specialized counselling for my child who is adopted?
- How do my values and attitudes affect my child?
- **What does the science say about this topic?**
  - Parents' values do influence their adolescents' attitudes and behaviours.
  - In close families, adolescents can also influence their parents' attitudes.
  - Parental religiosity, depending on how it is expressed, can have a number of positive health and behaviour outcomes for the children.
  - As always, authoritative parenting, in any situation, is associated with a variety of better child outcomes.
  - For divorcing parents, anything you can do to promote a collaborative relationship with the other parent will be an enormous gift to your child.
  - It is a good idea to wait about two years before starting start a new romantic relationship, after a divorce. If you do start a new relationship early, keep it low-key and make efforts not to involve your children.
  - Adopted children tend to do very well overall and do not normally require special treatment.
  - Be very wary of clinicians who promote special 'attachment therapy'. Opt instead for standard cognitive and behavioural treatments for children.
- **What do the authors advise?**
  - Be warm and loving and have firm rules which you discuss freely with your child.
  - Be prepared to compromise if your child offers a good rationale.
  - Arm yourself with good information, relax, and enjoy the experience.

Recommended reading for parents

Christensen, A. and Jacobson, N. (2000). *Reconcilable differences.* New York: Guilford Press.

Gottman, J. (2000). *Seven principles for making marriage work*. New York: Random House.

Heitler, S. (1997). *The power of two: Secrets to a strong and loving marriage*. Oakland, CA: New Harbinger Publications.

Who's minding the children?

Dixon

My wife and I are 'professional people'. By that I mean that from the time we were kids, we always planned on going to university, getting good jobs that were fulfilling, and having careers that provided the flexibility to do what we wanted to do, and get paid for doing it. The American syndicated columnist/author Harvey Mackay once wrote, 'Find something you love to do and you'll never have to work a day in your life.' This was a tenet that my wife and I aspired to. Today, both of us are active and contributing members of our communities, and of the child psychology discipline. We both have relatively well-regarded positions with leadership responsibilities, and our work bears on the lives of many people. As professional people enjoying professional lives, we are living in Mackay's world. So with so much going on in our professional lives, why would we ever want to have children?

When presented with that question, I usually deliver one or another tongue-in-cheek retort. I sometimes say that we had our two daughters to replace ourselves in the genetic pool. I muse that because our parents only *loaned* us their genes, we should reimburse the population upon completion of the terms of the loan. My other response is that we produced offspring to increase the chances that someone would care for us in our feeble years. Surely it is altogether too risky for old people to rely on the government or a profit-motivated insurance company for a warm bed and three square meals a day.

Flippant responses are fun, but an honest, rational response is harder to come by. I suppose we had children because that's what humans do. Living organisms are built to reproduce, perhaps driven to reproduce, and our production of kids was probably little more than a natural consequence of our being gifted with life ourselves. From an emotional standpoint, I'm sure our children were the products of our passionate desires to consummate our commitment and love for one another, and to show off our bond with one another to the world. And, of course, caring and providing for children were main reasons underlying our professional ambitions in the first place. So it was only logical that we carried over our professional interests into our personal lives.

Of course the *idea* of having children is a rather different matter than the *reality* of having children. Our idealistic musings notwithstanding, we learned soon after the birth of our first daughter that having a professional career would not mix easily with having a family. Even when Rachel was a newborn, we began devising strategies for mixing being good parents with being good professionals. As professional people, we identified with our careers. Asking us to give them up would have been like asking us to give up a limb. Besides, we grew up with the cultural message that we could have it all – good job, good family, good life – even if the roadmaps for getting there weren't exactly charted. Of course, our having it all would have been aided immeasurably by having the helping hands of our extended family nearby. But like so many professional couples, our careers drew us far afield from our homes of origin, and so childcare by our extended family was simply impossible.

Fortunately, the flexibility of our positions allowed us to resolve many of our logistical dilemmas. As a college professor, for example, I could take my daughter into work from time to time, and find a student or office worker to stay with her while I taught my classes. And my wife was able to schedule clients during afternoons and evenings, leaving her free to stay at home in the morning. We also had many community-based connections which turned up a number of desirable childcare opportunities. In the end, we were lucky and found a colleague who had a neighbour who was a retired grandmother with few daily responsibilities and commitments. This woman had raised her own family, enjoyed good health in both mind and body, and was willing to take on a new charge for short stints in the afternoon. For us, selecting her was a no-brainer. Very quickly after making the acquaintance of this kind woman, we began placing our daughter with her from 1:00 to 5:00 p.m. each working day. It was also providence that ours was the only child she minded. We hadn't fully realized our good fortune until we started getting emails and phone calls from friends and acquaintances asking whether this woman would take on their children. Greedily, we were relieved to learn that she wouldn't.

We look back on those days with fondness. But despite our privileges, our endeavours were not without challenge. For one thing, to accommodate our childcare arrangements, my wife and I rarely saw one another. I would go into work at 8 a.m., and return home at 5 p.m. with child in tow. My wife would leave for work at 1 p.m., drop our daughter off at childcare, and return home at 10 p.m. Thus, ironically, the very act of having a family to consummate our marriage and publicly express our bond, prevented us from being together more than a couple of hours per day; and much of this time was spent either getting ready for work or winding down from it. We were like two single-parent families under one roof. Yet for better or for worse, we endured. And we felt victorious that we never had to put our daughter in centre-based care!

These days I reflect on why we thought it was a victory that we avoided centre-based childcare. We must have believed that the benefits of avoiding centre-based childcare outweighed the personal costs; otherwise, why undertake the venture? Yet, I don't think we fancied any strong arguments against childcare, at least not well-articulated ones. And I am quite sure we were ignorant of the scientific literature on childcare, because that wasn't the focus of our professional training. I can only conclude that our opinions were based on stereotypes and innuendo, and that we acted in ignorance of the empirical evidence. Admittedly, we behaved in a decidedly non-scientific manner.

A science of childcare

Our purpose in including this chapter on the science of childcare was precisely so that other parents could avoid having to make childcare decisions in an evidentiary vacuum. Parents feel bad enough when they leave their children in the care of others, it seems the least we can do is inform them about the potential consequences of their decisions. It is ironic, I think, that millions of dollars and pounds have been awarded to childcare researchers by funding agencies for the sole purpose of investigating the outcomes of placing our children into the care of others, yet the average parent knows almost nothing of the results of these research projects.

But our hope as authors to provide a clear guiding light for parents to use to make informed childcare decisions was very soon dashed once the childcare literature was consulted. As it turns out, the science of childcare is anything *but* clear, and recommendations from various large-scale studies have done much to cloud and obfuscate the decision-making opportunities of parents. Perhaps the best description of the conclusions we can draw from modern state-of-the-art childcare science comes from psychologist Noam Schpancer (2006), who noted that 'Different types of children incur different types of effects in different types of settings at different times in different contexts.' As unfulfilling as this characterization of the literature is, it is strikingly accurate. The research really is all over the place, and it is very difficult to draw from it anything resembling advice to parents. Nevertheless, in the spirit of the savvy consumer being the informed consumer, we can use this space to dip into the literature to describe the kinds of findings that have been released in recent years.

But before we can do even this, we have to take a detour to understand some of the ground rules in childcare research. One of the first steps is knowing the nomenclature used in childcare research. For example, the term 'childcare' is sometimes called 'daycare', sometimes 'child-minding', sometimes 'infant care', and sometimes the research even includes information from 'preschools' and other 'pre-K' settings. For simplicity's sake, I will adopt the conventional 'childcare' moniker, and use it to refer to all settings in which children are not being watched, cared for, or supervised by the parent or other legal custodian/ guardian.

As well, it is important to make distinctions between the different types of groups doing the childcaring. A typical tactic employed by scientific studies is to compare the outcomes of children supervised daily by stay-at-home mums and dads to those of children in non-parental child-care arrangements. But as a category, non-parental care settings usually comprise highly disparate childcare arrangements. For example, non-parental care can be proffered by such heterogeneous providers as non-parental relatives in the child's home (e.g. grandparents), child-minders in the child's home (nannies), professional child-minders in the childminder's home (sometimes called family daycare), and both for-profit and non-profit childcare centres (e.g. nurseries and preschools; which may or may not focus on academic training). What is worse, sometimes care provided by fathers is lumped into the non-parental category, whereas other times it's included in the parental category. Obviously, when non-parental care settings are collapsed together all in a single group, it can be very difficult if not impossible to draw conclusions about the relative merits or deficiencies of non-parental care *as a group* vis-à-vis parental care; and it is nearly impossible to keep track of all the differences.

If this isn't already hard enough, to be informed we must also wade through myriads of possible 'outcomes' that are relevant to our childcare decision-making. One major goal of childcare research, indeed of most developmental research generally, is to identify the effects that various institutions, policies, and practices have on our children. It is standard practice to refer to these effects as 'outcomes'. Basically, we want to know if something is good or bad for our kids. So it shouldn't be asking too much when we turn to the science to find out whether childcare, in one form or another, is helpful or harmful to our children. In sum, what are the outcomes?

But here again, the science of childcare has only made things more confusing. The outcomes that have captured researchers' attention are all over the place. Some outcomes have been academic in nature, wherein researchers have examined whether childcare facilitates or impedes *cognitive development* in such domains as language proficiency, literacy, maths understanding, and general school readiness. Other research has focused on mental and behavioural health outcomes, and has looked at whether childcare makes children more or less aggressive, more or less popular, or more or less anxious. Still other endeavours have examined social-relational outcomes, and have explored whether non-parental childcare enhances or interferes with the quality of children's relationship with their parents. This latter research has focused in particular on what is called the 'mother–child attachment relationship'.

Finally, it seems that for every study that links childcare to a positive outcome, there is another study that links it to a negative one. Sometimes the difference between these two kinds of outcomes depends on factors such as the age and financial well-being of children at the time of childcare onset, as well as the quality and quantity of childcare in question. Sometimes a link that emerges for one type of non-parental childcare fails to hold true for other types of non-parental childcare. And our cloud of understanding darkens. I make these points not to depress parents as they wade through the multitude of factors that are likely to influence their childcare decisions, but instead to point out that even science doesn't at present have all the answers. It's not even clear that it knows all the questions. But science is dynamic and fluid, and in any case, it is the best resource we have to learn about child outcomes as they are related to childcare.

Worldwide studies

There are several major ongoing childcare studies at this time, and they can be found all over the world. I will list a few of them below, along with some identifying information that parents may be able to use in the future to find out about the latest conclusions being drawn by each study. One of the main conclusions we can draw from these major studies, especially since they are being conducted in many different countries and cultures, is that high-quality childcare (defined below) almost always produces better outcomes than low-quality childcare. But a second main conclusion we can draw is that, other than the quality care issue, it may not be possible to apply findings about childcare observed in one study to children drawn from different populations.

The NICHD Study of Early Child Care and Youth Development (USA)

The mother of all childcare studies is surely the American study funded by the United States National Institute of Child Health and Human Development (NICHD). Details about the study can be found at http://secc.rti.org. But in a nutshell, the NICHD study began collecting data in 1991 on 1,364 children across ten locations throughout the US. Currently in its IVth phase, the study continues to follow more than 1,000 of the original families as the children reach well into late adolescence. With thirty scientists involved in this massive study, they are too numerous to mention by name. But most child developmentalists would probably recognize Professor Jay Belsky, now at Birkbeck College, University of London, as one of the study's primary spiritual leaders. The study website presently lists over 130 peer-reviewed publications emerging from this very rich database, so one can imagine the sheer difficulty the study coordinators have in keeping track of and cataloguing all the various findings. A recently published 474-page book, *Child Care and Child Development*, does a yeoman's job of presenting the key findings for the one-stop shopper, but the technical tone of the tome surely renders much of it inaccessible to the average parent. Hence I reproduce some of the findings here in a fashion that lay parents may find more palatable.

One of the early claims to fame of the NICHD study was to endeavour a characterization of 'quality care' that could be used by parents to determine whether a childcare facility met some minimally acceptable standard. As well, since theirs was one of the first studies to undertake long-term childcare outcome research, coming up with a good, all-purpose definition of childcare quality was one of the first steps in their journey. What they came up with was a system that focused less on 'structural' aspects of the childcare environment, such as child-to-caregiver ratios and caregiver credentials, and more on the kinds of actual experiences children can expect to have in the setting. The researchers determined that nine elements of the caregiving environment were most strongly associated with positive outcomes. Seven of the elements derive from whether the caregiver:

1 responds to the child's vocalizations,
2 reads aloud to the child,
3 asks the child questions,
4 praises or speaks affectionately to the child,
5 teaches the child,
6 directs other positive talk to the child,
7 has close physical contact with the child.

And two of the elements reflect whether the child.

8 is unoccupied,
9 or is watching television.

Based on this list, the researchers developed an instrument called the 'Observational Record of the Caregiving Environment', or ORCE for short, which they hoped could eventually be used by parents. Presumably, an enquiring parent could obtain a copy of this instrument (which is reproduced in the book mentioned above), fill it out during a casual visit to a childcare facility, and compare it to the standards provided by the NICHD researchers (also reproduced in the book). As a result, each childcare facility the parent evaluates could be categorized as *poor*, *fair*, *good*, or *excellent*. The researchers found that in 'poor' programmes, 'sensitivity, responsiveness, and stimulation were not at all characteristic of the caregivers, and detachment and intrusiveness were very characteristic', whereas the opposite was true for 'excellent' programmes. Although it is hard for me to imagine a parent going to all this trouble to rate individual childcare facilities – indeed, I know of no large-scale efforts to distribute the ORCE to the public – I think their main point is an excellent one: parents should pay attention to the kinds of interpersonal interactions children in a childcare facility experience. After all, what good is a highly credentialled, award-winning childcare provider if in the end she doesn't engage children interpersonally?

Three other categories of research from this study should interest parents. One is the extent to which childcare influences cognitive outcomes such as language and intellectual development; the second is the extent to which childcare influences relationships between children and parents; and the third is the extent to which childcare contributes to children's 'acting-out' and problem behaviour. Data from the NICHD study bears on each of these issues. But it is important to keep in mind that the NICHD data are correlational, and as we describe in greater detail in Chapter 5 on the Mozart Effect, just because two factors are correlated does not mean that one causes the other; even if one happens earlier in time.

As it pertains to cognitive development, namely language and intellectual development, it appears that the amount and quality of certain aspects of childcare during the first two years of life are predictive of positive outcomes later on (as late as 10 or 11 years of age). Specifically, the more that caregivers are emotionally responsive and talk to children during infancy, the more those children show gains in language and intellectual outcomes in later childhood. This suggests that higher-quality childcare arrangements are associated with better cognitive gains than lower-quality childcare. But a follow-up question might be, how might childcare stand up to mum-care? Does attending non-parental childcare retard intellectual or language development in any way? Interestingly, according to the study, children in childcare generally did not fare more poorly than children in exclusive mum-care arrangements; and on some occasions such as when children came from economically disadvantaged homes, centre-based children actually showed advantages over children who had their own mothers as their primary caregivers. In sum, the NICHD dataset provides no evidence that childcare impacts negatively on the cognitive outcomes of children, suggesting instead that it may actually boost cognitive outcomes.

A second major concern for parents is the possibility that childcare might disrupt the normal parent–child attachment relationship. As a technical concept, 'attachment' refers to how closely connected mothers and their babies are and how well they can tolerate the absence of the other. Child psychologists believe that babies who are 'securely attached' do not like it when their mothers leave them, but will tolerate such absences because they know mothers will return even after a separation. These babies think of mum as reliable and responsive, and trust in her eventual return when she leaves. In contrast, 'insecurely attached' babies have failed to establish a notion of mum as reliable and responsive, and don't trust that she will return when she goes away. These babies may have established distrusting belief systems because their mothers have been reliably unreliable, or even worse, abusive. One worry, then, is whether a healthy, secure attachment relationship between a baby and his mother may be compromised when they are separated by childcare on a typical working day. Will too much separation lead a baby to become insecurely attached? A second worry is whether a baby may become emotionally attached to the childcare provider instead of the mother. Indeed, in an article by British scientist Penelope Leach, an English mother reported preferring centre care over single-minder care, for fear that her child might have developed too strong an attachment to the minder: 'If she is going to get one-to-one attention, I want it to be from myself . . . rather than a childminder.'

A review of articles from the NICHD study seems to indicate that, by and large, mother–child attachment is not linked to participation in childcare. At both 15 and 36 months, babies who were securely or insecurely attached were no more or less likely to have been childcare participants. The researchers uncovered some caveats to this general conclusion, however. For example, babies of mothers who were low in sensitivity and responsiveness were more securely attached when they were in high-quality childcare than when they were in low-quality childcare. So it was the double-whammy of having both (1) an unresponsive mother *and* (2) low-quality childcare, that produced the most negative of attachment outcomes.

The most recent and perhaps some of the most worrisome outcomes of the NICHD study are in the domain of problem behaviours. In both a 2003 study and a 2007 study, the NICHD group showed that the sheer amount of time infants spent in centre-based childcare, regardless of the quality of care and regardless of the income and educational levels of the parents, was predictive of the number of *problem behaviours* children exhibited throughout childhood, even as late as 10 or 11 years of age. By 'problem behaviour', I am referring to the kinds of things kids do that are viewed as problematic by adults. Problem behaviours include, among other things, being overly anxious or fearful, being aggressive or disrespectful to others, or engaging in conflictual interactions with teachers. Again, the finding that the total amount of time spent in childcare predicts the amount of problem behaviour exhibited doesn't mean that it was the childcare that *caused* the problem behaviour. The former is merely an indicator of the latter. But the association has nevertheless been troublesome to many. On a positive note, there also appears to be evidence that the positive effect of parenting quality on problem behaviours is stronger than the negative effect of childcare. In particular, the researchers found that high-quality parenting had the effect of reducing problem behaviour more so than centre-based childcare had of increasing it.

Before moving on to the other major childcare studies, let us summarize what we have found out. Participation in childcare predicts enhanced cognitive and language outcomes in children, but also increased problem behaviours (at least centre-based care does). If the correlations really were causal, we could conclude that childcare does both good and bad things to our children. But how could it do both? According to the NICHD group, the answer to this question is a mystery. The best candidate for an explanation at this time may be that care providers and primary school teachers may simply not have the time or training to work toward remedying problem behaviours, given that their focus is usually on academic performance In this regard, it may be in the public's best interest to ensure adequate training in the techniques of behaviour management, and to ensure adequate time and sufficient numbers of personnel during the school day to permit the care provider or teacher to stay on top of the problem behaviours, and to ameliorate them early on.

Families, Children and Child Care study and the Effective Provision of Preschool Education study (UK)

Two major English studies also have a bearing on our understanding of the impact of childcare on children's development. The first, titled the 'Families, Children, and Child Care' (FCCC) study focuses primarily on outcomes associated with childcare during infancy, as opposed to during preschool, and is following 1,201 children and their families. This study is being led by the research team of Professors Kathy Sylva, Alan Stein and Penelope Leach, and its website can be found at http://www.familieschildren childcare.org/

The second study, perhaps more ambitious in its inclusion of 3,000 children from 141 preschool centres from six types of provider in five English regions, is titled the 'Effective Provision of Preschool Education' (EPPE) study. It focuses primarily on five- to seven-year outcomes associated with enrolment in preschools at 3 and 4 years of age. Professor Kathy Sylva is also a principal researcher on this study, and is joined by several other colleagues, including Professors Edward Melhuish, Pam Sammons and Brenda Taggart. The website for this study can be found at http://

www.eppe.ioe.ac.uk, as can several research and technical papers that are free to the public and downloadable.

Data from the two English studies provide for a much needed contrast with the NICHD study, both because they allow us to look for similarities across the two cultures – and countries – and because they allow us an opportunity to contrast the differences. To be sure, there are a number of important differences in geographically separated cultures, even market-economy-motivated Western industrialized ones. As noted in the FCCC website:

1 In the UK, and much of Europe, most women with children work part-time. But in the US there is less part-time work, and almost none available in managerial and professional jobs.
2 Standards and settings vary from place to place. . . . US 'family child care' is not equivalent to 'childminding' in the UK.
3 Parental leaves vary considerably. Eighteen-month leaves are common in Germany, versus eighteen weeks in the UK and six weeks in the US.
4 In the US and UK, poor childcare is often blamed on lack of training or experience, low job satisfaction, and high turnover; but in Israel, childcare is generally very low in quality, even though the average age of caregivers is 43 years, most have more than ten years of experience and have been in the same centre for more than six years, and reportedly love their jobs.

These notable differences should inform and caution our efforts to generalize findings from any one culture to another. Despite the many differences between the US and UK systems, however, there remain some similarities in findings across the two studies. For one thing, as with the US study, results from the EPPE continue to show that childcare experiences during infancy are associated with (1) positive gains in cognition and language, but also (2) an increased likelihood of problem behaviours in later childhood.

However, because of its weightier focus on the impacts of preschool, as opposed to childcare *per se*, we can garner much more information from the EPPE than the NICHD study with respect to the unique opportunities that preschool-oriented, centre-based experience affords, as compared with care-only centres. As with the NICHD, the EPPE study examined both cognitive and social/behavioural outcomes. In terms of cognitive outcomes, the EPPE focused specifically on reading and maths. In terms of the social and behavioural domain, the study focused on four categories of outcome, namely *hyperactivity*, *self-regulation*, *antisocial behaviour*, and *prosocial behaviour*.

Almost without exception, the EPPE reveals the role of preschool in children's lives to be uniformly positive, cognitively and behaviourally, from the onset of preschool (about age 3) through to age 11 years. But the authors also point out that any preschool effects need to be interpreted against a backdrop of both the child's home learning environment and the kinds of parents children have. The research briefs (#RB007, #RB828) made available free and downloadable to the public on the EPPE website are concise, well-written summaries designed for the lay parent. However, some of the more noteworthy findings are worth reproducing here.

- Preschool experience, compared to none, enhances all-around development in children, and enhances prosocial behaviour at age 10 years.
- Duration of attendance is important; an earlier start is related to better intellectual development.
- Full-time attendance led to no better gains than part-time attendance.
- Disadvantaged children in particular can benefit significantly from good-quality preschool experiences, especially if they attend centres that cater to a mixture of children from different social backgrounds.
- High-quality schooling is related to better cognitive and social/behavioural development; higher-quality curricula is linked to increased self-regulation at age 10 years; higher-quality social-emotional relationships with the

staff is linked to reduced hyperactivity and enhanced prosocial behaviour at age 10 years.

- Settings that have staff with higher qualifications have children who make more progress.
- Quality indicators include warm interactive relationships with children, having a trained teacher as a manager and a good proportion of trained teachers on staff.
- Attending medium- or high-quality preschools helps protect a child against the disadvantage of later attending an ineffective primary school, at least in terms of 10-year hyperactivity, self-regulation, and prosocial behaviour.

Finally, have you ever worried that the type of non-parental childcare that you wished or hoped for did not match the type of childcare you ended up with? Well, you shouldn't have, since this is actually what happens more often than not with new parents. An interesting little study by Barnes and colleagues using the FCCC data revealed that most parents (57 per cent), in fact, *do not* wind up using the kind of non-parental childcare they had planned on or hoped to be using. Whether it be 'pie-in-the-sky' thinking or some other fallacy that misinformed their expectations, even though these parents didn't end up with their ideal childcare arrangement, their satisfaction with the childcare they ended up with was not negatively affected.

Other global childcare-focused longitudinal studies

Due to space limitations, it is not possible to review in much detail many of the other ongoing longitudinal studies on childcare. However, there are several. There is, for example, the Irish partner project of the EPPE, titled the 'Effective Pre-school Provision in Northern Ireland' (EPPNI). The study entails a longitudinal investigation of some 800+ Irish children aged 3 to 8 years. Findings from this study generally mirror those of the larger EPPE study.

The Australian study, 'Growing Up in Australia: The Longitudinal Study of Australian Children', designed and implemented by the Australian Institute of Family Studies in partnership with the Australian Government Department of Family and Community Services, is a whopper of a study, incorporating multiple waves of follow-up of 5,000 children. Data from this study are only now beginning to make it to press, and it is too early to know much about the impact of childcare on the cognitive and social/behavioural outcomes of Australian children. But an excerpt in an issue of the Australian journal *Family Matters* sounds intriguing. In it, author Linda Harrison writes, 'Overall, the research found that child care had a positive rather than a negative effect on children's social and emotional wellbeing.' A fuller account of the first article from the Growing Up in Australia study to target childcare can be found in volume 79 of *Family Matters*. In the meantime, check back frequently with the study's website: http://www.aifs.-gov.au/growingup/home.html.

In one of the only longitudinal childcare studies of non-English-speaking children, the 'Haifa Early Child Care Study' (Israel) has much to lend by way of comparison to the other studies reviewed. This study, which is smaller than the others at only 758 children, is nevertheless an important one because it is one of the few to reveal compromised parent–child attachment relationships for children who participate in centre-based childcare as compared with children in parental care. Unfortunately, few published articles have emerged from this study, and so compared with the other studies we have mentioned, relatively little is known about the cognitive and social-behavioural outcomes of children enrolled in urban Israeli childcare. The authors, headed up by Professor Nina Koren-Karie, also host no website for this study.

Nevertheless, the published work reveals a considerably impoverished childcare system, as compared to the US and UK systems, with consequent negative impacts on babies' attachments with their parents. Specifically, babies enrolled in the centre-based childcare systems were more likely to be insecurely attached to their parents than were babies receiving parental care. It is worrisome that the Israeli centres did not meet even a single criterion recommended by the NICHD Early Child Care Research Network. The NICHD recommends a child–staff ratio of 3:1, group sizes of no larger than six, and staff with formal, post-high school training in child development or early childhood education. However, the Israeli centres averaged child–staff ratios of 8:1, had group sizes that were never smaller than eight babies, and had relatively poorly trained staff, with about a third having no caregiver training at all, and a third with less than ten years of education of any sort.

What is more, the caregivers generally provided little more than 'primarily technical and custodial care', and forged inadequate personal connections with the children. Very rarely did the caregivers exhibit displays of emotional positivity. On the other hand, the caregivers didn't act especially negatively toward the babies, nor were they abusive. In general, the caregivers seemed content with their jobs. This latter fact may raise the most eyebrows because job contentedness comprises two of the NICHD characteristics thought to indicate high-quality care: (1) having low turnover rates among caregivers (most in the Haifa study had been working at the same facility for more than six years), and (2) having caregivers who were very happy with their jobs (Haifa personnel describe themselves as quite content). The bottom line in this paradoxical set of findings, as noted by Koren-Karie and her colleagues, is that caregivers' job stability and job satisfaction do not seem to overcome their lack of training and knowledge, the absence of which appears to prevent them from nurturing the babies, and showing them the level of emotional responsiveness babies need for healthy and secure emotional attachments with their parents.

Conclusions and recommendations

As we have talked about in other chapters throughout this book, we must be very careful not to draw causal conclusions from correlational data. The studies reviewed in this chapter, as well as the conclusions and recommendations derived from them, were based on correlational data exclusively. It is very tempting to conclude, for example, that the poor conditions that run rampant throughout the Israeli childcare centres are what *caused* the increased incidence of insecure attachment among the enrolled babies. But such a conclusion would not be allowed by scientific standards. There is simply no way to rule out the possibility that babies enrolled in the centres were in some fashion different from home-minded babies from the outset. The only way to eliminate the possibility of such group differences would be to conduct an experiment wherein babies from a single group were randomly assigned to a 'stay-at-home' group and a 'centre childcare group', and then to compare the outcomes of the two groups both before and after experiencing childcare. But obviously, this kind of random assignment is not generally possible.

Nevertheless, data from these studies are the only data we have, and it does not appear that a perfectly designed experiment is on the radar screen. With this in mind, we might then ask, what harm would there be in assuming that children's cognitive, attachment, and behavioural outcomes really do result from childcare? Would making such an assumption cause harm? If not, then perhaps working under that premise could do some good; at least until we get better or more complete data. Under a causal assumption, where do we stand? Well, if we believed that childcare *caused* the outcomes described above, then we would conclude that (1) the amount of time spent in childcare during infancy contributes to a slight increase in problem behaviours in later childhood, (2) non-responsive, mechanical custodial care in infancy leads to lowered levels of secure attachment between babies and parents, and (3) participating in childcare arrangements during infancy and toddlerhood, especially centre-based care with an academic curriculum, contributes to increases in cognitive and language development as well as primary school readiness.

Under these assumptions, what should be the take-home message for parents? As with all things, any recommendation should be taken with a dose of common sense in good measure. But we might venture some of the following recommendations:

- It is OK to use non-parental childcare, presuming that it meets minimal quality standards at worst, and high quality standards at best.
  - Grandparent care is trustworthy and reliable, but grandparents may not provide as much academic (or otherwise) stimulation as might other childcare arrangements.
  - Professionally certified childminders providing care in their own homes are likely to provide responsive, emotionally sensitive interactions with children, and their care may be excellent, but as with centre-based care:
    - Caution should be exercised, and efforts should be taken to observe the minder interacting with other children.
    - Minders may not provide an academic curriculum, and hence may not produce the kinds of cognitive and academic gains typical of high-quality, academically-oriented centre-based care.
  - Nanny care may be under greater personal control of the parents and, as such, parents should ensure the selection of a nanny who is capable of demonstrating genuine sensitive responsiveness toward her charges and, ideally, who can implement an adequate and age-appropriate academic curriculum as determined by the parents.
- For centre-based care, parents should look for seals of approval provided by local, regional, or national over-seeing bodies, who, through their approval process, have reviewed at least several of the major structural characteristics of high-quality centres. These can include, but are not limited to, such factors as:
  - low child–caregiver ratios
  - low staff turnover rates
  - high staff credentialling systems
  - stimulating and academically oriented physical environments as appropriate.
- For centre-based care, childminder care, and nanny care, parents should strive to observe the care providers in real-time interaction with children in an effort to see

how much the care providers participate in the mental and emotional lives of the children, in positive, responsive, and emotionally nurturing ways. Presumably, this would be the default kind of care provided by grandparents, but when in doubt, this should be observed as well.

- Recommendations from other parents, or discussions with other parents, may help parents work through the myriad of issues involved in decision-making about childcare; but other parents may be under different stressors and in different life circumstances from you, and what is good enough for them may not be good enough for you.
- It's OK if you don't end up with the non-parental childcare you had always hoped for; less than half of new parents do.

The Bottom Line

- **What are the key dilemmas parents have to struggle with on this topic?**
  - Does childcare cause harm?
  - Does childcare promote academic achievement?
  - Are some arrangements better (or worse) than others?
- **What does the science say about this topic?**
  - Despite massive investments of time and money, several ongoing nationalized research studies have failed to produce large-scale consistent and conclusive findings.
  - Positive and negative 'effects' are sometimes reported in one study, only to fail to be replicated in another study.
  - *Experiments* on the effects of childcare are nonexistent. It is therefore impossible to draw causal conclusions about the real effects of childcare on children.
  - Perhaps the strongest claims that can be made, based on the science to date, are that:
    - Spending a lot of time in childcare and/or preschool predicts better academic achievement.

- Spending a lot of time in childcare predicts more behaviour problems, but spending a lot of time in preschool predicts fewer behaviour problems.
- But a minimum level of care quality is needed before any positive effects can be expected to be found.
- Different childcare arrangements have different strengths and weaknesses.
  - Extended family members may promote strong attachment relationships, but focus less on academic curricula.
  - Centre-based facilities and professional childminders may promote academic achievement, but focus less on establishing personal relationships.
- **What do the authors advise?**
  - Parents should feel comfortable using professional childcare providers, assuming providers meet minimal levels of appropriate benchmarks for care quality, as established by both the parent and the relevant government entity.
  - Parents should perform background checks to the extent possible on professional providers; including reviewing all relevant credentials such as licences, certificates, and various government designations.
  - Parents should observe providers in action, both with their own children (if possible) and with other people's children.

References

Chapter 1

Buchan, William (1785). *Domestic medicine* (2nd edn). Digitized version retrieved from the internet April 2004. Retrieved from http://www.americanrevolution.org/medone.html

Getis., V. and Vinovskis, M. (1992). History of child care in the United States before 1950. In M. Lamb, K. Sternberg, C.P. Hwang and A. Broberg (eds), *Child care in context: Cross-cultural perspectives*. Hillsdale, NJ: Lawrence Erlbaum Associates.

Goelman, H. (1992). Day care in Canada. In M. Lamb, K. Sternberg, C.P. Hwang and A. Broberg (eds), *Child care in context: Cross-cultural perspectives*. Hillsdale, NJ: Lawrence Erlbaum Associates.

Greven, P. (1977). *The Protestant temperament: Patterns of child-rearing, religious experience, and the self in Early America*. New York: Alfred A. Knopf, pp. 14–42.

Hall, G.S. (1904). *Adolescence: Its psychology and its relations to physiology, anthropology, sociology, sex, crime, religion and education*, Vol. 2, Ch. 17. Retrieved from Classics in the History of Psychology website, www.psychclassics.yorku.ca

Hardyment, C. (1983). *Dream babies: Three centuries of good advice on child care*. London: Harper & Row.

Hrdy, S.B. (1999). *Mother Nature: A history of mothers, infants, and natural selection*. New York: Pantheon Books.

Hulbert, A. (2003). *Raising America: Experts, parents, and a century of advice about children*. New York: Alfred A. Knopf.

Ladd-Taylor, M. (1986). *Raising a baby the government way: Mothers' letters to the Children's Bureau, 1915–1932*. New Brunswick, NJ: Rutgers University Press.

Melhuish, E. and Moss, P. (1992). Day care in the United Kingdom in historical perspective. In M. Lamb, K. Sternberg, C.P. Hwang and A. Broberg (eds), *Child care in context: Cross-cultural perspectives*. Hillsdale, NJ: Lawrence Erlbaum Associates.

Mindell, J.A. (1997). *Sleeping through the night: How infants, toddlers, and their parents can get a good night's sleep*. New York: HarperCollins.

Moseley, J.B., O'Malley, K., Petersen, N.J., Menke, T.J., Brody, B.A., Kuykendall, D.H., Hollingsworth, J.C., Ashton, C.M. and Wray, N.R. (2002). A controlled trial of arthroscopic surgery for osteoarthritis of the knee, *New England Journal of Medicine*, 347, 81–88.

Roduit, C. (2009). Asthma at 8 years of age in children born by caesarean section. *Thorax*, 64, 107–113.

Thavagnamnam, S. *et al*. (2008). A meta-analysis of the association between Caesarian section and childhood asthma. *Clinical and Experimental Allergy*, 38, 629–633.

Chapter 2

Buckley, P., Rigda, R., Mundy, L. and McMillen, I.C. (2002). Interaction between bed sharing and other sleep environments during the first six months of life. *Early Human Development*, 66, 123–132.

Burnham, M., Goodlin-Jones, B., Gaylor, E. and Anders, T. (2002). Nighttime sleep-wake patterns and self-soothing from birth to one year of age: A longitudinal intervention study. *Journal of Child Psychology and Psychiatry*, 43, 713–725.

Kuhn, B. and Weidinger, D. (2000). Interventions for infant and toddler sleep disturbance: A review. *Child and Family Behaviour Therapy*, 22, 33–50.

Middlemiss, W. (2004). Infant sleep: A review of normative and problematic sleep and interventions. *Early Child Development and Care*, 174, 99–122.

Owens, J. (2004). Sleep in children: Cross-cultural perspectives. *Sleep and Biological Rhythms*, 2, 165–173.

Pinilla, T. and Birch, L. (1993). Help me make it through the night: Behavioral entrainment of breast-fed infants' sleep patterns. *Pediatrics*, 91, 436–444.

Ramchandani, P., Wiggs, L., Webb, V. and Stores, G. (2000). A systematic review of treatments for settling problems and night waking in young children. *British Medical Journal*, 320, 209–213.

Scher, A. and Blumberg, O. (1999). Night waking among 1-year-olds: A study of maternal separation anxiety. *Child: Care, Health, and Development*, 25, 323–334.

Sleep, J., Gilham, P., St James-Roberts, I. and Morris, S. (2002). A randomized controlled trial to compare alternative strategies for preventing infant crying and sleep problems in the first 12 weeks: The COSI study. *Primary Health Care Research and Development*, 3, 176–183.

Chapter 3

Allen, R. and Myers, A. (2006). Nutrition in toddlers. *American Family Physician*, 74, 1527–1532.

Bernard-Bonnin, A. (2006). Feeding problems of infants and toddlers. *Canadian Family Physician*, 52, 1247–1251.

Buescher, E. and Hair, P. (2001). Human milk anti-inflammatory component contents during acute mastitis. *Cellular Immunology*, 210, 87–95.

Chao, H. and Vandenplas, Y. (2007). Comparison of the effect of a cornstarch thickened formula and strengthened regular formula on regurgitation, gastric emptying and weight gain in infantile regurgitation. *Diseases of the Esophagus*, 20, 155–160.

Department of Health (2007). *Weaning: Starting solid food* (DH Publication No. 278960). London.

Filipiak, B., Zutavern, A., Koletzko, S., von Berg, A., Brockow, I., Grübl, A., Berdel, D., Reinhardt, D., Bauer, C., Wichmann, H., Heinrich, J. and the GINI-Group (2007). Solid food introduction in relation to eczema: results from a four-year prospective birth cohort study. *Journal of Pediatrics*, 151, 352–358.

Gabbe, S., Niebyl, J. and Simpson, J. (eds) (2007). *Normal and problem pregnancies* (5th edn). Philadelphia: Churchill Livingstone.

Garrison, M. and Christakis, D. (2000). A systematic review of treatments for infant colic. *Pediatrics*, 106, 184–190.

Greer, F., Sicherer, S., Burks, A., American Academy of Pediatrics Committee on Nutrition and American Academy of Pediatrics Section on Allergy and Immunology (2008). Effects of early nutritional interventions on the development of atopic disease in infants and children: the role of maternal dietary restriction, breastfeeding, timing of introduction of complementary foods, and hydrolyzed formulas. *Pediatrics*, 121, 183–191.

Howard, C., Howard, F., Lanphear, B., deBlieck, E., Eberly, S. and Lawrence, R. (1999). The effects of early pacifier use on breastfeeding duration. *Pediatrics*, 103, e33. Retrieved 18 June 2008 from http://pediatrics.aappublications.org/cgi/content/full/103/3/e33

Ingram, J. and Johnson, D. (2004). A feasibility study of an intervention to enhance family support for breast feeding in a deprived area in Bristol, UK. *Midwifery*, 20, 367–379.

Kramer, M. and Kakuma, R. (2004). The optimal duration of exclusive breastfeeding: a systematic review. *Advances in Experimental Medicine and Biology*, 554, 63–77.

Leaf, A.A. (2007). Vitamins for babies and young children. *Archives of Disease in Childhood*, 92, 160–164.

Moreland, J. and Coombs, J. (2000). Promoting and supporting breast-feeding. *American Family Physician*, 61, 2093–2100.

Savino, F. (2007). Focus on infantile colic. *Acta Pediatrica*, 96, 1259–1264.

Singhal, A., Cole, T., Fewtrell, M., Kennedy, K. *et al.* (2007). Promotion of faster weight gain in infants born small for gestational age: is there an adverse effect on later blood pressure? *Circulation*, 115, 213–220.

Spencer, J. (2008). Management of mastitis in breastfeeding women. *American Family Physician*, 78, 727–731.

Wagner, C., Hulsey, T., Fanning, D., Ebeling, M. and Hollis, B. (2006). High-dose vitamin D3 supplementation in a cohort of breastfeeding mothers and their infants: a 6-month follow-up pilot study. *Breastfeeding Medicine*, 1, 59–70.

Chapter 4

Butte, N. (2007). Dietary energy requirements in adolescents. Retrieved March 2008 from www.uptodate.com

Cooke, L. (2007). The importance of exposure for healthy eating in childhood: a review. *Journal of Human Nutrition and Dietetics*, 20, 294–301.

Demory-Luce, D. and Motil, K. (2007). Vegetarian diets for children. Retrieved March 2008 from www.uptodate.com

Duryea, T. (2007). Dietary recommendations for toddlers and preschool children. Retrieved March 2008 from www.uptodate.com

Flynn, M. *et al.* (2006). Reducing obesity and related chronic disease risk in children and youth: a synthesis of evidence with 'best practice' recommendations. *Obesity Reviews*, 7, 7–66.

Gidding, S. *et al.* (2005). Dietary recommendations for children and adolescents: a guide for practitioners. American Academy of Pediatrics. Retrieved January 2008 from www.pediatrics/org/cgi/doi/10.1542/peds.2005-2565

Reilly, J. and McDowell, Z. (2003). Physical activity interventions in the prevention and treatment of paediatric obesity: systematic review and critical appraisal. *Proceedings of the Nutrition Society*, 62, 611–619.

Schwartz, M. and Puhl, R. (2002). Childhood obesity: a societal problem to solve. *Obesity Reviews*, 4, 57–71.

Steinbeck, K. (2001). The importance of physical activity in the prevention of overweight and obesity in childhood: a review and an opinion. *Obesity Reviews*, 2, 117–130.

Viteri, F. and Gonzalez, H. (2002). Adverse outcomes of poor micronutrient status in childhood and adolescence. *Nutrition Reviews*, 60, S77–S83.

Chapter 5

Christakis, D.A. and Zimmerman, F.J. (2006). *The elephant in the living room: Make television work for your kids*. New York: Rodale Books.

Christakis, D.A., Zimmerman, F.J., DiGiuseppe, D.L. and McCarty, C.A. (2004). Early television exposure and subsequent attentional problems in children. *Pediatrics*, 113, 708–713.

Linebarger, D.L. and Walker, D. (2005). Infants' and toddlers' television viewing and language outcomes. *American Behavioral Scientist*, 48(5), 624–645.

Nantais, K.M. and Schellenberg, E.G. (1999). The Mozart effect: an artifact of preference. *Psychological Science*, 10, 370–373.

Pempek, T.A. (2008). *The impact of baby videos on parent–child interaction*. (Doctoral dissertation, ProQuest Information and Learning). Dissertation Abstracts International: Section B: The Sciences and Engineering, 68 (7-B).

Rauscher, F.H. (2002). Mozart and the mind: factual and fictional effects of musical enrichment. In J. Aronson (ed.), *Improving academic achievement: Impact of psychological factors on education*. New York: Academic Press, pp. 269–278.

Rauscher, F.H., Shaw, G.L. and Ky, K.N. (1993). Music and spatial task performance. *Nature*, 365, 611.

Rideout, V.J., Vandewater, E.A. and Wartella, E.A. (2003). *Zero to six: Electronic media in the lives of infants, toddlers, and preschoolers*. A Henry J. Kaiser Family Foundation study.

Sydney Morning Herald (2008). Parents bear pain for private schools. *Sydney Morning Herald*, 27 January. Sarah Price, education reporter.

Zimmerman, F.J., Christakis, D.A. and Meltzoff, A.N. (2007). Associations between media viewing and language development in children under age 2 years. *Journal of Pediatrics*, 151(4), 364–368.

Chapter 6

Caspi, A. and Silva, P.A. (1995). Temperamental qualities at age three predict personality traits in young adulthood: longitudinal evidence from a birth cohort. *Child Development*, 66, 486–498.

Caspi, A., Henry, B., McGee, R.O., Moffitt, T.E. and Silva, P.A. (1995). Temperamental origins of behavior problems: from age three to age fifteen. *Child Development*, 66, 55–68.

deVries, M.W. (1984). Temperament and infant mortality among the Masai of East Africa. *American Journal of Psychiatry*, 141, 1189–1194.

Dixon, W.E., Jr. and Shore, C. (1997). Temperamental predictors of linguistic style during multiword acquisition. *Infant Behavior and Development*, 20, 99–103.

Dixon, W.E., Jr. and Smith, P.H. (2000). Links between temperament and language acquisition. *Merrill-Palmer Quarterly*, 46, 417–440.

Engfer, A. (1992). Difficult temperament and child abuse. Notes on the validity of the child effect model. *Analise Psicologica*, 1, 51–61.

Maccoby, E.E., Snow, M.E. and Jacklin, C.N. (1984). Children's dispositions and mother–child interaction at 12 and 18 months: a short-term longitudinal study. *Developmental Psychology*, 20, 459–472.

Martin, G.C., Wertheim, E.H., Prior, M., Smart, D., Sanson, A. and Oberklaid, F. (2000). A longitudinal study of the role of childhood temperament in the development of eating concerns. *International Journal of Eating Disorders*, 27, 150–162.

Maziade, M., Cote, R., Boutin, P., Bernier, H. and Thivierge, J. (1987). Temperament and intellectual development: a longitudinal study from infancy to four years. *American Journal of Psychiatry*, 144, 144–150.

Prior, M., Smart, D., Sanson, A. and Oberklaid, F. (2000). Does shy-inhibited temperament in childhood lead to anxiety problems in adolescence? *Journal of the American Academy of Child and Adolescent Psychiatry*, 39, 461–468.

Smith, P.H., Dixon, W.E., Jr., Jankowski, J.J., Sanscrainte, M.M., Davidson, B.K. and Loboschefski, T. (1997). Longitudinal relationships between habituation and temperament in infancy. *Merrill-Palmer Quarterly*, 43, 291–304.

van den Boom, D.C. (1994). The influence of temperament and mothering on attachment and exploration: an experimental manipulation of sensitive responsiveness among lower-class mothers with irritable infants. *Child Development*, 65, 1457–1477.

Chapter 7

American Academy of Pediatrics Task Force on Circumcision (1999). Circumcision Policy Statement. *Pediatrics*, 103, 686–693.

Armon, K. and Elliott, E. (2000). Acute gastroenteritis. In E. Elliot, R. Davis, R. Gilbert, T. Klassen, S. Logan, C. Mellis and K. Williams (eds), *Evidence Based Pediatrics and Child Health*. London: BMJ Books, pp. 273–286.

Bedford, H. and Elliman, D. (2000). Concerns about immunisation. *British Medical Journal*, 320, 240–243.

Bohlke, K., Davis, R., Marcy, S., Braun, M. *et al.* (2003). Risk of anaphylaxis after vaccination of children and adolescents. *Pediatrics*, 112, 815–820.

Christakis, D., Harvey, E., Zerr, D., Feudtner, C. *et al.* (2000). A trade-off analysis of routine newborn circumcision. *Pediatrics*, 105, 246–249.

Halsey, N., Hyman, S. and the Conference Writing Panel (2001). Measles-mumps-rubella vaccine and autistic spectrum disorder: report from the New Challenges in Childhood Immunizations Conference convened in Oak Brook, Illinois, June 12–13, 2000. *Pediatrics*, 107, E84.

Kimmel, S. (2003). Immunizations: the importance of childhood, adolescent and adult immunizations. *CME Bulletin* (American Academy of Family Physicians), 2, 1–5.

Lerman, S. and Liao, J. (2001). Neonatal circumcision. *Pediatric Clinics of North America*, 48(6), 1539–1557.

Lieberman, J. (2003). Appropriate antibiotic use and why it is important: the challenges of bacterial resistance. *Pediatric Infectious Disease Journal*, 22, 1143–1151.

Liptak, G., Baker, S., Colletti, R., Croffie, J., DiLorenzo, C., Ector, W. and Nurko, S. (2000). Constipation. In E. Elliot, R. Davis, R. Gilbert, T. Klassen, S. Logan, C. Mellis and K. Williams (eds), *Evidence Based Pediatrics and Child Health*. London: BMJ Books, pp. 264–272.

Nurko, S., Baker, S., Colletti, R., Croffie, J., DiLorenzo, C., Ector, W. and Liptak, G. (2001). Managing constipation: evidence put to practice. *Contemporary Pediatrics*, 18, 56–65.

Salisbury, D., Ramsay, M. and Noakes, K. (eds) (2006). Immunisation against infectious disease. Retrieved 6 July 2008 from http://www.dh.gov.uk/en/Publichealth/Healthprotection/Immunisation/Greenbook/DH_4097254

Siegfried, N., Muller, M., Volmink, J., Deeks, J., Egger, M. *et al.* (2003). Male circumcision for prevention of heterosexual acquisition of HIV in men (Cochrane Review). *The Cochrane Library*, Issue 3. Oxford: Update Software.

Szabo, R. and Short, R. (2000). How does male circumcision protect against HIV infection? *British Medical Journal*, 310, 1592–1594.

Taylor, B., Miller, E., Farrington, C. *et al.* (1999). Autism and measles, mumps and rubella vaccine: no epidemiological evidence for a causal association. *Lancet*, 353, 2026–2029.

Vestergaard, M., Hviid, A., Madsen, K., Wohlfahrt, J., Thorsen, P., Schendel, D. *et al.* (2004). MMR vaccination and febrile seizures: evaluation of susceptible subgroups and long-term prognosis. *Journal of the American Medical Association*, 292, 351–357.

Wakefield, A., Murch, S., Anthony, A., Linnell, J., Casson, D., Malik, M. *et al.* (1998). Ileal-lymphoid-nodular hyperplasia, non-specific colitis, and pervasive developmental disorder in children. *Lancet*, 351, 637–641.

Chapter 8

Blum, N., Taubman, B. and Nemeth, N. (2003). Relationship between age at initiation of toilet training and duration of training: a prospective study. *Pediatrics*, 111, 810–814.

Brazelton, T.B., Christophersen, E.R., Frauman, A.C., Gorski, P.A., Poole, J.M., Stadtler, A.C. and Wright, C.L. (1999). Instruction, timeliness, and medical influences affecting toilet training. *Pediatrics*, 103, 1353–1358.

Foxx, R. and Azrin, N. (1973). Dry pants: a rapid method of toilet training children. *Behaviour Research and Therapy*, 11(4), 435–442.

Glazener, C., Evans, J.H.C. and Peto, R.E. (2004). Treating nocturnal enuresis in children: review of evidence. *Journal of Wound, Ostomy and Continence Nursing*, 31, 223–234.

Horn, I., Brenner, R., Rao, M. and Cheng, T. (2006). Beliefs about the appropriate age for initiating toilet training: are there racial and socioeconomic differences? *Journal of Pediatrics*, 149, 165–168.

Polaha, J., Warzak, W. and Dittmer-McMahon, K. (2002). Toilet training in primary care: current practice and recommendations from behavioral pediatrics. *Developmental and Behavioral Pediatrics*, 23, 424–429.

Schonwald, A., Sherritt, L., Stadtler, A. and Bridgemohan, C. (2004). Factors associated with difficult toilet training. *Pediatrics*, 113, 1753–1757.

Chapter 9

American Academy of Pediatrics. Committee on Psychosocial Aspects of Child and Family Health (1998). Guidance for effective discipline. *Pediatrics*, 101, 723–728.

Ateah, C., Secco, M. and Woodgate, R. (2003). The risks and

alternatives to physical punishment use with children. *Journal of Pediatric Health Care*, 17, 126–132.

Baer, D.M., Wolf, M.M. and Risley, T.R. (1968). Some current dimensions of applied behaviour analysis. *Journal of Applied Behaviour Analysis*, 1, 91–97.

Baer, D.M., Wolf, M.M. and Risley, T.R. (1987). Some still-current dimensions of applied behaviour analysis. *Journal of Applied Behaviour Analysis*, 20, 313–327.

Banks, J. (2002). Childhood discipline: challenges for clinicians and parents. *American Family Physician*, 66, 1447–1452.

Benjet, C. and Kazdin, A. (2003). Spanking children: the controversies, findings, and new directions. *Clinical Psychology Review*, 23, 197–224.

Berkowitz, C. (1996). Discipline. In C. Berkowitz, *Pediatrics: A primary care approach*. Philadelphia: Saunders, pp. 105–108.

Blum, N., Williams, G., Friman, P. and Christophersen, E. (1995). Disciplining young children: the role of verbal instructions and reasoning. *Pediatrics*, 96, 336–341.

Christophersen, E. (1992). Discipline. *Pediatric Clinics of North America*, 39, 395–411.

Eyberg, S.E., Nelson, M.M. and Boggs, S.R. (2008). Evidence-based psychosocial treatments for children and adolescents with disruptive behaviour. *Journal of Clinical Child Psychology*, 37, 215–237.

Herrenkohl, R. and Russo, M. (2001). Abusive early child rearing and early childhood aggression. *Child Maltreatment*, 6, 3–16.

Howard, B. (1996). Advising parents on discipline: what works. *Pediatrics*, 98, 809–815.

Illingworth, R. (1991). Discipline and punishment. In R. Illingworth, *The normal child: Some problems of the early years and their treatment* (10th edn). New York: Churchill Livingstone, pp. 245–254.

Larsen, M. and Tentis, E. (2003). The art and science of disciplining children. *Pediatric Clinics of North America*, 50, 817–840.

Leung, A., Robson, W. and Lim, S. (1992). Counseling parents about childhood discipline. *American Family Physician*, 45, 1185–1189.

McCord, J. (1996). Unintended consequences of punishment. *Pediatrics*, 98, 832–834.

Pinderhughes, E., Dodge, K., Bates, J., Pettit, G. and Zelli, A. (2000). Discipline responses: influences of parents' socioeconomic status, ethnicity, beliefs about parenting, stress, and cognitive-emotional processes. *Journal of Family Psychology*, 14, 380–400.

Shriver, M.D. and Allen, K.D. (2008). *Working with parents of noncompliant children: A guide to evidence-based parent training for practitioners and students*. Washington, DC: APA.

Skinner, B.F. (1953). *Science and human behaviour*. New York: Macmillan.

Smith, J. and Brooks-Gunn, J. (1997). Correlates and consequences of harsh discipline for young children. *Archives of Pediatric and Adolescent Medicine*, 151, 777–786.

Straus, M. (1996). Spanking and the making of a violent society. *Pediatrics*, 98, 837–842.

Straus, M., Sugarman, D. and Giles-Sims, J. (1997). Spanking by parents and subsequent antisocial behaviour of children. *Archives of Pediatric and Adolescent Medicine*, 151, 761–767.

Vaughan, V. and Litt, I. (1990). The preschool child. In V. Vaughan and I. Litt (eds), *Child and adolescent development: Clinical implications*. Philadelphia: Saunders, pp. 193–212.

Woodward, L., Taylor, E. and Dowdney, L. (1998). The parenting and family functioning of children with hyperactivity. *Journal of Child Psychology and Psychiatry*, 39, 161–169.

Chapter 10

Anderson, C.A. (2004). An update on the effects of playing violent video games. *Journal of Adolescence*, 27, 113–122.

Anderson, C.A. and Bushman, B.J. (2001). Effects of violent video games on aggressive behavior, aggressive cognition, aggressive affect, physiological arousal, and prosocial behavior: A meta-analytic review of the scientific literature. *Psychological Science*, 12, 353–359.

Anderson, C.A., Berkowitz, L., Donnerstein, E., Huesmann, L.R., Johnson, J.D., Linz, D., Malamuth, N.M. and Wartella, E. (2003). The influence of media violence on youth. *Psychological Science in the Public Interest*, 4, 81–110.

Bushman, B.J. and Anderson, C.A. (2001). Media violence and the American public: scientific facts versus media misinformation. *American Psychologist*, 56, 477–489.

Dixon, W.E., Jr. (2003). *Twenty studies that revolutionized child psychology*. Upper Saddle River, NJ: Prentice Hall.

Hosking, S., Young, K. and Regan, M. (2007). The effects of text messaging on young novice driver performance. In I.J. Faulks, M. Regan, M. Stevenson, J. Brown, A. Porter and J.D. Irwin (eds), *Distracted driving*. Sydney: Australasian College of Road Safety.

Huesmann, L.R. (2007). The impact of electronic media violence: scientific theory and research. *Journal of Adolescent Health*, 41, S6–S13.

Huesmann, L.R. and Taylor, L.D. (2003). The case against the case against media violence. In D. Gentile (ed.), *Media violence and children*. Westport, CT: Greenwood Press.

Mares, M.-L. and Woodard, IV, E.H. (2007). Positive effects of television on children's social interaction: a meta-analysis. In R.W. Preiss, B.M. Gayle, N. Burrell, M. Allen and J. Bryant (eds), *Mass media effects research: Advances through meta-analysis*. Mahwah, NJ: Erlbaum.

Paik, H. and Comstock, G. (1994). The effects of television violence on antisocial behavior: a meta-analysis. *Communication Research*, 21, 516–546.

Sherry, J.L. (2001). The effects of violent video games on aggression: a meta-analysis. *Human Communication Research*, 27, 409–431.

Smyth, J.M. (2007). Beyond self-selection in video game play: an experimental examination of the consequences of massively multiplayer online role-playing game play. *CyberPsychology & Behavior*, 10, 717–727.

Sprafkin, J.N., Liebert, R.M. and Poulos, R.W. (1975). Effects of a prosocial televised example on children's helping. *Journal of Experimental Child Psychology*, 20, 119–126

Chapter 11

Barber, J. and Delfabbro, P. (2000). Predictors of adolescent adjustment: parent–peer relationships and parent–child conflict. *Child and Adolescent Social Work Journal*, 17, 275–288.

Kumpfer, K. and Alvarado, R. (2003). Family-strengthening approaches for the prevention of youth problem behaviours. *American Psychologist*, 58, 457–465.

National Institute of Child Health and Human Development (2006). *Adventures in parenting: How responding, preventing, monitoring, mentoring, and modelling can help you be a successful parent*. Washington, DC: National Institutes of Health.

Nixon, R. (2002). Treatment of behaviour problems in pre-schoolers: a review of parent training programmes. *Clinical Psychology Review*, 22, 525–546.

Pennebaker, J. (1997). Writing about emotional experiences as a therapeutic process. *Psychological Science*, 8, 162–166.

Chapter 12

Fombonne, E. (1998). Increased rates of psychosocial disorders in youth. *European Archives of Psychiatry*, 248, 14–21.

Gershoff, E. (2002). Corporal punishment by parents and associated child behaviours and experiences: a meta-analytic and theoretical review. *Psychological Bulletin*, 128, 539–579.

Hutchings, J. and Appleton, P. (2002). Evaluation of two treatments for children with severe behaviour problems: Child behaviour and maternal mental health outcomes. *Behavioural and Cognitive Psychotherapy*, 30, 279–295.

Kane, P. and Garber, J. (2004). The relations among depression in fathers, children's psychopathology, and father–child conflict: a meta-analysis. *Clinical Psychology Review*, 24, 339–360.

Lin, D. *et al.* (1997). Maternal care, hippocampal glucocorticoid receptors, and hypothalamic-pituitary-adrenal responses to stress. *Science*, 277, 1659–1662.

Lochman, J. and van den Steenhoven, A. (2002). Family-based approaches to substance abuse prevention. *Journal of Primary Prevention*, 23, 49–114.

Sawyer, M. *et al.* (2001). The mental health of young people in Australia: key findings from the child and adolescent component of the national survey of mental health and well-being. *Australian and New Zealand Journal of Psychiatry*, 35, 806–814.

Skinner, B.F. (1957). *Verbal behavior*. Acton, MA: Copley Publishing Group.

Soutoullo, C. *et al.* (2005). Bipolar disorder in children and adolescents: international perspectives on epidemiology and phenomenology. *Bipolar Disorders*, 7, 497–506.

Strand, P. (2000). A modern behavioural perspective on child conduct disorder: integrating behavioural momentum and matching theory. *Child Psychology Review*, 20, 593–615.

Tiet, Q. *et al.* (2001). Relationship between specific adverse life events and psychiatric disorders. *Journal of Abnormal Child Psychology*, 29, 153–164.

Chapter 13

ADDitude Magazine.

American Psychiatric Association (2000). *The diagnostic and statistical manual of mental disorders* (4th edn) (DSM-IV). Washington, DC: American Psychiatric Association.

Barkley, R. (1994). *ADHD in the classroom: Strategies for teachers* (manual and DVD). Available from www.russellbarkley.org

Barkley, R. (2000). *Taking charge of ADHD: The complete authoritative guide for parents*. New York: Guilford Press.

Biederman, J. *et al.* (1999). Pharmacotherapy of attention-deficit/

hyperactivity disorder reduces risk for substance use disorder. *Paediatrics*, 104, 20.

Centers for Disease Control and Prevention (2007). Nonfatal traumatic brain injuries from sports and recreation activities: United States, 2001–2005. *Morbidity & Mortality Weekly Report*, 56(29).

Conoley, J. and Sheridan, S. (1996) Paediatric traumatic brain injury: challenges and interventions for families. *Journal of Learning Disabilities*, 29, 662–669.

Delaney, J.S. (2008). Canadian study examined more than 260 adolescents playing club soccer. *British Journal of Sports Medicine*, 42, 110–115.

Evans, R. (2008). Concussion and mild traumatic brain injury. Retrieved February 2009 from www.uptodate.com

Gray, M., Bain, J. and Willis, L. (2009). Protective headgear for soccer players: an overview. *The Sport Journal* (online). Retrieved 7 February 2009 from http://www.thesportjournal. org/article/protective-headgear-soccer-players-overview

Jones, K. (2007). Evaluation of the Incredible Years BASIC training programme for preschool children with conduct disorder and ADHD symptoms. Retrieved 8 February 2009 from www.incredibleyearswales.co.uk

MTA Cooperative Group (1999). A 14-month randomized clinical trial of treatment strategies for attention-deficit/hyperactivity disorder: multimodal treatment study of children with ADHD. *Archives of General Psychiatry*, 56, 1073–1086.

Reimers, C. and Brunger, B. (2006). *ADHD in the young child: Driven to redirection*. Plantation, FL: Specialty Press.

Senelick, R. and Dougherty, K. (2001). *Living with brain injury: A guide for families* (2nd edn). Birmingham, AL: Healthsouth Press.

Chapter 14

Anderson, S., Hastings, G. and MacFadyen, L. (2002). Strategic marketing in the UK tobacco industry. *The Lancet Oncology*, 3, 481–486.

Baker, J.G., Rosenthal, S.L., Leonhardt, D., Kollar, L.M., Succop, P.A., Burklow, K.A. *et al.* (1999). Relationship between perceived parental monitoring and young adolescent girls' sexual and substance use behaviors. *Journal of Pediatric and Adolescent Gynecology*, 12, 17–22.

Brown, J. and Witherspoon, E. (2002). The mass media and American adolescents' health. *Journal of Adolescent Health*, 31, 153–170.

Chromiak, J. and Antonio, J. (2002). Use of amino acids as growth hormone-releasing agents by athletes. *Nutrition*, 18, 683–684.

Crosby, R., DiClemente, R., Wingood, G., Harrington, K., Davies, S., Hook, E. *et al.* (2002). Low parental monitoring predicts subsequent pregnancy among African-American adolescent females. *Journal of Pediatric and Adolescent Gynecology*, 15, 43–46.

Dempsey, R., Mazzone, M. and Meurer, L. (2002). Does oral creatine supplementation improve strength? A meta-analysis. *Journal of Family Practice*, 51, 945–951.

Eaton, D., Kann, L., Kinchen, S., Shanklin, S., Ross, J. *et al.* (2008). Youth risk behavior survey – United States, 2007. *MMWR Surveillance Summaries*, 57(SS04), 1–131.

Gross, R. and Duke, P. (1980). The effect of early versus late physical maturation on adolescent behavior. *Pediatric Clinics of North America*, 27, 71–77.

Kmietowicz, Z. (2002). US and UK are top in teenage pregnancy rates. *British Medical Journal*, 321, 1354.

Kobus, K. (2003). Peers and adolescent smoking. *Addiction*, 98(suppl. 1), 37–55.

Komro, K., McCarty, M., Forster, J., Blaine, T. *et al.* (2003). Parental, family, and home characteristics associated with cigarette smoking among adolescents. *American Journal of Health Promotion*, 17, 291–299.

Lammers, C., Ireland, M., Resnick, M. and Blum, R. (2000). Influences on adolescents' decision to postpone onset of sexual intercourse: a survival analysis of virginity among youths aged 13 to 18 years. *Journal of Adolescent Health*, 26, 42–48.

McCrystal, P., Percy, A. and Higgins, K. (2007). Frequent cannabis use among 14/15 year olds in Northern Ireland. *Drug and Alcohol Dependence*, 88, 19–27.

Munro, H., Davis, M. and Hughes, G. (2004). Adolescent sexual health. In *National statistics: The health of children and young people*. London: Office for National Statistics.

Resnick, M., Bearman, P., Blum, R., Bauman, K., Harris, K., Jones, J. *et al.* (1997). Protecting adolescents from harm: findings from the National Longitudinal Study on Adolescent Health. *Journal of the American Medical Association*, 278, 823–832.

Romer, D., Stanton, B., Galbraith, J., Feigelman, S., Black, M. and Xiaoming, L. (1999). Parental influence on adolescent sexual behavior in high-poverty settings. *Archives of Pediatric and Adolescent Medicine*, 153, 1055–1062.

Rowan, S. (2004). Drug-use, smoking and drinking. In *National statistics: The health of children and young people*. London: Office for National Statistics.

Smetana, J. (1995). Parenting styles and conceptions of parental authority during adolescence. *Child Development*, 66, 299–316.

Stanton, B., Xiaoming, L., Galbraith, J., Cornick, G., Feigelman, S., Kaljee, L. *et al.* (2000). Parental underestimates of adolescent risk behavior: a randomized, controlled trial of a parental monitoring intervention. *Journal of Adolescent Health*, 26, 18–26.

Steinberg, L., Fletcher, A. and Darling, N. (1994). Parental monitoring and peer influences on adolescent substance use. *Pediatrics*, 93, 1060–1064.

Strasburger, V.C. and Brown, R.T. (1991). *Adolescent medicine: A practical guide*. Boston: Little, Brown & Co.

Williams, R., McDermitt, D., Bertrand, L. and Davis, R. (2003). Parental awareness of adolescent substance use. *Addictive Behaviors*, 28, 803–809.

Xiaoming, L., Feigelman, S. and Stanton, B. (2000). Perceived parental monitoring and health risk behaviors among urban low-income African-American children and adolescents. *Journal of Adolescent Health*, 27, 43–48.

Xiaoming, L., Stanton, B. and Feigelman, S. (2000). Impact of perceived parental monitoring on adolescent risk behavior over 4 years. *Journal of Adolescent Health*, 27, 49–56.

Chapter 15

Ahrons, C. (2006). Family ties after divorce: long-term implications for children. *Family Process*, 46, 53–65.

Amato, P. (2000). The consequences of divorce for adults and children. *Journal of Marriage and the Family*, 62, 1269–1287.

American Psychological Association (2004). APA Policy Statement: Sexual orientation, parents, & children. Retrieved January 2008 from http://www.apa.org/pi/lgbc/policy/parents.html

Barth, R., Crea, T., John, K., Thoburn, J. and Quinton, D. (2005). Beyond attachment theory and therapy: towards sensitive and evidence-based interventions with foster and adoptive families in distress. *Child and Family Social Work*, 10, 257–268.

Bohman, M. (1996). Predisposition to criminality: Swedish adoption studies in retrospect. *Ciba Foundation Symposium*, 194, 99–109.

Braver, S., Ellman, I. and Fabricius, W. (2003). Relocation after divorce and children's best interests: new evidence and legal considerations. *Journal of Family Psychology*, 17, 206–219.

Brodzinsky, D. (1993). Long-term outcomes in adoption. *The Future of Children*, 3(1), 153–166.

Burke, S., McIntosh, J. and Gridley, H. (2007). Parenting after separation: a position statement prepared for the Australian Psychological Society. Australian Psychological Society, August 2007, retrieved January 2008 from www.psychology.org.au

Chaffin, M. *et al.* (2006). Report of the APSAC task force on attachment therapy, reactive attachment disorder, and attachment problems. *Child Maltreatment*, 11, 76–89.

Chaoyang, L., Pentz, M. and Chih-Ping, C. (2002). Parental substance use as a modifier of adolescent substance use risk. *Addiction*, 97, 1537–1550.

Children's Research Centre (n.d.). A study of intercountry adoption outcomes in Ireland: summary report. Retrieved January 2008 from http:// www.adoptionboard.ie/booklets/Intercountry _Adoption_Outcomes_Ireland_summary.pdf

Ginther, D. and Pollak, R. (2004). Family structure and children's educational outcomes: blended families, stylized facts, and descriptive regressions. *Demography*, 41, 671–696.

Kelly, J. (2005). Developing beneficial parenting plan models for children following separation and divorce. *Journal of the American Academy of Matrimonial Lawyers*, 19, 237–254.

Kelly, J. (2006). Children's living arrangements following separation and divorce: insights from empirical and clinical research. *Family Process*, 46, 35–52.

Kelly, J. and Emery, R. (2003). Children's adjustment following divorce: risk and resilience perspectives. *Family Relations*, 52, 352–362.

Leung, P., Erich, S. and Kanenberg, H. (2005). A comparison of family functioning in gay/lesbian, heterosexual, and special needs adoptions. *Children and Youth Services Review*, 27, 1031–1044.

Levitt, S. and Dubner, S. (2005). *Freakonomics: A rogue economist explores the hidden side of everything*. New York: HarperCollins.

Manlove, J., Terry-Humen, E., Ikramullah, E. and Moore, K. (2006). The role of parent religiosity in teens' transition to sex and contraception. *Journal of Adolescent Health*, 39, 578–587.

Najman, J. *et al.* (1997). Impact of family type and family quality on child behaviour problems: a longitudinal study. *Journal of the American Academy of Child and Adolescent Psychiatry*, 36, 1357–1365.

Nelson, B., Patience, T. and MacDonald, D. (1999). Adolescent risk behaviour and the influence of parents and education. *Journal of the American Board of Family Practitioners*, 12, 436–443.

Pinquart, M. and Silbereisen, R. (2004). Transmission of values from adolescents to their parents: the role of value content and authoritative parenting. *Adolescence*, 39, 83–100.

Regnerus, M. (2003). Religion and positive adolescent outcomes: a review of research and theory. *Review of Religious Research*, 44, 394–413.

Rosenthal, J. (1993). Outcomes of adoption of children with special needs. *The Future of Children*, 3(1), 78–88.

Silverman, A. (1993). Outcomes of transracial adoption. *The Future of Children*, 3(1), 104–118.

Snider, J.B., Clements, A. and Vazsonyi, A. (2004). Late adolescent perceptions of parent religiosity and parenting processes. *Family Process*, 43, 489–502.

Stanley, S. and Fincham, F. (2002). The effects of divorce on children. *Couples Research and Therapy Newsletter* (AABT-SIG), 8, 7–10.

Wight, D., Williamson, L. and Henderson, M. (2006). Parental influences on young people's sexual behaviour: a longitudinal analysis. *Journal of Adolescence*, 29, 473–494.

Wills, T., Sandy, J., Yaeger, A. and Shinar, O. (2001). Family risk factors and adolescent substance use: moderation effects for temperament dimensions. *Developmental Psychology*, 37, 283–297.

Chapter 16

Barnes, J., Leach, P., Sylva, K., Stein, A., Malmberg, L.-K. and FCCC Team (2006). Infant care in England: mothers' aspirations, experiences, satisfaction and caregiver relationships. *Early Child Development and Care*, 176, 553–573.

Belsky, J., Vandell, D.L., Burchinal, M., Clarke-Steward, K.A., McCartney, K., Owen, M.T. and NICHD Early Child Care Research Network (2007). Are there long-term effects of early child care. *Child Development*, 78, 681–701.

Koren-Karie, N., Sagi-Schwartz, A. and Egoz-Mizrachi, N. (2005). The emotional quality of childcare centers in Israel: the Haifa study of early childcare. *Infant Mental Health Journal*, 26, 110–126.

Leach, P., Barnes, J., Nichols, M., Goldin, J., Stein, A., Sylva, K., Malmberg, L.-E. and FCCC Team (2006). Child care before 6 months of age: a qualitative study of mothers' decisions and feelings about employment and non-maternal care. *Infant and Child Development*, 15, 471–502.

Leach, P., Barnes, J., Malmberg, L.-E., Sylva, K., Stein, A. and FCCC Team (2008). The quality of different types of child care at 10 and 18 months: a comparison between types and factors related to quality. *Early Child Development and Care*, 2, 177–209.

NICHD Early Child Care Research Network (2003). Does amount

of time spent in child care predict socioemotional adjustment during the transition to kindergarten? *Child Development*, 74, 976–1005.

NICHD Early Child Care Research Network (2005). *Child Care and Child Development: Results from the NICHD Study of Early Child Care and Youth Development*. New York: Guilford Press.

Schpancer, N. (2006). The effects of daycare: persistent questions, elusive answers. *Early Childhood Quarterly*, 21, 227–237.

Index

Locators for figures/tables appear in *italic*
Locators for main headings which also have subheadings refer to general information about the topic.

59156904R00209

Made in the USA
Lexington, KY
27 December 2016